FOUR COMEDIES

LYSISTRATA

THE ACHARNIANS

THE CONGRESSWOMEN

THE FROGS

Four Comedies by Aristophanes

Lysistrata

The Acharnians

The Congresswomen
Translated by Douglass Parker

The Frogs
Translated by Richmond Lattimore

Ann Arbor Paperbacks
The University of Michigan Press

Second printing 1971

First edition as an Ann Arbor Paperback 1969

Copyright © by William Arrowsmith 1961, 1962, 1964, 1967, 1969

Published in the United States of America by
The University of Michigan Press and simultaneously
in Don Mills, Canada, by Longmans Canada Limited

Manufactured in the United States of America

Lysistrata

Translated by Douglass Parker
with sketches by Ellen Raskin

CONTENTS

HAVERLY
CONIVGI CARISSIMAE
ΔΕΙΝΗΙ ΜΑΛΑΚΗΙ ΣΕΜΝΗΙ ΑΓΑΝΗΙ
SAEPE STVPEFACTVS SEMPER ADMIRATVS
HVNC LIBRVM INTERPRES

D. D. D. D. L. M.

Introduction

The Play

Lysistrata was first performed at Athens in the year 411 B.C., probably during the Lenaia. Of the achievement of that first production, we know nothing at all; of more recent developments, we are better informed.

Regular translation, frequent adaptation, persistent production, and occasional confiscation—these are the signs of success, making *Lysistrata* today's popular favorite among Aristophanes' surviving comedies. A not altogether joyous eminence. Even the most rabid advocate of the wide circulation of the classics-in-any-form must blanch slightly at the broadcast misconception that this play is a hoard of applied lubricity. Witness its latest American publication, bowdlerized-in-reverse, nestled near some choice gobbets from Frank Harris' autobiography in a slick and curious quarterly called *Eros,* now under indictment. If this be success, there is scant comfort in it.* What profit in outwearing time's ravages, only to win through to a general snigger? Both Aristophanes and his audience deserve better.

Happily, they do receive it. *Lysistrata* is Aristophanes' most popular play, not because it is his most obscene (it is not) nor his most prurient (he is never prurient), but because, to a present-day reader or viewer, it is his most comprehensible, capable of assimilation with the least violence to preconceptions. Indeed, when we examine its preoccupation with sex, the source of its notoriety, we find the treatment rather more soothing than shocking. Those facets of the subject at which we, uneasy in our daintiness, are wont to boggle, have nearly disappeared. Gone, almost, is the homosexuality (now a clinical matter, hardly the object of fun); gone the scatology (so uncomfortable in Monuments of the Western Tradition). *Lysistrata* centers on what has become for us the last refuge of genteel ribaldry—heterosexual intercourse. If the presentation is more explicit than we usually expect on a stage, we can

---

* Some, however: It is refreshing to conjecture what treatment Harris might have received from Aristophanes, who is by most standards quite orthodox in matters sexual. Compare his remarks on Ariphrades, especially at *Knights* 1280 ff.

still understand it and conclude with the comforting generality that the Greeks were, after all, just like us.

They were not, of course. They invested sex with little transcendental significance, and nothing could have been more foreign to them than the two most current misconstructions of *Lysistrata*—the mid-Victorian ("Brute Man Saved from Himself by the Love of a Good Woman") and the Reichian ("Happy Ganglia Make the Whole World Kin"). *Lysistrata* concurs with Aristophanes' other briefs for peace, *The Acharnians* and *The Peace,* in its basically hedonistic approach: To the discomforts of war are opposed the joys of fulfilled desire. Admittedly, there have been changes. The earlier plays interweave a triad of desires —Wine, Food, and Sex; here, the first two members of the triad are muted (though not dispensed with entirely), and the third is explored to the full.

Predictably, this exploration of single theme rather than cluster is preferred by certain critics to Aristophanes' normal practice in that it generates something curiously close to the modern notion of a plot. Abetting this is the split Chorus, which not only performs its normal function of a control which limits and defines the main action, but parallels that action with one of its own: gaffer loses crone, gaffer gets crone. Put the parts together, let individual action be succeeded by the appropriate choral action, and the result seems positively Well-Made. Though objection is occasionally raised to a presumed lack of connection between the sex-strike and the seizure of the Akropolis, anyone who considers the terms in which that seizure is first defined—the old men's attack on the locked gates with logs they cannot lift, with fires they cannot light—will hardly be persuaded. And just as well. The connection is not just a structural ploy, but central to the play's meaning. The Akropolis, the heart of the city, is fused with the objects of desire, and its restoration is Love Achieved.

Love, not merely Sex—a vital distinction. If *Lysistrata* is not an exaltation of rut, neither is it a nihilistic satire which undercuts all human progress, all collective action, by cynically opposing to it the basic animality of the individual. Upsetting as it may seem to us, the heirs of a Puritan ethic, Aristophanes' hedonism is rarely anarchic. Certainly not here. The fundamental relationship is not blind sexual gratification, the force that drives the water through the rocks, any rocks, but love in its civic manifestation—the bond between husband and wife. Once this is established and identified with the City itself, Aristophanes can and does develop it into other areas. He can turn it around to show the wife and mother's proper share in the State, broaden it into a plea for Panhellenism, push it beyond sex entirely (in the split Choruses) to its irreducible residue. The neural itch is only the beginning; the goal is a united City and a unified Hellas at peace, the gift of Aphrodite. Significantly, the play ends with, not an orgy, but an invocation by Spartans and Athenians of the whole pantheon. *Eros* and *sophia*, sex and wisdom, join as the civilizing force of love.

Nobility of conception, of course, does not confer dignity of execution, and the basic ridiculousness of sex is rarely lost sight of. It is precisely this tension between intent and accomplishment, a tension all too visible in this most phallic of all comedies, that makes the play work. No character is exempt. Not even the heroine, whose somewhat prissy idealism cracks wide open for a moment at line 715 in the inclusive cry *binêtiômen*—"we want to get laid." *Lysistrata* is a great play, not a so-so tract.

Still, there does exist a minority view. The play's technical excellences are unquestionable: tight formal unity, economy of movement, realism in characterizations, range of feeling. They are also rather un-Aristophanic excellences, and the specialist who prefers earlier, comparatively messy pieces may perhaps be forgiven. Certainly one point must be conceded him: At spots in *Lysistrata*, particularly during debates, Aristophanes' linguistic exuberance deserts him. I do not mean eloquence, but wit, the constant subterranean interplay of sound and sense which elsewhere makes poetry of argumentation. Whether this comes from haste, or from despair, or from the lack of balance which accompanies an overpowering desire to convince—the same lack that, to my mind, deforms the end of *The Clouds*—I cannot say. For whatever reason, it constitutes a blemish.

But a minor blemish on a major work, one tough-minded about sex, tough-minded about war. *Lysistrata*'s greatness ultimately resides in its sheer nerve, its thoroughgoing audacity in confronting, after twenty years of conflict, an Athens poised between external and internal disasters, between the annihilation of her Sicilian expeditionary force in 413 and the overthrow of her constitution in 411. With an astigmatism born of centuries, we are only too liable to misconstrue it, by refusing to see the heroine whole, by regarding the women's revolt as more possibility than fantasy, by giving way to sentimentality. But somehow we cannot do it much harm. Even when he writes like someone else, Aristophanes, servant of the Muses and Aphrodite, is Aristophanes still.

Translation

In general, the principles of this translation remain those guiding my versions of *The Acharnians* and *The Wasps*. It is interpretive rather than literal. It cannot be used as a by-the-line crib, but aims at recreating in American English verse what I conceive to have been Aristophanes' essential strategies in Greek. To do this, fields of metaphor have often been changed, jokes added in compensation for jokes lost, useless proper names (primarily those of chorus members and supernumeraries) neglected. Not all of these changes have been indicated in the notes. Some particular points:

Obscenity: Though its workings may seem rococo at times, this version tries to be unblushing, and thus avoid the second greatest sin against Aristophanes, coyness. However, there is one area of compromise that must be justified: The language of the women has been slightly muted, not in the interest of propriety, but to make their characters viable to a modern audience. Lysistrata, for example, has more than a little of the *grande dame* about her, also an intriguing reluctance to refer directly to the relations between the sexes. When she must so refer, it is incongruous and funny—but a literal Englishing of *peous*, the last word in line 124 (here rendered, "Then here's the program: Total Abstinence from SEX!"), either by "penis" or by some curt Saxonism, would stretch the only available stereotype till it shattered, and reduced her assimilated social rank disastrously for the play.

Proper Names: Such is the power of tradition that the name of the heroine, and hence of the play, is here presented in its Latin form rather than in the straight transliteration from the Greek—"Lysistrate"— which would follow the normal practice for this series. But, in any case, the Latin rules for accent should hold, and the name be pronounced LySIStrata. Pronunciations of other principals: KleoNIky, MYRrhiny, LAMpito, KiNEEsias.

Staging: Those who hold that the Theater of Dionysos possessed, in the fifth century B.C., a stage raised above the level of the orchestra (i.e., of the Chorus' dancing area) will find ample proof of their contention in *Lysistrata;* those who maintain that such a raised stage was a fourth-century innovation will find it easy to discount such proof; I prefer to avoid the hassle altogether, though I lean to the fourth-century theory. But all the setting that is really needed is a building, center, with double doors, representing the entrance to the Akropolis, or Propylaia, on whose roof Lysistrata and her women can appear after the coup d'état. The prologue might profit slightly in the direction of literality by the presence of Lysistrata's house, right, and Kleonike's house, left. The first entrance of the Chorus of Men might gain (in the absence of parodoi) by a climbable hill; squeamish audiences might be helped over the Kinesias-Myrrhine encounter if it took place inside a Cave of Pan, Myrrhine appearing (rather than disappearing) briefly to obtain her props. All these are matters of individual taste, and affect the translation not at all. But one principle is at work throughout and must be observed: *Characters and Chorus do not normally mingle.* It is important to note certain applications of this general rule for this play: The Chorus of Women *at no time* enters the Akropolis, nor does it attack the Commissioner and his Skythians; these are the actions of different women, the younger women (most of them supers) who have joined in the oath toward the end of the Prologue. In my reading of the play, I see only one exception to the rule, and it is more apparent than actual: The abortive storming of the Akropolis by the united Chorus in the last scene, an attempt repulsed by the torch-bearing Commissioner.

Text

I have worked most closely with Coulon's Budé text of 1928 and its immediate source, Wilamowitz' edition of 1927, supplementing them with little profit by the text of Cantarella (1956) and with great profit by those of Rogers (second edition, 1911) and Van Leeuwen (1903). But these worthies, singly or collectively, are not to be held responsible for certain features of the Greek underlying my translation. The characteristic weakness of the manuscripts of Aristophanes—their inability to answer with any certainty the recurrent question, "Who's talking?"— breaks out in its most virulent form in this most susceptible play; the translator, trying desperately to make dramatic sense of everything, must formulate his own replies. I have indicated in the notes my major departures from Coulon. Certain of these, particularly the continued presence of the Commissioner and Kinesias after their respective frustrations, may seem violent in the extreme. I can only state here that they are not arbitrary, but proceed from a reasoned examination of the problems involved.

Some minor solutions *are* arbitrary, of course, and scarcely susceptible of proof, as in line 122, where I have distributed between Kleonike and Myrrhine two words assigned by the manuscripts to Kleonike alone, for a purely pragmatic reason: it plays better that way. Again, my answer to the hackneyed query, "What woman delivers lines 447-448?"—to make Ismenia the Theban, heretofore mute, the speaker of two lines in Attic Greek—is an impossible solution to an impossible problem. Its only virtue is to bring in a previously introduced character without breaking the pattern—which, at that, is better than assigning the lines to the leader of the Women's Chorus.

This seeming disrespect for received writ has had its disturbing consequences, primarily an itch to fiddle further. The oath, for example: In the manuscripts, Lysistrata administers it (212 ff.) to the bibulous Kleonike as representative of the assembled women. In view of subsequent developments, might the responsions not better be made by

Myrrhine, who will illustrate the practical applications of the oath? Or, to take the Commissioner, whose part I have already fattened considerably: Certain tricks of speech, coupled with his determination at 1011-1012 to make the necessary arrangements, suggest that he, rather than the Chorus (or Koryphaios), might be the official greeter of both the Spartan and the Athenian delegations, beginning the iambs at 1074 (p. 74, "Men of Sparta, I bid you welcome!"). But, though the will to refrain comes hard, I have, for the moment, stopped.

Acknowledgments

My thanks go to the University of California, for typing grants; to Eleanore Stone, who fearlessly and impeccably typed and proofread the present version; to colleagues at Riverside, especially William Sharp, who enlightened me on drama; to colleagues in Washington, especially Kenneth Reckford, who enlightened me on Aristophanes. More than thanks to William Arrowsmith, who has taught me more about translation than I shall ever know; and to my wife, the dedicatee of this volume, who taught me about women without being a traitor to her sex.

DOUGLASS PARKER

Characters of the Play

LYSISTRATA ⎫
KLEONIKE ⎬ *Athenian women*
MYRRHINE ⎭
LAMPITO, *a Spartan woman*
ISMENIA, *a Boiotian girl*
KORINTHIAN GIRL
POLICEWOMAN
KORYPHAIOS OF THE MEN
CHORUS OF OLD MEN *of Athens*
KORYPHAIOS OF THE WOMEN
CHORUS OF OLD WOMEN *of Athens*
COMMISSIONER *of Public Safety*
FOUR POLICEMEN
KINESIAS, *Myrrhine's husband*
CHILD *of Kinesias and Myrrhine*
SLAVE
SPARTAN HERALD
SPARTAN AMBASSADOR
FLUTE-PLAYER
ATHENIAN WOMEN
PELOPONNESIAN WOMEN
PELOPONNESIAN MEN
ATHENIAN MEN

SCENE: *A street in Athens. In the background,
the Akropolis; center, its gateway, the Propylaia.
The time is early morning.* Lysistrata is discovered
alone, pacing back and forth in furious impatience.*

LYSISTRATA
Women!
Announce a debauch in honor of Bacchos,
a spree for Pan, some footling fertility fieldday,
and traffic stops—the streets are absolutely clogged
with frantic females banging on tambourines. No urging
for an orgy!
        But *today*—there's not one woman here.

Enter Kleonike.

Correction: one. Here comes my next door neighbor.
—Hello, Kleonike.*

KLEONIKE
        Hello to *you,* Lysistrata.
—But what's the fuss? Don't look so barbarous, baby;
knitted brows just aren't your style.

LYSISTRATA
        It doesn't
matter, Kleonike—I'm on fire right down to the bone.
I'm positively ashamed to be a woman—a member
of a sex which can't even live up to male slanders!
To hear our husbands talk, we're *sly:* deceitful,
always plotting, monsters of intrigue. . . .

KLEONIKE

Proudly.

        That's us!

LYSISTRATA
And so we agreed to meet today and plot
an intrigue that really deserves the name of monstrous. . .
and WHERE are the women?
        Slyly asleep at home—
they won't get up for anything!

KLEONIKE
        Relax, honey.
They'll be here. You know a woman's way is hard—
mainly the way out of the house: fuss over hubby,
wake the maid up, put the baby down, bathe him,
feed him. . .

LYSISTRATA

        Trivia. They have more fundamental business
to engage in.

KLEONIKE

        Incidentally, Lysistrata, just why are you
calling this meeting? Nothing teeny, I trust?

LYSISTRATA
Immense.

KLEONIKE

        Hmmm. And pressing?

LYSISTRATA

                Unthinkably tense.

KLEONIKE
Then where IS everybody?

LYSISTRATA

        Nothing like that. If it were,
we'd already be in session. Seconding motions.
—No, *this* came to hand some time ago. I've spent
my nights kneading it, mulling it, filing it down. . . .

KLEONIKE
Too bad. There can't be very much left.

LYSISTRATA

              Only this:
the hope and salvation of Hellas lies with the WOMEN!

KLEONIKE
Lies with the women? Now *there's* a last resort.

LYSISTRATA
It lies with us to decide affairs of state
and foreign policy.

        The Spartan Question: Peace
or Extirpation?

KLEONIKE

      How *fun!*

        I cast an Aye for Extirpation!

LYSISTRATA
The Utter Annihilation of every last Boiotian?

KLEONIKE
AYE!—I mean Nay. Clemency, please, for those scrumptious
eels.*

LYSISTRATA

     And as for Athens. . . I'd rather not put
the thought into words. Just fill in the blanks, if you will.
—To the point: If we can meet and reach agreement
here and now with the girls from Thebes and the Peloponnese,
we'll form an alliance and save the States of Greece!

KLEONIKE

Us? Be practical. Wisdom from women? There's nothing
cosmic about cosmetics—and Glamor is our only talent.
All we can do is *sit,* primped and painted,
made up and dressed up,

Getting carried away in spite of her argument.

                          ravishing in saffron wrappers,
peekaboo peignoirs, exquisite negligees, those chic,
expensive little slippers that come from the East. . .

LYSISTRATA

Exactly. You've hit it. I see our way to salvation
in just such ornamentation—in slippers and slips, rouge
and perfumes, negligees and decolletage. . . .

KLEONIKE

                              How so?

LYSISTRATA

So effectively that not one husband will take up his spear
against another. . .

KLEONIKE

           Peachy!
                  I'll have that kimono
dyed. . .

LYSISTRATA

     . . . or shoulder his shield. . .

KLEONIKE

                             . . .squeeze into that daring
negligee. . .

LYSISTRATA

     . . .or unsheathe his sword!

KLEONIKE

                               . . .and buy those slippers!

LYSISTRATA

Well, now. Don't you think the girls should be here?

KLEONIKE

Be here? Ages ago—they should have flown!

She stops.

But no. You'll find out. These are authentic Athenians:
no matter what they do, they do it late.

LYSISTRATA

But what about the out-of-town delegations? There isn't
a woman here from the Shore; none from Salamis. . .

KLEONIKE

That's quite a trip. They usually get on board
at sunup. Probably riding at anchor now.

LYSISTRATA

I thought the girls from Acharnai would be here first.
I'm especially counting on them. And they're not here.

KLEONIKE

I think Theogenes' wife is under way.
When I went by, she was hoisting her sandals. . .*

Looking off right.

But look!

Some of the girls are coming!

*Women enter from the right. Lysistrata looks off to the left where more—a ragged lot—
are straggling in.*

LYSISTRATA

And more over here!

KLEONIKE

Where did you find *that* group?

LYSISTRATA

They're from the outskirts.*

KLEONIKE

Well, that's something. If you haven't done anything else,
you've really ruffled up the outskirts.

Myrrhine enters guiltily from the right.

MYRRHINE

Oh, Lysistrata,

we aren't late, are we?

Well, *are* we?

Speak to me!

LYSISTRATA

What is it, Myrrhine? Do you want a medal for tardiness?
Honestly, such behavior, with so much at stake. . .

MYRRHINE

I'm sorry. I couldn't find my girdle in the dark.
And anyway, we're here now. So tell us all about it,
whatever it is.

KLEONIKE
                    No, wait a minute. Don't
begin just yet. Let's wait for those girls from Thebes
and the Peloponnese.

LYSISTRATA
                    Now *there* speaks the proper attitude.

Lampito, a strapping Spartan woman, enters left, leading a pretty Boiotian girl (Ismenia)
and a huge, steatopygous Korinthian.
        And here's our lovely Spartan.
                            Hel*lo,* Lampito
dear.
            Why, darling, you're simply ravishing! Such
a blemishless complexion—so clean, so out-of-doors!
And will you look at that figure—the pink of pefection!

KLEONIKE
I'll bet you could strangle a bull.

LAMPITO
                            I calklate so.*
Hit's fitness whut done it, fitness and dancin'. You know
the step?

Demonstrating.
                    Foot it out back'ards an' toe yore twitchet.

The women crowd around Lampito.

KLEONIKE
What unbelievably beautiful bosoms!

LAMPITO
                                Shuckins,
whut fer you tweedlin' me up so? I feel like a heifer
come fair-time.

LYSISTRATA

Turning to Ismenia.
                    And who is this young lady here?

LAMPITO
Her kin's purt-near the bluebloodiest folk in Thebes—
the First Fam'lies of Boiotia.

LYSISTRATA

As they inspect Ismenia.
                                Ah, picturesque Boiotia:
her verdant meadows, her fruited plain. . .

KLEONIKE

Peering more closely.
                                        Her sunken
garden where no grass grows. A cultivated country.

LYSISTRATA

Gaping at the gawking Korinthian.

And who is *this*—er—little thing?

LAMPITO

She hails
from over by Korinth, but her kinfolk's quality—mighty
big back there.

KLEONIKE

On her tour of inspection.

She's mighty big back *here*.

LAMPITO

The womenfolk's all assemblied. Who-all's notion
was this-hyer confabulation?

LYSISTRATA

Mine.

LAMPITO

Git on with the give-out.
I'm hankerin' to hear.

MYRRHINE

Me, too! I can't imagine
what could be so important. Tell us about it!

LYSISTRATA

Right away.
—But first, a question. It's not
an involved one. Answer yes or no.

A pause.

MYRRHINE

Well, ASK it!

LYSISTRATA

It concerns the fathers of your children—your husbands, absent
on active service. I know you all have men
abroad.
—Wouldn't you like to have them home?

KLEONIKE

My husband's been gone for the last five months! Way up
to Thrace, watchdogging military waste.* It's horrible!

MYRRHINE

Mine's been posted to Pylos for seven whole months!

LAMPITO

My man's no sooner rotated out of the line
than he's plugged back in. Hain't no discharge in this war!

14

KLEONIKE
And lovers can't be had for love or money,
not even synthetics. Why, since those beastly Milesians
revolted and cut off the leather trade, that handy
do-it-yourself kit's *vanished* from the open market!

LYSISTRATA
If I can devise a scheme for ending the war,
I gather I have your support?

KLEONIKE
You can count on me!
If you need money, I'll pawn the shift off my back—

Aside.

and drink up the cash before the sun goes down.

MYRRHINE
Me, too! I'm ready to split myself right up
the middle like a mackerel, and give you half!

LAMPITO
Me, too! I'd climb Taygetos Mountain plumb
to the top to git the leastes' peek at Peace!

LYSISTRATA
Very well, I'll tell you. No reason to keep a secret.

Importantly, as the women cluster around her.
We can force our husbands to negotiate Peace,
Ladies, by exercising steadfast Self-Control—
By Total Abstinence. . .

A pause.

KLEONIKE
From WHAT?

MYRRHINE
Yes, what?

LYSISTRATA
You'll do it?

KLEONIKE
Of course we'll do it! We'd even *die!*

LYSISTRATA
Very well,
then here's the program:
Total Abstinence
from SEX!

The cluster of women dissolves.
—Why are you turning away? Where are you going?

Moving among the women.

—What's this? Such stricken expressions! Such gloomy gestures!
—Why so pale?
                    —Whence these tears?
                                        —What IS this?
Will you do it or won't you?
                    Cat got your tongue?

KLEONIKE

Afraid I can't make it. Sorry.
                                On with the War!

MYRRHINE

Me neither. Sorry.
                    On with the War!

LYSISTRATA

                                This from
my little mackerel? The girl who was ready, a minute
ago, to split herself right up the middle?

KLEONIKE

Breaking in between Lysistrata and Myrrhine.

Try something else. Try anything. If you say so,
I'm willing to walk through fire barefoot.
                                        But not
to give up SEX—there's nothing like it, Lysistrata!

LYSISTRATA

To Myrrhine.

And you?

MYRRHINE

            Me, too! I'll walk through fire.

LYSISTRATA

                                Women!
Utter sluts, the entire sex! Will-power,
nil. We're perfect raw material for Tragedy,
the stuff of heroic lays. "Go to bed with a god
and then get rid of the baby"—that sums us up!

Turning to Lampito.

—Oh, Spartan, be a dear. If *you* stick by me,
just you, we still may have a chance to win.
Give me your vote.

LAMPITO

                    Hit's right onsettlin' fer gals
to sleep all lonely-like, withouten no humpin'.
But I'm on yore side. We shore need Peace, too.

LYSISTRATA
You're a darling—the only woman here
worthy of the name!

KLEONIKE
                    Well, just suppose we *did,*
as much as possible, abstain from. . . what you said,
you know—not that we *would*—could something like that
bring Peace any sooner?

LYSISTRATA
                    Certainly. Here's how it works:
We'll paint, powder, and pluck ourselves to the last
detail, and stay inside, wearing those filmy
tunics that set off everything we *have*—
                              and then
slink up to the men. They'll snap to attention, go absolutely
mad to love us—
                    but we won't let them. We'll Abstain.
—I imagine they'll conclude a treaty rather quickly.

LAMPITO

Nodding.

Menelaos he tuck one squint at Helen's bubbies
all nekkid, and plumb threw up.

Pause for thought.

                              Throwed up his sword.

KLEONIKE
Suppose the men just leave us flat?

LYSISTRATA
                              In that case,
we'll have to take things into our own hands.

KLEONIKE
There simply isn't any reasonable facsimile!
—Suppose they take us by force and drag us off
to the bedroom against our wills?

LYSISTRATA
                              Hang on to the door.

KLEONIKE
Suppose they beat us?

LYSISTRATA
                    Give in—but be bad sports.
Be nasty about it—they don't enjoy these forced
affairs. So make them suffer.
                              Don't worry; they'll stop
soon enough. A married man wants harmony—
cooperation, not rape.

17

KLEONIKE

Well, I suppose so. . . .

Looking from Lysistrata to Lampito.

If *both* of you approve this, then so do we.

LAMPITO

Hain't worried over our menfolk none. We'll bring 'em
round to makin' a fair, straightfor'ard Peace
withouten no nonsense about it. But take this rackety
passel in Athens: I misdoubt no one could make 'em
give over thet blabber of theirn.

LYSISTRATA

They're our concern.
Don't worry. We'll bring them around.

LAMPITO

Not likely.
Not long as they got ships kin still sail straight,
an' thet fountain of money up thar in Athene's temple.*

LYSISTRATA

That point is quite well covered:
We're taking over
the Akropolis, including Athene's temple, today.
It's set: Our oldest women have their orders.
They're up there now, pretending to sacrifice, waiting
for us to reach an agreement. As soon as we do,
they seize the Akropolis.

LAMPITO

The way you put them thengs,
I swear I can't see how we kin possibly lose!

LYSISTRATA

Well, now that it's settled, Lampito, let's not lose
any time. Let's take the Oath to make this binding.

LAMPITO

Just trot out thet-thar Oath. We'll swear it.

LYSISTRATA

Excellent.
—Where's a policewoman?

*A huge girl, dressed as a Skythian archer (the Athenian police) with bow and circular
shield, lumbers up and gawks.*

—What are *you* looking for?

Pointing to a spot in front of the women.

Put your shield down here.

The girl obeys.

No, hollow *up!*

The girl reverses the shield. Lysistrata looks about brightly.
—Someone give me the entrails.

A dubious silence.

KLEONIKE

Lysistrata, what kind
of an Oath are we supposed to swear?

LYSISTRATA

The Standard.
Aischylos used it in a play, they say—the one where
you slaughter a sheep and swear on a shield.

KLEONIKE

Lysistrata,
you *do not* swear an Oath for *Peace* on a *shield!*

LYSISTRATA

What Oath do you want?

Exasperated.

Something bizarre and expensive?
A fancier victim—"Take one white horse and disembowel"?

KLEONIKE

White horse? The symbolism's too obscure.*

LYSISTRATA

Then how
do we swear this oath?

KLEONIKE

Oh, *I* can tell you
that, if you'll let me.
First, we put an enormous
black cup right here—hollow up, of course.
Next, into the cup we slaughter a jar of Thasian
wine, and swear a mighty Oath that we won't. . .
dilute it with water.

LAMPITO

To Kleonike.

Let me corngratulate you—
that were the beatenes' Oath I ever heerd on!

LYSISTRATA

Calling inside.

Bring out a cup and a jug of wine!

*Two women emerge, the first staggering under the weight of a huge black cup, the second
even more burdened with a tremendous wine jar. Kleonike addresses them.*

KLEONIKE

You darlings!
What a tremendous display of pottery!

Fingering the cup.

A girl
could get a glow just *holding* a cup like this!

She grabs it away from the first woman, who exits.

LYSISTRATA

Taking the wine jar from the second serving woman (who exits), she barks at Kleonike.
Put that down and help me butcher this boar!

Kleonike puts down the cup, over which she and Lysistrata together hold the jar of wine (the "boar"). Lysistrata prays.

O Mistress Persuasion,
O Cup of Devotion,
Attend our invocation:
Accept this oblation,
Grant our petition,
Favor our mission.

Lysistrata and Kleonike tip up the jar and pour the gurgling wine into the cup. Myrrhine, Lampito, and the others watch closely.

MYRRHINE

Such an attractive shade of blood. And the spurt—
pure Art!

LAMPITO

Hit shore do smell mighty purty!

Lysistrata and Kleonike put down the empty wine jar.

KLEONIKE

Girls, let me be the first

Launching herself at the cup.

to take the Oath!

LYSISTRATA

Hauling Kleonike back.

You'll have to wait your turn like everyone else.
—Lampito, how do we manage with this mob?

Cumbersome.
—Everyone place her right hand on the cup.

The women surround the cup and obey.

I need a spokeswoman. One of you to take
the Oath in behalf of the rest.

The women edge away from Kleonike, who reluctantly finds herself elected.

The rite will conclude
with a General Pledge of Assent by all of you, thus
confirming the Oath. Understood?

Nods from the women. Lysistrata addresses Kleonike.

Repeat after me:

LYSISTRATA
I will withhold all rights of access or entrance

KLEONIKE
I will withhold all rights of access or entrance

LYSISTRATA
From every husband, lover, or casual acquaintance

KLEONIKE
from every husband, lover, or casual acquaintance

LYSISTRATA
Who moves in my direction in erection.

—Go on.

KLEONIKE
who m-moves in my direction in erection.

Ohhhhh!
—Lysistrata, my knees are shaky. Maybe I'd better...

LYSISTRATA
I will create, imperforate in cloistered chastity,

KLEONIKE
I will create, imperforate in cloistered chastity,

LYSISTRATA
A newer, more glamorous, supremely seductive me

KLEONIKE
a newer, more glamorous, supremely seductive me

LYSISTRATA
And fire my husband's desire with my molten allure—

KLEONIKE
and fire my husband's desire with my molten allure—

LYSISTRATA
But remain, to his panting advances, icily pure.

KLEONIKE
but remain, to his panting advances, icily pure.

LYSISTRATA
If he should force me to share the connubial couch,

KLEONIKE
If he should force me to share the connubial couch,

LYSISTRATA
I refuse to return his stroke with the teeniest twitch.

KLEONIKE
I refuse to return his stroke with the teeniest twitch.

LYSISTRATA
I will not lift my slippers to touch the thatch

KLEONIKE
I will not lift my slippers to touch the thatch

LYSISTRATA
Or submit sloping prone in a hangdog crouch.

KLEONIKE
or submit sloping prone in a hangdog crouch.

LYSISTRATA
**If I this oath maintain,
may I drink this glorious wine.**

KLEONIKE
*If I this oath maintain,
may I drink this glorious wine.*

LYSISTRATA
**But if I slip or falter,
let me drink water.**

KLEONIKE
*But if I slip or falter,
let me drink water.*

LYSISTRATA
—And now the General Pledge of Assent:
WOMEN

A-MEN!

LYSISTRATA
Good. I'll dedicate the oblation.

She drinks deeply.

KLEONIKE

Not too much,
darling. You know how anxious we are to become
allies and friends.

Not to mention *staying* friends.

*She pushes Lysistrata away and drinks. As the women take their turns at the cup, loud
cries and alarums are heard offstage.*

LAMPITO
What-all's that bodacious ruckus?

LYSISTRATA

Just what I told you:
It means the women have taken the Akropolis. Athene's
Citadel is ours!

It's time for you to go,
Lampito, and set your affairs in order in Sparta.

Indicating the other women in Lampito's group.
> Leave these girls here as hostages.

Lampito exits left. Lysistrata turns to the others.
> Let's hurry inside
> the Akropolis and help the others shoot the bolts.

KLEONIKE
> Don't you think the men will send reinforcements
> against us as soon as they can?

LYSISTRATA
> So where's the worry?
> The men can't burn their way in or frighten us out.
> The Gates are ours—they're proof against fire and fear—
> and they open only on our conditions.

KLEONIKE
> Yes!
> That's the spirit—let's deserve our reputations:

As the women hurry off into the Akropolis.
> UP THE SLUTS!
> WAY FOR THE OLD IMPREGNABLES!

The door shuts behind the women, and the stage is empty.

A pause, and the Chorus of Men shuffles on from the left in two groups, led by their Koryphaios. They are incredibly aged Athenians; though they may acquire spryness later in the play, at this point they are sheer decrepitude. Their normally shaky progress is impeded by their burdens: each man not only staggers under a load of wood across his shoulders, but has his hands full as well—in one, an earthen pot containing fire (which is in constant danger of going out); in the other, a dried vinewood torch, not yet lit. Their progress toward the Akropolis is very slow.

KORYPHAIOS OF MEN
To the right guide of the First Semichorus, who is stumbling along in mild agony.
> Forward, Swifty, keep 'em in step! Forget your shoulder.
> I know these logs are green and heavy—but duty, boy, duty!

SWIFTY
Somewhat inspired, he quavers into slow song to set a pace for his group.
> I'm never surprised. At my age, life
> is just one damned thing after another.
> And yet, I never thought my wife
> was anything more than a home-grown bother.
> But now, dadblast her,
> she's a National Disaster!

FIRST SEMICHORUS OF MEN
> What a catastrophe—

MATRIARCHY!
They've brought Athene's statue* to heel,
they've put the Akropolis under a seal,
they've copped the whole damned commonweal . . .
What is there left for them to steal?

KORYPHAIOS OF MEN

To the right guide of the Second Semichorus—a slower soul, if possible, than Swifty.
Now, Chipper, speed's the word. The Akropolis, on the double!
Once we're there, we'll pile these logs around them, and convene
a circuit court for a truncated trial. Strictly impartial:
With a show of hands, we'll light a spark of justice under
every woman who brewed this scheme. We'll burn them all
on the first ballot—and the first to go is Ly. . .

Pause for thought.

is Ly. . .

Remembering and pointing at a spot in the audience.
is *Lykon's* wife—and there she is, right over there!*

CHIPPER

Taking up the song again.
I won't be twitted, I won't be guyed,
I'll teach these women not to trouble us!
Kleomenes the Spartan tried
expropriating our Akropolis*
some time ago—
ninety-five years or so—

SECOND SEMICHORUS OF MEN
but he suffered damaging losses
when he ran across US!
He breathed defiance—and more as well:
No bath for six years—you could tell.
We fished him out of the Citadel
and quelled his spirit—but not his smell.

KORYPHAIOS OF MEN
That's how I took him. A savage siege:
Seventeen ranks
of shields were massed at that gate, with blanket infantry cover.
I slept like a baby.
So when mere women (who gall the gods
and make Euripides sick) try the same trick, should I
sit idly by?
Then demolish the monument I won at Marathon!

FIRST SEMICHORUS OF MEN

Singly.

     —The last lap of our journey!
     —I greet it with some dismay.
     —The danger doesn't deter me,
            —but
it's uphill
    —all the way.
—Please, somebody,
     —find a jackass
to drag these logs
       —to the top.
    —I ache to join the fracas,
         —but
my shoulder's aching
       —to stop.

SWIFTY

    Backward there's no turning.
    Upward and onward, men!
    And keep those firepots burning, or
    we make this trip again.

CHORUS OF MEN

Blowing into their firepots, which promptly send forth clouds of smoke.
     With a puff (pfffff). . . .
     and a cough (hhhhhh). . . .
    The smoke! I'll choke! Turn it off!

SECOND SEMICHORUS OF MEN

Singly.

    —Damned embers.
        —Should be muzzled.
   —There oughta be a law.
   —They jumped me
       —when I whistled
          —and then
they gnawed my eyeballs
      —raw.
—There's lava in my lashes.
—My lids are oxidized.
—My brows are braised.
       —These ashes are
volcanoes
    —in disguise.

CHIPPER

This way, men. And remember,
the Goddess needs our aid.
So don't be stopped by cinders. Let's
press on to the stockade!

CHORUS OF MEN

Blowing again into their firepots, which erupt as before.

With a huff (hfffff). . . .
and a chuff (chffff). . . .
Drat that smoke. Enough is enough!

KORYPHAIOS OF MEN

*Signalling the Chorus, which has now tottered into position before the Akropolis gate, to
stop, and peering into his firepot.*

Praise be to the gods, it's awake. There's fire in the old fire yet.
—Now the directions. See how they strike you:

First, we deposit
these logs at the entrance and light our torches. Next, we crash
the gate. When that doesn't work, we request admission. Politely.
When *that* doesn't work, we burn the damned door down, and
smoke
these women into submission.

That seem acceptable? Good.
Down with the load. . .ouch, that smoke! Sonofabitch!

*A horrible tangle results as the Chorus attempts to deposit the logs. The Koryphaios turns
to the audience.*

Is there a general in the house? We have a logistical problem. . . .

No answer. He shrugs.

Same old story. Still at loggerheads over in Samos.*

With great confusion, the logs are placed somehow.

That's better. The pressure's off. I've got my backbone back.

To his firepot.

What, pot? You forgot your part in the plot?

Urge that smudge
to be hot on the dot and scorch my torch.

Got it, pot?

Praying.

Queen Athene, let these strumpets
crumple before our attack.
Grant us victory, male supremacy. . .
and a testimonial plaque.

*The men plunge their torches into firepots and arrange themselves purposefully before the
gate. Engaged in their preparations, they do not see the sudden entrance, from the right,*

of the Chorus of Women, led by their Koryphaios. These wear long cloaks and carry pitchers of water. They are very old—though not so old as the men—but quite spry. In their turn, they do not perceive the Chorus of Men.

KORYPHAIOS OF WOMEN

Stopping suddenly.

What's this—soot? And smoke as well? I may be all wet,
but this might mean fire. Things look dark, girls; we'll have to dash.

They move ahead, at a considerably faster pace than the men.

FIRST SEMICHORUS OF WOMEN

Singly.

Speed! Celerity!   Save our sorority
from arson. Combustion.   And heat exhaustion.
Don't let our sisterhood   shrivel to blisterhood.
    Fanned into slag by hoary typhoons.
    By flatulent, nasty, gusty baboons.
      We're late! Run!
      The girls might be done!

Tutte.

Filling my pitcher   was absolute torture:
The fountains in town   are so *crowded* at dawn,
glutted with masses   of the lower classes
blatting and battering,   shoving, and shattering
jugs. But I juggled   my burden, and wriggled
away to extinguish   the igneous anguish
    of neighbor, and sister, and daughter—
    Here's Water!

SECOND SEMICHORUS OF WOMEN

Singly.

Get wind of the news?   The gaffers are loose.
The blowhards are off   with fuel enough
to furnish a bathhouse.   But the finish is pathos:
    They're scaling the heights with a horrid proposal.
    They're threatening women with rubbish disposal!
      How ghastly—how gauche!
      burned up with the trash!

Tutte.

Preserve me, Athene,   from gazing on any
matron or maid   auto-da-fé'd.
Cover with grace   these redeemers of Greece
from battles, insanity,   Man's inhumanity.
Gold-browed goddess,   hither to aid us!
Fight as our ally,   join in our sally
    against pyromaniac slaughter—
    Haul Water!

KORYPHAIOS OF WOMEN

Noticing for the first time the Chorus of Men, still busy at their firepots, she cuts off a member of her Chorus who seems about to continue the song.

Hold it. What have we here? You don't catch true-blue patriots
red-handed. These are authentic degenerates, male, taken
in flagrante.

KORYPHAIOS OF MEN

Oops. Female troops. This could be upsetting.
I didn't expect such a flood of reserves.

KORYPHAIOS OF WOMEN

Merely a spearhead.
If our numbers stun you, watch that yellow streak spread. We
represent just one percent of one percent of This Woman's Army.

KORYPHAIOS OF MEN

Never been confronted with such backtalk. Can't allow it. Somebody
pick up a log and pulverize that brass.

Any volunteers?

There are none among the male chorus.

KORYPHAIOS OF WOMEN

Put down the pitchers, girls. If they start waving that lumber,
we don't want to be encumbered.

KORYPHAIOS OF MEN

Look, men, a few sharp jabs
will stop that jawing. It never fails.

The poet Hipponax
swears by it.*

Still no volunteers. The Koryphaios of Women advances.

KORYPHAIOS OF WOMEN

Then step right up. Have a jab at me.
Free shot.

KORYPHAIOS OF MEN

Advancing reluctantly to meet her.

Shut up! I'll peel your pelt. I'll pit your pod.

KORYPHAIOS OF WOMEN

The name is Stratyllis. I dare you to lay one finger on me.

KORYPHAIOS OF MEN

I'll lay on you with a fistful. Er—any specific threats?

KORYPHAIOS OF WOMEN

Earnestly.

I'll crop your lungs and reap your bowels, bite by bite,
and leave no balls on the body for other bitches to gnaw.*

KORYPHAIOS OF MEN

Retreating hurriedly.

Can't beat Euripides for insight. And I quote:

No creature's found

so lost to shame as Woman.*

Talk about realist playwrights!

KORYPHAIOS OF WOMEN

Up with the water, ladies. Pitchers at the ready, place!

KORYPHAIOS OF MEN

Why the water, you sink of iniquity? More sedition?

KORYPHAIOS OF WOMEN

Why the fire, you walking boneyard? Self-cremation?

KORYPHAIOS OF MEN

I brought this fire to ignite a pyre and fricassee your friends.

KORYPHAIOS OF WOMEN

I brought this water to douse your pyre. Tit for tat.

KORYPHAIOS OF MEN

You'll douse my fire? Nonsense!

KORYPHAIOS OF WOMEN

You'll see, when the facts soak in.

KORYPHAIOS OF MEN

I have the torch right here. Perhaps I should barbecue *you*.

KORYPHAIOS OF WOMEN

If you have any soap, I could give you a bath.

KORYPHAIOS OF MEN

A bath from those

polluted hands?

KORYPHAIOS OF WOMEN

Pure enough for a blushing young bridegroom.

KORYPHAIOS OF MEN

Enough of that insolent lip.

KORYPHAIOS OF WOMEN

It's merely freedom of speech.

KORYPHAIOS OF MEN

I'll stop that screeching!

KORYPHAIOS OF WOMEN

You're helpless outside of the jury-box.

KORYPHAIOS OF MEN

Urging his men, torches at the ready, into a charge.

Burn, fire, burn!

KORYPHAIOS OF WOMEN

As the women empty their pitchers over the men.

And cauldron bubble.

KORYPHAIOS OF MEN

Like his troops, soaked and routed.

Arrrgh!

KORYPHAIOS OF WOMEN

Goodness.

What seems to be the trouble? Too hot?

KORYPHAIOS OF MEN

Hot, hell! Stop it!

What do you think you're doing?

KORYPHAIOS OF WOMEN

If you must know, I'm gardening.

Perhaps you'll bloom.

KORYPHAIOS OF MEN

Perhaps I'll fall right off the vine!

I'm withered, frozen, shaking. . .

KORYPHAIOS OF WOMEN

Of course. But, providentially,

you brought along your smudgepot.

The sap should rise eventually.

Shivering, the Chorus of Men retreats in utter defeat.

A Commissioner of Public Safety* enters from the left, followed quite reluctantly by a squad of police—four Skythian archers. He surveys the situation with disapproval.

COMMISSIONER

Fire, eh? Females again—spontaneous combustion
of lust. Suspected as much.

Rubadubdubbing, incessant
incontinent keening for wine, damnable funeral
foofaraw for Adonis resounding from roof to roof—
heard it all before. . .

Savagely, as the Koryphaios of Men tries to interpose a remark.

and WHERE?

The ASSEMBLY!

Recall, if you can, the debate on the Sicilian Question:
That bullbrained demagogue Demostratos (who will rot, I trust)
rose to propose a naval task force.

His wife,
writhing with religion on a handy roof, bleated
a dirge:

"BEREFT! OH WOE OH WOE FOR ADONIS!"
And so of course Demostratos, taking his cue,
outblatted her:
  "A DRAFT! ENROLL THE WHOLE OF
 ZAKYNTHOS!"
His wife, a smidgin stewed, renewed her yowling:
"OH GNASH YOUR TEETH AND BEAT YOUR BREASTS
FOR ADONIS!"
And so of course Demostratos (that god-detested blot,
that foul-lunged son of an ulcer) gnashed tooth and nail
and voice, and bashed and rammed his program through.
And THERE is the Gift of Women:
  MORAL CHAOS!

KORYPHAIOS OF MEN
Save your breath for actual felonies, Commissioner;
see what's happened to us! Insolence, insults,
these we pass over, but not lese-majesty:
  We're flooded
with indignity from those bitches' pitchers—like a bunch
of weak-bladdered brats. Our cloaks are sopped. We'll sue!

COMMISSIONER
Useless. Your suit won't hold water. Right's on their side.
For female depravity, gentlemen, WE stand guilty—
we, their teachers, preceptors of prurience, accomplices
before the fact of fornication. We sowed them in sexual
license, and now we reap rebellion.
  The proof?
Consider. Off we trip to the goldsmith's to leave
an order:
  "That bangle you fashioned last spring for my wife
 is sprung. She was thrashing around last night, and the prong
 popped out of the bracket. I'll be tied up all day—I'm
 boarding the ferry right now—but my wife'll be home.
 If you get the time, please stop by the house in a bit
 and see if you can't do something—anything—to fit
 a new prong into the bracket of her bangle."
  And bang.
Another one ups to a cobbler—young, but no apprentice,
full kit of tools, ready to give his awl—
and delivers this gem:
  "My wife's new sandals are tight.
 The cinch pinches her pinkie right where she's sensitive.
 Drop in at noon with something to stretch her cinch
 and give it a little play."

And a cinch it is.
Such hanky-panky we have to thank for today's
Utter Anarchy: I, a Commissioner of Public
Safety, duly invested with extraordinary powers
to protect the State in the Present Emergency, have secured
a source of timber to outfit our fleet and solve
the shortage of oarage. I need the money immediately. . .
and WOMEN, no less, have locked me out of the Treasury!

Pulling himself together.

—Well, no profit in standing around.

To one of the archers.

Bring
the crowbars. I'll jack these women back on their pedestals!
—WELL, you slack-jawed jackass? What's the attraction?
Wipe that thirst off your face. I said *crow*bar, not saloon!
—All right, men, all together. Shove those bars
underneath the gate and HEAVE!

Grabbing up a crowbar.

I'll take this side.
And now let's root them out, men, ROOT them out.
One, Two. . .

The gates to the Akropolis burst open suddenly, disclosing Lysistrata. She is perfectly composed and bears a large spindle. The Commissioner and the Police fall back in consternation.

LYSISTRATA

Why the moving equipment?
I'm quite well motivated, thank you, and here I am.
Frankly, you don't need crowbars nearly so much as brains.

COMMISSIONER

Brains? O name of infamy! Where's a policeman?

He grabs wildly for the First Archer and shoves him toward Lysistrata.

Arrest that woman!
Better tie her hands behind her.

LYSISTRATA

By Artemis, goddess of the hunt, if he lays a finger
on me, he'll rue the day he joined the force!

She jabs the spindle viciously at the First Archer, who leaps, terrified, back to his comrades.

COMMISSIONER

What's this—retreat? Never! Take her on the flank.

The First Archer hangs back. The Commissioner grabs the Second Archer.

—Help him.

—Will the two of you kindly TIE HER UP?

He shoves them toward Lysistrata. Kleonike, carrying a large chamber pot, springs out of the entrance and advances on the Second Archer.

KLEONIKE

By Artemis, goddess of the dew,* if you so much
as touch her, I'll stomp the shit right out of you!

The two Archers run back to their group.

COMMISSIONER

Shit? Shameless! Where's another policeman?

He grabs the Third Archer and propels him toward Kleonike.

Handcuff *her* first. Can't stand a foul-mouthed female.

Myrrhine, carrying a large, blazing lamp, appears at the entrance and advances on the Third Archer.

MYRRHINE

By Artemis, bringer of light, if you lay a finger
on her, you won't be able to stop the swelling!

The Third Archer dodges her swing and runs back to the group.

COMMISSIONER

Now what? Where's an officer?

Pushing the Fourth Archer toward Myrrhine.

Apprehend that woman!
I'll see that *somebody* stays to take the blame!

Ismenia the Boiotian, carrying a huge pair of pincers, appears at the entrance and advances on the Fourth Archer.

ISMENIA*

By Artemis, goddess of Tauris, if you go near
that girl, I'll rip the hair right out of your head!

The Fourth Archer retreats hurriedly.

COMMISSIONER

What a colossal mess: Athens' Finest—
finished!

Arranging the Archers.

—Now, men, a little *esprit de corps.* Worsted
by women? Drubbed by drabs?

Never!

Regroup,
reform that thin red line.
Ready?
CHARGE!

He pushes them ahead of him.

LYSISTRATA
I warn you. We have four battalions behind us—
full-armed combat infantrywomen, trained
from the cradle. . .

COMMISSIONER
Disarm them, Officers! Go for the hands!

LYSISTRATA
Calling inside the Akropolis.

MOBILIZE THE RESERVES!

A horde of women, armed with household articles, begins to pour from the Akropolis.
Onward, you ladies from hell!
Forward, you market militia, you battle-hardened
bargain hunters, old sales campaigners, grocery
grenadiers, veterans never bested by an overcharge!
You troops of the breadline, doughgirls—
INTO THE FRAY!

Show them no mercy!
Push!
Jostle!
Shove!
Call them nasty names!
Don't be ladylike.
The women charge and rout the Archers in short order.
Fall back—don't strip the enemy! The day is ours!
The women obey, and the Archers run off left. The Commissioner, dazed, is left muttering to himself.

COMMISSIONER
Gross ineptitude. A sorry day for the Force.

LYSISTRATA
Of course. What did you expect? We're not slaves;
we're freeborn Women, and when we're scorned, we're full
of fury. Never Underestimate the Power of a Woman.

COMMISSIONER
Power? You mean Capacity. I should have remembered
the proverb: *The lower the tavern, the higher the dudgeon.*

KORYPHAIOS OF MEN

Why cast your pearls before swine, Commissioner? I know you're
a civil

servant, but don't overdo it. Have you forgotten the bath
they gave us—in public,
fully dressed,
totally soapless?
Keep rational discourse for *people!*

He aims a blow at the Koryphaios of Women, who dodges and raises her pitcher.

KORYPHAIOS OF WOMEN

I might point out that lifting
one's hand against a neighbor is scarcely civilized behavior—
and entails, for the lifter, a black eye.
I'm really peaceful by nature,
compulsively inoffensive—a perfect doll. My ideal is a well-bred
repose that doesn't even stir up dust. . .

Swinging at the Koryphaios of Men with the pitcher.

unless some no-good lowlife
tries to rifle my hive and gets my dander up!

The Koryphaios of Men backs hurriedly away, and the Chorus of Men goes into a worried dance.

CHORUS OF MEN

Singly.

O Zeus, what's the use of this constant abuse?
How do we deal with this female zoo?
Is there no solution to Total Immersion?
What can a poor man DO?

Tutti.

Query the Adversary!
Ferret out their story!
What end did they have in view,
to seize the city's sanctuary,
snatch its legendary eyrie,
snare an area so very
terribly taboo?

KORYPHAIOS OF MEN

To the Commissioner.

Scrutinize those women! Scour their depositions—assess
their rebuttals!
Masculine honor demands this affair be probed to the
bottom!

COMMISSIONER

Turning to the women from the Akropolis.

All right, you. Kindly inform me, dammit, in your own words:
What possible object could you have had in blockading the
    Treasury?

LYSISTRATA

We thought we'd deposit the money in escrow and withdraw you
    men
from the war.

COMMISSIONER

          The money's the cause of the war?

LYSISTRATA

                  And all our internal
disorders—the Body Politic's chronic bellyaches: What causes
Peisandros' frantic rantings, or the raucous caucuses of the Friends
of Oligarchy?* The chance for graft.
              But now, with the money up there,
they can't upset the City's equilibrium—or lower its balance.

COMMISSIONER

And what's your next step?

LYSISTRATA

             Stupid question. We'll budget the money.

COMMISSIONER

You'll budget the money?

LYSISTRATA

           Why should you find that so shocking?
We budget the household accounts, and you don't object at all.

COMMISSIONER

That's different.

LYSISTRATA

      Different? How?

COMMISSIONER

         The War Effort needs this money!

LYSISTRATA

Who needs the War Effort?

COMMISSIONER

        Every patriot who pulses to save
all that Athens holds near and dear. . .

LYSISTRATA

        Oh, *that*. Don't worry.
We'll save you.

COMMISSIONER

You will save us?

LYSISTRATA

Who else?

COMMISSIONER

But this is unscrupulous!

LYSISTRATA

We'll save you. You can't deter us.

COMMISSIONER

Scurrilous!

LYSISTRATA

You seem disturbed.
This makes it difficult. But, still—we'll save you.

COMMISSIONER

Doubtless illegal!

LYSISTRATA

We deem it a duty. For friendship's sake.

COMMISSIONER

Well, forsake this friend:
I DO NOT WANT TO BE SAVED, DAMMIT!

LYSISTRATA

All the more reason.
It's not only Sparta; now we'll have to save you from *you*.

COMMISSIONER

Might I ask where you women conceived this concern about War
and Peace?

LYSISTRATA

Loftily.

We shall explain.

COMMISSIONER

Making a fist.

Hurry up, and you won't
get hurt.

LYSISTRATA

Then *listen*. And do try to keep your hands to yourself.

COMMISSIONER

Moving threateningly toward her.

I can't. Righteous anger forbids restraint, and decrees. . .

KLEONIKE

Brandishing her chamber pot.

Multiple fractures?

40

COMMISSIONER

Retreating.

> Keep those croaks for yourself, you old crow!

To Lysistrata.

> All right, lady, I'm ready. Speak.

LYSISTRATA

> I shall proceed:

When the War began, like the prudent, dutiful wives that we are,
we tolerated you men, and endured your actions in silence. (Small
   wonder—
you wouldn't let us say boo.)

> You were not precisely the answer

to a matron's prayer—we knew you too well, and found out more.
Too many times, as we sat in the house, we'd hear that you'd done it
again—manhandled another affair of state with your usual
staggering incompetence. Then, masking our worry with a nervous
   laugh,
we'd ask you, brightly, "How was the Assembly today, dear?
   Anything
in the minutes about Peace?" And my husband would give
his stock reply.
"What's that to you? Shut up!" And I did.

KLEONIKE

Proudly.

> *I* never shut up!

COMMISSIONER

I trust you were shut up. Soundly.

LYSISTRATA

> Regardless, *I* shut up.

And then we'd learn that you'd passed another decree, fouler
than the first, and we'd ask again: "Darling, how *did* you manage
anything so idiotic?" And my husband, with his customary glare,
would tell me to spin my thread, or else get a clout on the head.
And of course he'd quote from Homer:

> *Ye menne must husband ye warre.* *

COMMISSIONER

Apt and irrefutably right.

LYSISTRATA

> *Right,* you miserable misfit?

To keep us from giving advice while you fumbled the City away
in the Senate? Right, indeed!

> But this time was really too much:

Wherever we went, we'd hear you engaged in the same conversation:

"What Athens needs is a Man."*

"But there isn't a Man in the country."

"You can say that again."

There was obviously no time to lose.
We women met in immediate convention and passed a unanimous
resolution: To work in concert for safety and Peace in Greece.
We have valuable advice to impart, and if you can possibly
deign to emulate our silence, and take your turn as audience,
we'll rectify you—we'll straighten you out and set you right.

COMMISSIONER

You'll set *us* right? You go too far. I cannot permit
such a statement to. . .

LYSISTRATA

Shush.

COMMISSIONER

I categorically decline to shush
for some confounded woman, who wears—as a constant reminder
of congenital inferiority, an injunction to public silence—a veil!
Death before such dishonor!

LYSISTRATA

Removing her veil.

If that's the only obstacle. . .
I feel you need a new panache,
so take the veil, my dear Commissioner, and drape it thus—

and SHUSH!

*As she winds the veil around the startled Commissioner's head, Kleonike and Myrrhine,
with carding-comb and wool-basket, rush forward and assist in transforming him into a
woman.*

KLEONIKE

Accept, I pray, this humble comb.

MYRRHINE

Receive this basket of fleece as well.

LYSISTRATA

Hike up your skirts, and card your wool,
and gnaw your beans—and stay at home!
While we rewrite Homer:
Yᵉ WOMEN must WIVE yᵉ warre!

To the Chorus of Women, as the Commissioner struggles to remove his new outfit.
Women, weaker vessels, arise!

Put down your pitchers.
It's our turn, now. Let's supply our friends with some moral support.

The Chorus of Women dances to the same tune as the Men, but with much more confidence.

CHORUS OF WOMEN

Singly.

> Oh, yes! I'll dance to bless their success.
> Fatigue won't weaken my will. Or my knees.
> I'm ready to join in any jeopardy,
> > with girls as good as *these!*

Tutte.

> A tally of their talents
> convinces me they're giants
> of excellence. To commence:
> there's Beauty, Duty, Prudence, Science,
> Self-Reliance, Compliance, Defiance,
> and Love of Athens in balanced alliance
> > with Common Sense!

KORYPHAIOS OF WOMEN

To the women from the Akropolis.

> Autochthonous daughters of Attika, sprung from the soil that bore
> your mothers, the spiniest, spikiest nettles known to man,
> prove your mettle and attack! Now is no time to dilute your
> anger. You're running ahead of the wind!

LYSISTRATA

> We'll wait for the wind
> from heaven. The gentle breath of Love and his Kyprian mother
> will imbue our bodies with desire, and raise a storm to tense
> and tauten these blasted men until they crack. And soon
> we'll be on every tongue in Greece—the *Pacifiers.**

COMMISSIONER

> That's quite
> a mouthful. How will you win it?

LYSISTRATA

> First, we intend to withdraw
> that crazy Army of Occupation from the downtown shopping section.

KLEONIKE

Aphrodite be praised!

LYSISTRATA

> The pottery shop and the grocery stall
> are overstocked with soldiers, clanking around like those maniac
> > Korybants,
> armed to the teeth for a battle.

COMMISSIONER

> A Hero is Always Prepared!

LYSISTRATA
I suppose he is. But it does look silly to shop for sardines
from behind a shield.

KLEONIKE
                 I'll second that. I saw
a cavalry captain buy vegetable soup on horseback. He carried
the whole mess home in his helmet.
                              And then that fellow from Thrace,
shaking his buckler and spear—a menace straight from the stage.
The saleslady was stiff with fright. He was hogging her ripe figs—
    free.

COMMISSIONER
I admit, for the moment, that Hellas' affairs are in one hell of
a snarl. But how can you set them straight?

LYSISTRATA
                           Simplicity itself.

COMMISSIONER
Pray demonstrate.

LYSISTRATA
               It's rather like yarn. When a hank's in a tangle,
we lift it—so—and work out the snarls by winding it up
on spindles, now this way, now that way.
                      That's how we'll wind up the War,
if allowed: We'll work out the snarls by sending Special
    Commissions—
back and forth, now this way, now that way—to ravel these tense
international kinks.

COMMISSIONER
              I lost your thread, but I know there's a hitch.
Spruce up the world's disasters with spindles—typically woolly
female logic.

LYSISTRATA
          If *you* had a scrap of logic, you'd adopt
our wool as a master plan for Athens.

COMMISSIONER
                   What course of action
does the wool advise?

LYSISTRATA
           Consider the City as fleece, recently
shorn. The first step is Cleansing: Scrub it in a public bath,
and remove all corruption, offal, and sheepdip.
                     Next, to the couch
for Scutching and Plucking: Cudgel the leeches and similar vermin

loose with a club, then pick the prickles and cockleburs out.
As for the clots—those lumps that clump and cluster in knots
and snarls to snag important posts*—you comb these out,
twist off their heads, and discard.

> Next, to raise the City's
nap, you card the citizens together in a single basket
of common weal and general welfare. Fold in our loyal
Resident Aliens, all Foreigners of proven and tested friendship,
and any Disenfranchised Debtors. Combine these closely with the
  rest.
Lastly, cull the colonies settled by our own people:
these are nothing but flocks of wool from the City's fleece,
scattered throughout the world. So gather home these far-flung
flocks, amalgamate them with the others.

> Then, drawing this blend
of stable fibers into one fine staple, you spin a mighty
bobbin of yarn—and weave, without bias or seam, a cloak
to clothe the City of Athens!

COMMISSIONER

> This is too much! The City's
died in the wool, worsted by the distaff side—by women
who bore no share in the War. . . .

LYSISTRATA

> None, you hopeless hypocrite?
The quota we bear is double. First, we delivered our sons
to fill out the front lines in Sicily . . .

COMMISSIONER

> Don't tax me with that memory.

LYSISTRATA

Next, the best years of our lives were levied. Top-level strategy
attached our joy, and we sleep alone.

> But it's not the matrons
like us who matter. I mourn for the virgins, bedded in single
blessedness, with nothing to do but grow old.

COMMISSIONER

> Men *have* been known
to age, as well as women.

LYSISTRATA

> No, not as well as—better.
A man, an absolute antique, comes back from the war, and he's
  barely
doddered into town before he's married the veriest nymphet.
But a woman's season is brief; it slips, and she'll have no husband,
but sit out her life groping at omens—and finding no men.

45

COMMISSIONER
Lamentable state of affairs. Perhaps we can rectify matters:

*To the audience.**

TO EVERY MAN JACK, A CHALLENGE:
ARISE!

Provided you can. . .

LYSISTRATA
Instead, Commissioner, why not simply curl up and *die?*
Just buy a coffin; here's the place.

*Banging him on the head with her spindle.**
I'll knead you a cake for the wake—and *these*

Winding the threads from the spindle around him.
make excellent wreaths. So Rest In Peace.

KLEONIKE

Emptying the chamber pot over him.
Accept these tokens of deepest grief.

MYRRHINE

Breaking her lamp over his head.
A final garland for the dear deceased.

LYSISTRATA
May I supply any last request?
Then run along. You're due at the wharf:
Charon's anxious to sail—
you're holding up the boat for Hell!

COMMISSIONER
This is monstrous—maltreatment of a public official—
maltreatment of ME!
I must repair directly
to the Board of Commissioners, and present my colleagues concrete
evidence of the sorry specifics of this shocking attack!

He staggers off left. Lysistrata calls after him.

LYSISTRATA
You won't haul us into court on a charge of neglecting
the dead, will you? (How like a man to insist
on his rights—even his last ones.) Two days between death
and funeral, that's the rule.
Come back here early
day after tomorrow, Commissioner:
We'll lay you out.

Lysistrata and her women re-enter the Akropolis. The Koryphaios of Men advances to address the audience.

KORYPHAIOS OF MEN
Wake up, Athenians! Preserve your freedom—the time is Now!
To the Chorus of Men.
Strip for action, men. Let's cope with the current mess.
The men put off their long mantles, disclosing short tunics underneath, and advance toward the audience.

CHORUS OF MEN
This trouble may be terminal; it has a loaded odor,
an ominous aroma of constitutional rot.
My nose gives a prognosis of radical disorder—
it's just the first installment of an absolutist plot!
The Spartans are behind it:
they must have masterminded
some morbid local contacts (engineered by Kleisthenes).
Predictably infected,
these women straightway acted
to commandeer the City's cash. They're feverish to freeze
my be-all,
my end-all. . .
my *payroll!**

KORYPHAIOS OF MEN
The symptoms are clear. Our birthright's already nibbled. And
oh, so
daintily: WOMEN ticking off troops* for improper etiquette.
WOMEN propounding their featherweight views on the fashionable
use
and abuse of the shield. And (if any more proof were needed)
WOMEN
nagging us to trust the Nice Spartan, and put our heads
in his toothy maw—to make a dessert and call it Peace.
They've woven the City a seamless shroud, bedecked with the
legend
DICTATORSHIP.
But I won't be hemmed in. I'll use their weapon
against them, and uphold the right by sneakiness.
With knyf under cloke,
gauntlet in glove, sword in olivebranch,
Slipping slowly toward the Koryphaios of Women.
I'll take up my post
in Statuary Row, beside our honored National Heroes,
the natural foes of tyranny: Harmodios,
Aristogeiton,
and Me.*

Next to her.

> Striking an epic pose, so, with the full approval
> of the immortal gods,
>
> > I'll bash this loathsome hag in the jaw!

He does, and runs cackling back to the Men. She shakes a fist after him.

KORYPHAIOS OF WOMEN

Mama won't know her little boy when he gets home!

To the Women, who are eager to launch a full-scale attack.

> Let's not be hasty, fellow. . . hags. Cloaks off first.

The Women remove their mantles, disclosing tunics very like those of the Men, and advance toward the audience.

CHORUS OF WOMEN

> We'll address you, citizens, in beneficial, candid,
> > patriotic accents, as our breeding says we must,
> since, from the age of seven, Athens graced me with a splendid
> > string of civic triumphs to signalize her trust:
> > > I was Relic-Girl quite early,
> > > > then advanced to Maid of Barley;
> in Artemis' "Pageant of the Bear" I played the lead.
> > To cap this proud progression,*
> > I led the whole procession
> at Athene's Celebration, certified and pedigreed
> > > —that cachet
> > > so distingué—
> > > a *Lady!*

KORYPHAIOS OF WOMEN

To the audience.

> I trust this establishes my qualifications. I may, I take it, address
> the City to its profit? Thank you.
> > > I admit to being a woman—
> but don't sell my contribution short on that account. It's better
> than the present panic. And my word is as good as my bond,
> because I hold stock in Athens—stock I paid for in sons.

To the Chorus of Men.

> —But you, you doddering bankrupts, where are your shares in the
> > State?

Slipping slowly toward the Koryphaios of Men.

> Your grandfathers willed you the Mutual Funds from the Persian
> > War*—
> and where are they?

48

Nearer.

You dipped into capital, then lost interest . . .
and now a pool of your assets won't fill a hole in the ground.
All that remains is one last potential killing—Athens.
Is there any rebuttal?

The Koryphaios of Men gestures menacingly. She ducks down, as if to ward off a blow, and removes a slipper.

Force is a footling resort. I'll take
my very sensible shoe, and paste you in the jaw!

She does so, and runs back to the women.

CHORUS OF MEN

Their native respect for our manhood is small,
and keeps getting smaller. Let's bottle their gall.
The man who won't battle has no balls at all!

KORYPHAIOS OF MEN

All right, men, skin out of the skivvies. Let's give them a whiff
of Man, full strength. No point in muffling the essential Us.

The men remove their tunics.

CHORUS OF MEN

A century back, we soared to the Heights*
and beat down Tyranny there.
Now's the time to shed our moults
and fledge our wings once more,
to rise to the skies in our reborn force,
and beat back Tyranny here!

KORYPHAIOS OF MEN

No fancy grappling with these grannies; straightforward strength.
The tiniest
toehold, and those nimble, fiddling fingers will have their foot
in the door, and we're done for.
*No amount of know-how can lick
a woman's knack.*

They'll want to build ships . . . next thing we
know,
we're all at sea, fending off female boarding parties.
(Artemisia fought us at Salamis. Tell me, has anyone caught her
yet?)

But we're *really* sunk if they take up horses. Scratch
the Cavalry:
A woman is an easy rider with a natural seat.

Take her over the jumps bareback, and she'll never slip
her mount. (That's how the Amazons nearly took Athens. On
   horseback.
Check on Mikon's mural down in the Stoa.)
                                     Anyway,
the solution is obvious. Put every woman in her place—stick her
in the stocks.
                  To do this, first snare your woman around the neck.

He attempts to demonstrate on the Koryphaios of Women. After a brief tussle, she works loose and chases him back to the Men.

CHORUS OF WOMEN

      The beast in me's eager and fit for a brawl.
      Just rile me a bit and she'll kick down the wall.
      You'll bawl to your friends that you've no balls at all.

KORYPHAIOS OF WOMEN

All right, ladies, strip for action. Let's give them a whiff
of *Femme Enragée*—piercing and pungent, but not at all tart.

The women remove their tunics.

CHORUS OF WOMEN

      We're angry. The brainless bird who tangles
          with *us* has gummed his last mush.
      In fact, the coot who even heckles
          is being daringly rash.
      So look to your nests, you reclaimed eagles—
          whatever you lay, we'll squash!

KORYPHAIOS OF WOMEN

Frankly, you don't faze me. *With* me, I have my friends—
Lampito from Sparta; that genteel girl from Thebes, Ismenia—
committed to me forever. *Against* me, *you*—permanently
out of commission. So do your damnedest.
                             Pass a law.
Pass seven. Continue the winning ways that have made your name
a short and ugly household word.
                    Like yesterday:
I was giving a little party, nothing fussy, to honor
the goddess Hekate. Simply to please my daughters, I'd invited
a sweet little thing from the neighborhood—flawless pedigree,
   perfect
taste, a credit to any gathering—a Boiotian eel.
But she had to decline. Couldn't pass the border. You'd passed a
   law.

Not that you care for my party. You'll overwork your right of
>passage
till your august body is overturned,

>>>>and you break your silly neck!

She deftly grabs the Koryphaios of Men by the ankle and upsets him. He scuttles back to the Men, who retire in confusion.

Lysistrata emerges from the citadel, obviously distraught.

KORYPHAIOS OF WOMEN

Mock-tragic.

>*Mistress, queen of this our subtle scheme,*
>*why burst you from the hall with brangled brow?*

LYSISTRATA

>*Oh, wickedness of woman! The female mind*
>*does sap my soul and set my wits a-totter.*

KORYPHAIOS OF WOMEN
>*What drear accents are these?*

LYSISTRATA

>>*The merest truth.*

KORYPHAIOS OF WOMEN
>*Be nothing loath to tell the tale to friends.*

LYSISTRATA
>*'Twere shame to utter, pain to hold unsaid.*

KORYPHAIOS OF WOMEN
>*Hide not from me affliction which we share.*

LYSISTRATA
>*In briefest compass,*

Dropping the paratragedy.

>>we want to get laid.

KORYPHAIOS OF WOMEN

>>>By Zeus!

LYSISTRATA
No, no, not HIM!

>>Well, that's the way things are.
I've lost my grip on the girls—they're mad for men!
But sly—they slip out in droves.

>>>A minute ago,
I caught one scooping out the little hole
that breaks through just below Pan's grotto.*

>>>>One
had jerry-rigged some block-and-tackle business
and was wriggling away on a rope.

Another just flat
deserted.

Last night I spied one mounting a sparrow,
all set to take off for the nearest bawdyhouse. I hauled
her back by the hair.

And excuses, pretexts for overnight
passes? I've heard them all.

Here comes one. Watch.

To the First Woman, as she runs out of the Akropolis.
—You, there! What's your hurry?

FIRST WOMAN

I have to get home.
I've got all this lovely Milesian wool in the house,
and the moths will simply batter it to bits!

LYSISTRATA

I'll bet.

Get back inside.

FIRST WOMAN

I swear I'll hurry right back!
—Just time enough to spread it out on the couch?

LYSISTRATA
Your wool will stay unspread. And you'll stay here.

FIRST WOMAN
Do I have to let my piecework *rot?*

LYSISTRATA

Possibly.

The Second Woman runs on.

SECOND WOMAN
Oh dear, oh goodness, what shall I do—my flax!
I left and forgot to peel it!

LYSISTRATA

Another one.
She suffers from unpeeled flax.

—Get back inside!

SECOND WOMAN
I'll be right back. I just have to pluck the fibers.

LYSISTRATA
No. No plucking. You start it, and everyone else
will want to go and do their plucking, too.

The Third Woman, swelling conspicuously, hurries on, praying loudly.

THIRD WOMAN
O Goddess of Childbirth, grant that I not deliver
until I get me from out this sacred precinct!

LYSISTRATA
What sort of nonsense is *this?*

THIRD WOMAN
      I'm due—any second!

LYSISTRATA
You weren't pregnant yesterday.

THIRD WOMAN
      Today I am—
a miracle!
   Let me go home for a midwife, *please!*
I may not make it!

LYSISTRATA
Restraining her.
      You can do better than that.
Tapping the woman's stomach and receiving a metallic clang.
What's this? It's hard.

THIRD WOMAN
      I'm going to have a boy.

LYSISTRATA
Not unless he's made of bronze. Let's see.
She throws open the Third Woman's cloak, exposing a huge bronze helmet.
Of all the brazen. . . You've stolen the helmet from Athene's
statue! Pregnant, indeed!

THIRD WOMAN
      I am *so* pregnant!

LYSISTRATA
Then why the helmet?

THIRD WOMAN
      I thought my time might come
while I was still on forbidden ground. If it did,
I could climb inside Athene's helmet and have
my baby there.
    The pigeons do it all the time.

LYSISTRATA
Nothing but excuses!
Taking the helmet.
      This is your baby. I'm afraid
you'll have to stay until we give it a name.

THIRD WOMAN
But the Akropolis is *awful*. I can't even sleep! I saw
the snake that guards the temple.

LYSISTRATA
                                    That snake's a fabrication.*

THIRD WOMAN
I don't care *what* kind it is—I'm *scared!*

The other women, who have emerged from the citadel, crowd around.

KLEONIKE
And those goddamned holy owls! All night long,
tu-wit, tu-wu—they're hooting me into my grave!

LYSISTRATA
Darlings, let's call a halt to this hocus-pocus.
You miss your men—now isn't that the trouble?

Shamefaced nods from the group.

Don't you think they miss you just as much?
I can assure you, their nights are every bit
as hard as yours. So be good girls; endure!
Persist a few days more, and Victory is ours.
It's fated: a current prophecy declares that the men
will go down to defeat before us, provided that *we*
maintain a United Front.

Producing a scroll.

                                    I happen to have
a copy of the prophecy.

KLEONIKE
                        Read it!

LYSISTRATA
                                Silence, *please*:

Reading from the scroll.

**But when the swallows, in flight from the
    hoopoes, have flocked to a hole
on high, and stoutly eschew their
    accustomed perch on the pole,
yea, then shall Thunderer Zeus to
    their suff'ring establish a stop,
by making the lower the upper. . .**

KLEONIKE
Then *we'll* be lying on top?

54

LYSISTRATA

But should these swallows, indulging their
  lust for the perch, lose heart,
dissolve their flocks in winged dissension,
  and singly depart
the sacred stronghold, breaking the
  bands that bind them together—
then know them as lewd, the pervertedest
  birds that ever wore feather.

KLEONIKE

There's nothing obscure about *that* oracle. Ye gods!

LYSISTRATA

Sorely beset as we are, we must not flag
or falter. So back to the citadel!

As the women troop inside.

                    And if we fail
that oracle, darlings, our image is absolutely *mud!*

She follows them in. A pause, and the Choruses assemble.

CHORUS OF MEN

                    I have a simple
                    tale to relate you,
                    a sterling example
                    of masculine virtue:

            The huntsman bold Melanion
              was once a harried quarry.
            The women in town tracked him down
              and badgered him to marry.

            Melanion knew the cornered male
              eventually cohabits.
            Assessing the odds, he took to the woods
              and lived by trapping rabbits.

            He stuck to the virgin stand, sustained
              by rabbit meat and hate,
          and never returned, but ever remained
              an alfresco celibate.

            Melanion is our ideal;
              his loathing makes us free.
            Our dearest aim is the gemlike flame
              of his misogyny.

OLD MAN

            Let me kiss that wizened cheek. . . .

OLD WOMAN

Threatening with a fist.
> A wish too rash for that withered flesh.

OLD MAN
> and lay you low with a highflying kick.

He tries one and misses.

OLD WOMAN
> Exposing an overgrown underbrush.

OLD MAN
> A hairy behind, historically, means
>> masculine force: Myronides
> harassed the foe with his mighty mane,
>> and furry Phormion swept the seas
>> of enemy ships, never meeting his match—
>> such was the nature of his thatch.

CHORUS OF WOMEN
>> I offer an anecdote
>> for your opinion,
>> an adequate antidote
>> for your Melanion:

>> Timon, the noted local grouch,
>> put rusticating hermits
> out of style by building his wilds
>> inside the city limits.

>> He shooed away society
>> with natural battlements:
> his tongue was edgèd; his shoulder, frigid;
>> his beard, a picket fence.

>> When random contacts overtaxed him,
>> he didn't stop to pack,
> but loaded curses on the male of the species,
>> left town, and never came back.

>> Timon, you see, was a misanthrope
>> in a properly narrow sense:
> his spleen was vented only on men. . .
>> *we* were his dearest friends.

OLD WOMAN

Making a fist.
>> Enjoy a chop to that juiceless chin?

OLD MAN

Backing away.

> I'm jolted already. Thank you, no.

OLD WOMAN

> Perhaps a trip from a well-turned shin?

She tries a kick and misses.

OLD MAN

> Brazenly baring the mantrap below.

OLD WOMAN

At least it's *neat*. I'm not too sorry
   to have you see my daintiness.
My habits are still depilatory;
   age hasn't made me a bristly mess.
      Secure in my smoothness, I'm never in doubt—
         though even down is out.

Lysistrata mounts the platform and scans the horizon. When her gaze reaches the left, she stops suddenly.

LYSISTRATA

Ladies, attention! Battle stations, please!
And quickly!

A general rush of women to the battlements.

KLEONIKE

> What is it?

MYRRHINE

> > What's all the shouting for?

LYSISTRATA

A MAN!

Consternation.

> Yes, it's a man. And he's coming this way!.
Hmm. Seems to have suffered a seizure. Broken out
with a nasty attack of love.

Prayer, aside.

> > O Aphrodite,
> > Mistress all-victorious,
> > mysterious, voluptuous,
> > you who make the crooked straight. . .
> > don't let this happen to US!

KLEONIKE

I don't care who he is—*where is he?*

LYSISTRATA

Pointing.

> > Down there—
just flanking that temple—Demeter the Fruitful.

KLEONIKE

My.

Definitely a man.

MYRRHINE

Craning for a look.

I wonder who it can be?

LYSISTRATA

See for yourselves. —Can anyone identify him?

MYRRHINE

Oh lord, I can.

That is my husband—Kinesias.*

LYSISTRATA

To Myrrhine.

Your duty is clear.

Pop him on the griddle, twist
the spit, braize him, baste him, stew him in his own
juice, do him to a turn. Sear him with kisses,
coyness, caresses, *everything*—

but stop where Our Oath

begins.

MYRRHINE

Relax. I can take care of this.

LYSISTRATA

Of course

you can, dear. Still, a little help can't hurt, now
can it? I'll just stay around for a bit
and—er—poke up the fire.

—Everyone else inside!

*Exit all the women but Lysistrata, on the platform, and Myrrhine, who stands near the
Akropolis entrance, hidden from her husband's view. Kinesias staggers on, in erection and
considerable pain, followed by a male slave who carries a baby boy.*

KINESIAS

OUCH!!

Omigod.

Hypertension, twinges. . . . I can't hold out much more.
I'd rather be dismembered.

How long, ye gods, how long?

LYSISTRATA

Officially.

WHO GOES THERE?

WHO PENETRATES OUR POSITIONS?

KINESIAS

Me.

LYSISTRATA
　　　A Man?

KINESIAS
　　　　　　　Every inch.

LYSISTRATA
　　　　　　　　　　Then inch yourself out
of here. Off Limits to Men.

KINESIAS
　　　　　　　　　　This *is* the limit.
Just who are *you* to throw me out?

LYSISTRATA
　　　　　　　　　　The Lookout.

KINESIAS
Well, look here, Lookout. I'd like to see Myrrhine.
How's the outlook?

LYSISTRATA
　　　　　　　　Unlikely. Bring Myrrhine
to you? The idea!
　　　　　　　Just by the by, who are you?

KINESIAS
A private citizen. Her husband, Kinesias.

LYSISTRATA
　　　　　　　　　　　　No!
Meeting you—I'm overcome!
　　　　　　　　　　Your name, you know,
is not without its fame among us girls.

Aside.

—Matter of fact, we have a name for *it*.—
I swear, you're never out of Myrrhine's mouth.
She won't even nibble a quince, or swallow an egg,
without reciting, "Here's to Kinesias!"

KINESIAS
　　　　　　　　　　For god's sake,
will you. . .

LYSISTRATA
Sweeping on over his agony.
　　　　　　　Word of honor, it's true. Why, when
we discuss our husbands (you know how women are),
Myrrhine refuses to argue. She simply insists:
"Compared with Kinesias, the rest have *nothing!*" Imagine!

KINESIAS
Bring her out here!

LYSISTRATA

Really? And what would I
get out of this?

KINESIAS

You see my situation. I'll raise
whatever I can. This can all be yours.

LYSISTRATA

Goodness.
It's really her place. I'll go and get her.

She descends from the platform and moves to Myrrhine, out of Kinesias' sight.

KINESIAS

Speed!
—Life is a husk. She left our home, and happiness
went with her. Now pain is the tenant. Oh, to enter
that wifeless house, to sense that awful emptiness,
to eat that tasteless, joyless food—it makes
it hard, I tell you.
Harder all the time.

MYRRHINE

Still out of his sight, in a voice to be overheard.

Oh, I *do* love him! I'm mad about him! But he
doesn't want my love. Please don't make me see him.

KINESIAS

Myrrhine darling, why do you *act* this way?
Come down here!

MYRRHINE

Appearing at the wall.

Down there? Certainly not!

KINESIAS

It's me, Myrrhine. I'm begging you. Please come down.

MYRRHINE

I don't see why you're begging me. You don't need me.

KINESIAS

I don't need you? I'm at the end of my rope!

MYRRHINE

I'm leaving.

She turns. Kinesias grabs the boy from the slave.

KINESIAS

No! Wait! At least you'll have to listen
to the voice of your child.

To the boy, in a fierce undertone.

—(Call your mother!)

Silence.

. . . to the voice
of your very own child. . .

—(Call your mother, brat!)

CHILD

MOMMYMOMMYMOMMY!

KINESIAS

Where's your maternal instinct? He hasn't been washed
or fed for a week. How can you be so pitiless?

MYRRHINE

Him I pity. Of all the pitiful excuses
for a father. . . .

KINESIAS

Come down here, dear. For the baby's sake.

MYRRHINE

Motherhood! I'll have to come. I've got no choice.

KINESIAS

Soliloquizing as she descends.

It may be me, but I'll swear she looks years younger—
and gentler—her eyes caress me. And then they flash:
that anger, that verve, that high-and-mighty air!
She's fire, she's ice—and I'm stuck right in the middle.

MYRRHINE

Taking the baby.

Sweet babykins with such a nasty daddy!
Here, let Mummy kissums. Mummy's little darling.

KINESIAS

The injured husband.

You should be ashamed of yourself, letting those women
lead you around. Why do you DO these things?
You only make me suffer and hurt your poor,
sweet self.

MYRRHINE

Keep your hands away from me!

KINESIAS

But the house, the furniture, everything we own—you're letting
it go to hell!

MYRRHINE

Frankly, I couldn't care less.

KINESIAS
But your weaving's unraveled—the loom is full of chickens!
You couldn't care less about *that?*

MYRRHINE
I certainly couldn't.

KINESIAS
And the holy rites of Aphrodite? Think how long
that's been.
Come on, darling, let's go home.

MYRRHINE
I absolutely refuse!
Unless you agree to a truce
to stop the war.

KINESIAS
Well, then, if that's your decision,
we'll STOP the war!

MYRRHINE
Well, then, if that's your decision,
I'll come back—*after* it's done.
But, for the present,
I've sworn off.

KINESIAS
At least lie down for a minute.
We'll talk.

MYRRHINE
I know what you're up to—NO!
—And yet. . . . I really can't say I don't love you. . .

KINESIAS
You love me?
So what's the trouble? *Lie down.*

MYRRHINE
Don't be disgusting.
In front of the baby?

KINESIAS
Er. . . no. Heaven Forfend.

Taking the baby and pushing it at the slave.
—Take this home.

The slave obeys.
—Well, darling, we're rid of the kid. . .
let's go to bed!

MYRRHINE
                        Poor dear.
                                        But where does one do
this sort of thing?

KINESIAS
                        Where? All we need is a little
nook. . . . We'll try Pan's grotto. Excellent spot.

MYRRHINE

With a nod at the Akropolis.
I'll have to be pure to get back in *there*. How can I
expunge my pollution?

KINESIAS
                                Sponge off in the pool next door.

MYRRHINE
I did swear an Oath. I'm supposed to perjure myself?

KINESIAS
Bother the Oath. Forget it—I'll take the blame.

A pause.

MYRRHINE
Now I'll go get us a cot.

KINESIAS
                        No! Not a cot!
The ground's enough for us.

MYRRHINE
                                I'll get the cot.
For all your faults, I refuse to put you to bed
in the dirt.

She exits into the Akropolis.

KINESIAS
                She certainly loves me. That's nice to know.

MYRRHINE

Returning with a rope-tied cot.
Here. You hurry to bed while I undress.

Kinesias lies down.
Gracious me—I forgot. We need a mattress.

KINESIAS
Who wants a mattress? Not me!

MYRRHINE
                                Oh, yes, you do.
It's perfectly squalid on the ropes.

KINESIAS

                                    Well, give me a kiss
to tide me over.

MYRRHINE

                    Voilà.

She pecks at him and leaves.

KINESIAS

                    OoolaLAlala!
—Make it a quick trip, dear.

MYRRHINE

Entering with the mattress, she waves Kinesias off the cot and lays the mattress on it.
                              Here we are.
Our mattress. Now hurry to bed while I undress.

Kinesias lies down again.
            Gracious me—I forgot. You don't have a pillow.

KINESIAS

I do *not* need a pillow.

MYRRHINE

                    I know, but *I* do.

She leaves.

KINESIAS

What a lovefeast! Only the table gets laid.*

MYRRHINE

Returning with a pillow.
            Rise and shine!

Kinesias jumps up. She places the pillow.
                    And now I have everything I need.

KINESIAS

Lying down again.
            You certainly do.

                        Come here, my little jewelbox!

MYRRHINE

Just taking off my bra.
                        Don't break your promise:
no cheating about the Peace.

KINESIAS

                              I swear to god,
I'll die first!

MYRRHINE

Coming to him.

                    Just look. You don't have a blanket.

66

KINESIAS
I didn't plan to go camping—I want to make love!

MYRRHINE
Relax. You'll get your love. I'll be right back.

She leaves.

KINESIAS
Relax? I'm dying a slow death by dry goods!

MYRRHINE
Returning with the blanket.

Get up!

KINESIAS
Getting out of bed.

I've been up for hours. I was up before I was up.

Myrrhine spreads the blanket on the mattress, and he lies down again.

MYRRHINE
I presume you want perfume?

KINESIAS

Positively NO!

MYRRHINE
Absolutely *yes*—whether you want it or not.

She leaves.

KINESIAS
Dear Zeus, I don't ask for much—but please let her spill it.

MYRRHINE
Returning with a bottle.

Hold out your hand like a good boy.

Now rub it in.

KINESIAS
Obeying and sniffing.

This is to quicken desire? Too strong. It grabs
your nose and bawls out: *Try again tomorrow.*

MYRRHINE
I'm *awful!* I brought you that rancid Rhodian brand.

She starts off with the bottle.

KINESIAS
This is just *lovely*. Leave it, woman!

MYRRHINE

Silly!

She leaves.

KINESIAS
God damn the clod who first concocted perfume!

MYRRHINE

Returning with another bottle.

Here, try this flask.

KINESIAS

Thanks—but you try mine.
Come to bed, you witch—

*and please stop bringing
things!*

MYRRHINE

That is exactly what I'll do.
There go my shoes.

Incidentally, darling, you *will*
remember to vote for the truce?

KINESIAS

I'LL THINK IT OVER!

Myrrhine runs off for good.

That woman's laid me waste—destroyed me, root
and branch!

I'm scuttled,

gutted,

up the spout!

And Myrrhine's gone!

In a parody of a tragic kommos.

Out upon't! But how? But where?
Now I have lost the fairest fair,
how screw my courage to yet another
sticking-place? Aye, there's the rub—
And yet, this wagging, wanton babe
must soon be laid to rest, or else. . .
Ho, Pandar!

Pandar!

I'd hire a nurse.

KORYPHAIOS OF MEN

Grievous your bereavement, cruel
the slow tabescence of your soul.
I bid my liquid pity mingle.

Oh, where the soul, and where, alack!
the cod to stand the taut attack
of swollen prides, the scorching tensions
that ravine up the lumbar regions?

His morning lay
has gone astray.

KINESIAS

In agony.

O Zeus, reduce the throbs, the throes!

KORYPHAIOS OF MEN

I turn my tongue to curse the cause
of your affliction—that jade, that slut,
that hag, that ogress. . .

KINESIAS

No! Slight not
my light-o'-love, my dove, my sweet!

KORYPHAIOS OF MEN

Sweet!
O Zeus who rul'st the sky,
snatch that slattern up on high,
crack thy winds, unleash thy thunder,
tumble her over, trundle her under,
juggle her from hand to hand;
twirl her ever near the ground—
drop her in a well-aimed fall
on our comrade's tool! That's all.

Kinesias exits left.
A Spartan Herald enters from the right, holding his cloak together in a futile attempt to conceal his condition.

HERALD

This Athens? Where-all kin I find the Council of Elders
or else the Executive Board? I brung some news.

The Commissioner,* swathed in his cloak, enters from the left.

COMMISSIONER

And what are you—a man? a signpost? a joint-stock
company?

HERALD

A herald, sonny, a honest-to-Kastor
herald. I come to chat 'bout thet-there truce.

COMMISSIONER

. . .carrying a concealed weapon? Pretty underhanded.

HERALD

Twisting to avoid the Commissioner's direct gaze.

Hain't done no sech a thang!

COMMISSIONER

Very well, stand still.
Your cloak's out of crease—hernia? Are the roads that bad?

SPARTAN

I swear this feller's plumb tetched in the haid!

COMMISSIONER

Throwing open the Spartan's cloak, exposing the phallus.

You clown,

you've got an erection!

SPARTAN

Wildly embarrassed.

Hain't got no sech a thang!
You stop this-hyer foolishment!

COMMISSIONER

What *have* you got there, then?

SPARTAN

Thet-thur's a Spartan *epistle.** In code.

COMMISSIONER

I have the key.

Throwing open his cloak.

Behold another Spartan *epistle.* In code.

Tiring of teasing.

Let's get down to cases. I know the score,
so tell me the truth.

How are things with you in Sparta?

HERALD

Thangs is up in the air. The whole Alliance
is purt-near 'bout to explode. We-uns'll need barrels,
'stead of women.

COMMISSIONER

What was the cause of this outburst?
The great god Pan?

HERALD

Nope. I'll lay 'twere Lampito,
most likely. She begun, and then they was off
and runnin' at the post in a bunch, every last little gal
in Sparta, drivin' their menfolk away from the winner's
circle.

COMMISSIONER

How are you taking this?

HERALD

Painful-like.
Everyone's doubled up worse as a midget nursin'
a wick in a midnight wind come moon-dark time.
Cain't even tetch them little old gals on the moosey
without we all agree to a Greece-wide Peace.

70

COMMISSIONER
Of course!
                    A universal female plot—all Hellas
risen in rebellion—I should have known!
                                        Return
to Sparta with this request:
                            Have them despatch us
a Plenipotentiary Commission, fully empowered
to conclude an armistice. I have full confidence
that I can persuade our Senate to do the same,
without extending myself. The evidence is at hand.

HERALD
I'm a-flyin', Sir! I hev never heered your equal!

Exeunt hurriedly, the Commissioner to the left, the Herald to the right.

KORYPHAIOS OF MEN
        The most unnerving work of nature,*
        the pride of applied immorality,
        is the common female human.
        No fire can match, no beast can best her.
        O Unsurmountability,
        thy name—worse luck—is Woman.

KORYPHAIOS OF WOMEN
        After such knowledge, why persist
        in wearing out this fecklesss
        war between the sexes?
        When can I apply for the post
        of ally, partner, and general friend?

KORYPHAIOS OF MEN
        I won't be ployed to revise, re-do,
        amend, extend, or bring to an end
        my irreversible credo:
        Misogyny Forever!
        —The answer's never.

KORYPHAIOS OF WOMEN
        All right. Whenever you choose.
        But, for the present, I refuse
        to let you look your absolute worst,
        parading around like an unfrocked freak:
        I'm coming over and get you dressed.

She dresses him in his tunic, an action (like others in this scene) imitated by the members
of the Chorus of Women toward their opposite numbers in the Chorus of Men.

KORYPHAIOS OF MEN
>This seems sincere. It's not a trick.
>Recalling the rancor with which I stripped,
>I'm overlaid with chagrin.

KORYPHAIOS OF WOMEN
>Now you resemble a man,
>not some ghastly practical joke.
>And if you show me a little respect
>(and promise not to kick), I'll extract
>the beast in you.

KORYPHAIOS OF MEN
Searching himself.
>What beast in me?

KORYPHAIOS OF WOMEN
>That insect. There. The bug that's stuck
>in your eye.

KORYPHAIOS OF MEN
Playing along dubiously.
>This gnat?

KORYPHAIOS OF WOMEN
>Yes, nitwit!

KORYPHAIOS OF MEN
>Of course.
>That steady, festering agony. . . .
>You've put your finger on the source
>of all my lousy troubles. Please
>roll back the lid and scoop it out.
>I'd like to see it.

KORYPHAIOS OF WOMEN
>All right, I'll do it.
Removing the imaginary insect.
>Although, of all the impossible cranks. . . .
>Do you sleep in a swamp? Just look at this.
>I've never seen a bigger chigger.

KORYPHAIOS OF MEN
>Thanks.
>Your kindness touches me deeply. For years,
>that thing's been sinking wells in my eye.
>Now you've unplugged me. Here come the tears.

KORYPHAIOS OF WOMEN
  I'll dry your tears, though I can't say why.
Wiping away the tears.
  Of all the irresponsible boys. . . .
  And I'll kiss you.
   KORYPHAIOS OF MEN
    Don't you kiss me!
   KORYPHAIOS OF WOMEN
  What made you think you had a choice?
She kisses him.

   KORYPHAIOS OF MEN
  All right, damn you, that's enough of that ingrained palaver.
  I can't dispute the truth or logic of the pithy old proverb:
    Life with women is hell.
    Life without women is hell, too.
  And so we conclude a truce with you, on the following terms:
  in future, a mutual moratorium on mischief in all its forms.
  Agreed? —Let's make a single chorus and start our song.
The two Choruses unite and face the audience.

   CHORUS OF MEN*
    We're not about to introduce
    the standard personal abuse—
     the Choral Smear
    Of Present Persons (usually,
    in every well-made comedy,
     inserted here).
    Instead, in deed and utterance, we
    shall now indulge in philanthropy
     because we feel
    that members of the audience
    endure, in the course of current events,
     sufficient hell.
    Therefore, friends, be rich! Be flush!
    Apply to us, and borrow cash
     in large amounts.
    The Treasury stands behind us—there—
    and we can personally take care
     of small accounts.
    Drop up today. Your credit's good.
    Your loan won't have to be repaid
     in full until
    the war is over. And then, your debt
    is only the money you actually get—
     nothing at all.

CHORUS OF WOMEN
>Just when we meant to entertain
>some madcap gourmets from out of town
>>—such flawless taste!—
>the present unpleasantness intervened,
>and now we fear the feast we planned
>>will go to waste.
>The soup is waiting, rich and thick;
>I've sacrificed a suckling pig
>>—the pièce de résistance—
>whose toothsome cracklings should amaze
>the most fastidious gourmets—
>>you, for instance.
>To everybody here, I say
>take potluck at my house today
>>with me and mine.
>Bathe and change as fast as you can,
>bring the children, hurry down,
>>and walk right in.
>Don't bother to knock. No need at all.
>My house is yours. Liberty Hall.
>>What are friends for?
>Act self-possessed when you come over;
>it may help out when you discover
>>I've locked the door.

A delegation of Spartans enters from the right, with difficulty. They have removed their cloaks, but hold them before themselves in an effort to conceal their condition.

KORYPHAIOS OF MEN
>What's this? Behold the Spartan ambassadors,
>>dragging their beards,
>pussy-footing along. It appears they've developed
>>a hitch in the crotch.

Advancing to greet them.
>Men of Sparta, I bid you welcome!
>>>>And now
>to the point: What predicament brings you among us?

SPARTAN
>We-uns is up a stump. Hain't fit fer chatter.

Flipping aside his cloak.
>Here's our predicament. Take a look for yourselfs.

KORYPHAIOS OF MEN
>Well, I'll be damned—a regular disaster area.
>Inflamed. I imagine the temperature's rather intense?

SPARTAN
Hit ain't the heat, hit's the tumidity.
                                                    But words
won't help what ails us. We-uns come after Peace.
Peace from any person, at any price.

Enter the Athenian delegation from the left, led by Kinesias.* They are wearing cloaks, but are obviously in as much travail as the Spartans.

KORYPHAIOS OF MEN
Behold our local Sons of the Soil, stretching
their garments away from their groins, like wrestlers. Grappling
with their plight. Some sort of athlete's disease, no doubt.
An outbreak of epic proportions.
                                        Athlete's foot?
No. Could it be athlete's. . . ?

KINESIAS
Breaking in.

                                        Who can tell us
how to get hold of Lysistrata? We've come as delegates
to the Sexual Congress.

Opening his cloak.

                                    Here are our credentials.

KORYPHAIOS OF MEN
Ever the scientist, looking from the Athenians to the Spartans and back again.
The words are different, but the malady seems the same.

To Kinesias.

Dreadful disease. When the crisis reaches its height,
what do you take for it?

KINESIAS
                            Whatever comes to hand.
But now we've reached the bitter end. It's Peace
or we fall back on Kleisthenes.
                                    And he's got a waiting list.

KORYPHAIOS OF MEN

To the Spartans.

Take my advice and put your clothes on. If someone
from that self-appointed Purity League* comes by, you may
be docked. They do it to the statues of Hermes, they'll do it
to you.

KINESIAS
Since he has not yet noticed the Spartans, he interprets the warning as meant for him, and hurriedly pulls his cloak together, as do the other Athenians.
                Excellent advice.

SPARTAN

                                    Hit shorely is.

Hain't nothing to argue after. Let's git dressed.

As they put on their cloaks, the Spartans are finally noticed by Kinesias.

KINESIAS

Welcome, men of Sparta! This is a shameful
disgrace to masculine honor.

SPARTAN

                               Hit could be worser.

Ef them Herm-choppers seed us all fired up,
they'd *really* take us down a peg or two.

KINESIAS

Gentlemen, let's descend to details. Specifically,
why are you here?

SPARTAN

                        Ambassadors. We come to dicker
'bout thet-thur Peace.

KINESIAS

                     Perfect! Precisely our purpose.

Let's send for Lysistrata. Only she can reconcile
our differences. There'll be no Peace for us without her.

SPARTAN

We-uns ain't fussy. Call Lysistratos, too, if you want.

The gates to the Akropolis open, and Lysistrata emerges, accompanied by her handmaid, Peace—a beautiful girl without a stitch on. Peace remains out of sight by the gates until summoned.

KORYPHAIOS OF MEN

Hail, most virile of women! Summon up all your experience:
Be terrible and tender,
                  lofty and lowbrow,
                                 severe and demure.
Here stand the Leaders of Greece, enthralled by your charm.
They yield the floor to you and submit their claims for your
   arbitration.

LYSISTRATA

Really, it shouldn't be difficult, if I can catch them
all bothered, before they start to solicit each other.
I'll find out soon enough. Where's Peace?
                                 —Come here.

Peace moves from her place by the gates to Lysistrata. The delegations goggle at her.
        Now, dear, first get those Spartans and bring them to me.
        Take them by the hand, but don't be pushy about it,
        not like our husbands (no savoir-faire at all!).

Be a lady, be proper, do just what you'd do at home:
if hands are refused, conduct them by the handle.

Peace leads the Spartans to a position near Lysistrata.

And now a hand to the Athenians—it doesn't matter
where; accept any offer—and bring *them* over.

Peace conducts the Athenians to a position near Lysistrata, opposite the Spartans.

You Spartans move up closer—right *here*—

To the Athenians.

                    and *you*
stand over *here*.

          —And now attend my speeech.

This the delegations do with some difficulty, because of the conflicting attractions of Peace, who is standing beside her mistress.

I am a woman—but not without some wisdom:
my native wit is not completely negligible,
and I've listened long and hard to the discourse of my elders—
my education is not entirely despicable.

                    Well,
now that I've got you, I intend to give you hell,
and I'm perfectly right. Consider your actions:

                    At festivals,
in Pan-Hellenic harmony, like true blood-brothers, you share
the selfsame basin of holy water, and sprinkle
altars all over Greece—Olympia, Delphoi,
Thermopylai. . . (I could go on and on, if length
were my only object.)

                But now, when the Persians sit by
and wait, in the very presence of your enemies, you fight
each other, destroy *Greek* men, destroy *Greek* cities!
—Point One of my address is now concluded.

KINESIAS

Gazing at Peace.

I'm destroyed, if this is drawn out much longer!

LYSISTRATA

Serenely unconscious of the interruption.

—Men of Sparta, I direct these remarks to you.
Have you forgotten that a Spartan suppliant once came
to beg assistance from Athens? Recall Perikleidas:
Fifty years ago, he clung to our altar,
his face dead-white above his crimson robe, and pleaded
for an army. Messene was pressing you hard in revolt,
and to this upheaval, Poseidon, the Earthshaker, added
another.

But Kimon took four thousand troops
from Athens—an army which saved the state of Sparta.
Such treatment have you received at the hands of Athens,
you who devastate the country that came to your aid!

KINESIAS

Stoutly; the condemnation of his enemy has made him forget the girl momentarily.
You're right, Lysistrata. The Spartans are clearly in the wrong!

SPARTAN

Guiltily backing away from Peace, whom he has attempted to pat.
Hit's wrong, I reckon, but that's the purtiest behind. . .

LYSISTRATA

Turning to the Athenians.
—Men of Athens, do you think I'll let *you* off?
Have you forgotten the Tyrant's days,* when you wore
the smock of slavery, when the Spartans turned to the spear,
cut down the pride of Thessaly, despatched the friends
of tyranny, and dispossessed your oppressors?

                                         Recall:
On that great day, your only allies were Spartans;
your liberty came at their hands, which stripped away
your servile garb and clothed you again in Freedom!

SPARTAN

Indicating Lysistrata.
Hain't never seed no higher type of woman.

KINESIAS

Indicating Peace.
Never saw one I wanted so much to top.

LYSISTRATA

Oblivious to the byplay, addressing both groups.
With such a history of mutual benefits conferred
and received, why are you fighting? Stop this wickedness!
Come to terms with each other! What prevents you?

SPARTAN

We'd a heap sight druther make Peace, if we was indemnified
with a plumb strategic location.

Pointing at Peace's rear.
                                We'll take thet butte.

LYSISTRATA
Butte?

SPARTAN
>The Promontory of Pylos—Sparta's Back Door.
We've missed it fer a turrible spell.

Reaching.

>>Hev to keep our

hand in.
KINESIAS

Pushing him away.

>The price is too high—you'll never take that!

LYSISTRATA
Oh, let them have it.

KINESIAS

>>What room will we have left

for maneuvers?
LYSISTRATA

>>Demand another spot in exchange.

KINESIAS
Surveying Peace like a map as he addresses the Spartan.
>Then you hand over to us—uh, let me see—
let's try Thessaly*—

Indicating the relevant portions of Peace.

>>First of all, Easy Mountain. . .
then the Maniac Gulf behind it. . .

>>>and down to Megara

for the legs. . .
SPARTAN

>>You cain't take all of thet! Yore plumb

out of yore mind!
LYSISTRATA

To Kinesias.

>>Don't argue. Let the legs go.

Kinesias nods. A pause. General smiles of agreement.
KINESIAS

Doffing his cloak.

>I feel an urgent desire to plow a few furrows.

SPARTAN

Doffing his cloak.

>Hit's time to work a few loads of fertilizer in.

LYSISTRATA
Conclude the treaty and the simple life is yours.
If such is your decision, convene your councils,
and then deliberate the matter with your allies.

KINESIAS
Deliberate? Allies?
                              We're over-extended already!
Wouldn't every ally approve of our position—
Union Now?

SPARTAN
                         I know I kin speak for ourn.

KINESIAS
And I for ours.
                    They're just a bunch of gigolos.

LYSISTRATA
I heartily approve.
                        Now first attend to your purification,
then we, the women, will welcome you to the Citadel
and treat you to all the delights of a home-cooked banquet.
Then you'll exchange your oaths and pledge your faith,
and every man of you will take his wife
and depart for home.

Lysistrata and Peace enter the Akropolis.

KINESIAS
                              Let's hurry!

SPARTAN
                                   Lead on, everwhich
way's yore pleasure.

KINESIAS
                        This way, then—and HURRY!

The delegations exeunt at a run.

CHORUS OF WOMEN
                    I'd never stint on anybody.
                    And now I include, in my boundless bounty,
                         the younger set.
                    Attention, you parents of teenage girls
                    about to debut in the social whirl.
                         Here's what you get:
                    Embroidered linens, lush brocades,
                    a huge assortment of ready-mades,
                         from mantles to shifts;
                    plus bracelets and bangles of solid gold—
                    every item my wardrobe holds—
                         absolute gifts!
                    Don't miss this offer. Come to my place,
                    barge right in, and make your choice.

You can't refuse.
Everything there must go today.
Finders keepers—cart it away!
How can you lose?
Don't spare me. Open all the locks.
Break every seal. Empty every box.
Keep ferreting—
And your sight's considerably better than mine
if you should possibly chance to find
a single thing.

CHORUS OF MEN

Troubles, friend? Too many mouths
to feed, and not a scrap in the house
to see you through?
Faced with starvation? Don't give it a thought.
Pay attention; I'll tell you what
I'm gonna do.
I overbought. I'm overstocked.
Every room in my house is clogged
with flour (best ever),
glutted with luscious loaves whose size
you wouldn't believe. I need the space;
do me a favor:
Bring gripsacks, knapsacks, duffle bags,
pitchers, cisterns, buckets, and kegs
around to me.
A courteous servant will see to your needs;
he'll fill them up with A-1 wheat—
and all for free!
—Oh. Just one final word before
you turn your steps to my front door:
I happen to own
a dog. Tremendous animal.
Can't stand a leash. And bites like hell—
better stay home.

*The united Chorus flocks to the door of the Akropolis.**

KORYPHAIOS OF MEN

Banging at the door.
Hey, open up in there!

The door opens, and the Commissioner appears. He wears a wreath, carries a torch, and is slightly drunk. He addresses the Koryphaios.

COMMISSIONER

You know the Regulations.
Move along!

He sees the entire Chorus.

—And why are YOU lounging around?
I'll wield my trusty torch and scorch the lot!

The Chorus backs away in mock horror. He stops and looks at his torch.

—*This* is the bottom of the barrel. A cheap burlesque bit.
I refuse to do it. I have my pride.

With a start, he looks at the audience, as though hearing a protest. He shrugs and addresses the audience.

—No choice, eh?
Well, if that's the way it is, we'll take the trouble.
Anything to keep you happy.

The Chorus advances eagerly.

KORYPHAIOS OF MEN

Don't forget us!
We're in this, too. Your trouble is ours!

COMMISSIONER

Resuming his character and jabbing with his torch at the Chorus.

Keep moving!
Last man out of the way goes home without hair!
Don't block the exit. Give the Spartans some room.
They've dined in comfort; let them go home in peace.

*The Chorus shrinks back from the door. Kinesias, wreathed and quite drunk, appears at the door. He speaks his first speech in Spartan.**

KINESIAS

Hain't never seed sech a spread! Hit were splendiferous!

COMMISSIONER

I gather the Spartans won friends and influenced people?

KINESIAS

And *we've* never been so brilliant. It was the wine.

COMMISSIONER

Precisely.

The reason? A sober Athenian is just
non compos. If I can carry a little proposal
I have in mind, our Foreign Service will flourish,
guided by this rational rule:

No Ambassador
Without a Skinful.

Reflect on our past performance:

Down to a Spartan parley we troop, in a state
of disgusting sobriety, looking for trouble. It muddles
our senses: we read between the lines; we hear,
not what the Spartans say, but what we suspect
they might have been about to be going to say.
We bring back paranoid reports—cheap fiction, the fruit
of temperance. Cold-water diplomacy, pah!

                                        Contrast
this evening's total pleasure, the free-and-easy
give-and-take of friendship: If we were singing,
            Just Kleitagora and me,
            Alone in Thessaly,
and someone missed his cue and cut in loudly,
            Ajax, son of Telamon,
            He was one hell of a man—
no one took it amiss, or started a war;
we clapped him on the back and gave three cheers.

During this recital, the Chorus has sidled up to the door.
            —Dammit, are you back here again?

Waving his torch.

                                    Scatter!
Get out of the road! Gangway, you gallowsbait!

KINESIAS
Yes, everyone out of the way. They're coming out.

*Through the door emerge the Spartan delegation, a flutist, the Athenian delegation,
Lysistrata, Kleonike, Myrrhine, and the rest of the women from the citadel, both Athenian and Peloponnesian. The Chorus splits into its male and female components and draws
to the sides to give the procession room.*

SPARTAN
To the flutist.

Friend and kinsman, take up them pipes a yourn.
I'd like fer to shuffle a bit and sing a right sweet
song in honor of Athens and us'uns, too.

COMMISSIONER
To the flutist.

Marvelous, marvelous—come, take up your pipes!

To the Spartan.

I certainly love to see you Spartans dance.

The flutist plays, and the Spartan begins a slow dance.

SPARTAN

            Memory,
            send me
            your Muse,
            who knows

our glory,
knows Athens'—
Tell the story:
At Artemision
like gods, they stampeded
the hulks of the Medes, and
beat them.

And Leonidas
leading us—
the wild boars
whetting their tusks.
And the foam flowered,
flowered and flowed,
down our cheeks
to our knees below.
The Persians there
like the sands of the sea—

Hither, huntress,
virgin, goddess,
tracker, slayer,
to our truce!
Hold us ever
fast together;
bring our pledges
love and increase;
wean us from the
fox's wiles—

Hither, huntress!
Virgin, hither!

LYSISTRATA*

Surveying the assemblage with a proprietary air.
Well, the preliminaries are over—very nicely, too.
So, Spartans,

Indicating the Peloponnesian women who have been hostages.
take these girls back home. And *you*

To the Athenian delegation, indicating the women from the Akropolis.
take *these* girls. Each man stand by his wife, each wife
by her husband. Dance to the gods' glory, and thank them
for the happy ending. And, from now on, please be careful.
Let's not make the same mistakes again.

The delegations obey; the men and women of the chorus join again for a rapid ode.

CHORUS
> Start the chorus dancing,
> Summon all the Graces,
> Send a shout to Artemis in invocation.
> Call upon her brother,
> healer, chorus master,
> Call the blazing Bacchus, with his maddened muster.
>
> Call the flashing, fiery Zeus, and
> call his mighty, blessed spouse, and
> call the gods, call all the gods,
> to witness now and not forget
> our gentle, blissful Peace—the gift,
> the deed of Aphrodite.
> Ai!
> Alalai! Paion!
> Leap you! Paion!
> Victory! Alalai!
> Hail! Hail! Hail!

LYSISTRATA
Spartan, let's have another song from you, a new one.

SPARTAN
> Leave darlin' Taygetos,
> Spartan Muse! Come to us
> once more, flyin'
> and glorifyin'
> *Spartan* themes:
> the god at Amyklai,
> bronze-house Athene,
> Tyndaros' twins,
> the valiant ones,
> playin' still by Eurotas' streams.
>
> Up! Advance!
> Leap to the dance!
>
> Help us hymn Sparta,
> lover of dancin',
> lover of foot-pats,
> where girls go prancin'
> like fillies along Eurotas' banks,
> whirlin' the dust, twinklin' their shanks,
> shakin' their hair
> like Maenads playin'
> and jugglin' the thyrsis,
> in frenzy obeyin'

Leda's daughter, the fair, the pure
Helen, the mistress of the choir.

Here, Muse, here!
Bind up your hair!

Stamp like a deer! Pound your feet!
Clap your hands! Give us a beat!

Sing the greatest,
sing the mightiest,
sing the conqueror,
sing to honor her—

Athene of the Bronze House!
Sing Athene!

Exeunt omnes, dancing and singing.

Notes

page 9. *early morning:* The play's two time scales should be noted. By one, its action encompasses a day, beginning at dawn and lasting until after sundown; by the other, its events logically occupy a period of weeks, if not months—not that this sort of logic has much to do with the case. At no point is the play stopped to indicate the passage of time.

9. *Kleonike:* This is to adopt Wilamowitz' conjecture for the *Kalonike* of the manuscripts, without accepting his views on the character's age. Kleonike's actions approach those of the stock bibulous old woman too closely to indicate a sweet young thing. She is older than Lysistrata, who fits comfortably on the vague borderline between "young matron" and "matron." Quite a bit younger are Myrrhine and Lampito.

10. *those scrumptious eels:* The constant Athenian gustatory passion, rendered sharper by the War's embargo: eels from Lake Kopaïs in Boiotia.

12. *hoisting her sandals:* This rendering follows, with Coulon, Van Leeuwen's emendation at 64—τἀκάτειον "sail"—while suggesting that the pun plays on the unmetrical reading of the Ravennas, τἀκάτιον "skiff," as a name applied to a woman's shoe. It is tempting to return to an old proposal of Biset and read τἀκάτιον ἀνῄρετο.

12. *from the outskirts:* Literally, "from Anagyrous," a rural deme of Attika which took its name from the plant *anagyros* "the stinking bean-trefoil." Kleonike's riposte puns on this by reference to an old proverb: "Well, the *anagyros* certainly seems to have been disturbed" ="you've really stirred up a stink"="the fat's in the fire." Here, as often when geographical names are involved, it is more important to render the fact of a pun than the specifics of the original.

13. *I calklate so:* In employing a somewhat debased American mountain dialect to render the Laconic Greek of Lampito and her countrymen, I have tried to evoke something like the Athenian attitude toward their perennial enemies. They regarded the Spartans as formidably old-fashioned bumpkins, imperfectly civilized, possessed of a determined indifference to more modern value systems.

14. *Military waste:* Or perhaps treason. The Greek refers to a General Eukrates, who may be the brother of the illustrious and ill-starred

Nikias. If so, he was put to death by the Thirty Tyrants in 404.

page 18. *in Athene's temple:* In the Opisthodomos, at the back of the Parthenon, was kept the reserve fund of one thousand silver talents established at the beginning of the War twenty years before. Since the fund had been dipped into during the previous year, Lampito's expression constitutes more than a normal exaggeration.

19. *The symbolism's too obscure:* This sentence may seem a startling expansion of the word *poi* (literally, "Whither?"; here, "What is the point of . . . ?"), but is in a good cause—an attempt to explain and motivate the darkest white horse in literature. The sequence is this: Lysistrata, annoyed at the interruption, sarcastically proposes a gaudy sacrifice; Kleonike, whose mind is proof against sarcasm, points out that it has nothing to do with the matter at hand. For the rationale, I am indebted to Wilamowitz, though he assigned the lines (191-93) differently. Other explanations, in terms of Amazons, genitalia, or lovemaking blueprints, are, albeit venerable, obscure in themselves. One sympathizes with Rogers, who translated, "grey mare."

26. *Athene's statue:* Not one of Pheidias' colossal statues, but the old wooden figure of Athene Polias ("Guardian of the City") in the Erechtheion.

26. *right over there:* I have given the Koryphaios a bad memory and placed the object of his anger in the audience to point up what is happening. Rhodia, wife of the demagogue Lykon, was a real person, frequently lampooned for her morals. In a not unusual breaking of the dramatic illusion, her name occurs here as a surprise for the expected "Lysistrata." Some commentators, disliking surprises, have decided that Lysistrata is the wife of someone named Lykon—thus managing to ruin a joke and import an obscurity without the change of a word.

26. *expropriating our Akropolis:* Kleomenes' occupation of the Akropolis in 508, high point of his unsuccessful bid to help establish the Athenian aristocrats, lasted rather less than the six years which the Chorus seems to remember. The actual time was two days.

28. *at loggerheads over in Samos:* Most of the Athenian fleet was at the moment based in Samos, practically the only Ionian ally left to Athens, in order to make ready moves against those states who had defected to Sparta in 412 after the Sicilian fiasco.

30. *Hipponax swears by it:* The Greek refers to one Boupalos, a Chian sculptor mercilessly lampooned by the testy poet until, as a doubtful tradition has it, he hanged himself. The only surviving verse of Hipponax which bears on the subject ("Hold my clothes; I'll sock Boupalos in the jaw") does little to establish the tradition—or, indeed, to dispel the feeling that Hipponax was about as effective a boxer as the Koryphaios.

30. *for other bitches to gnaw:* I here adopt John Jackson's transposition of line 363 to follow 367 (*Marginalia Scaenica,* p. 108).

page 31. *so lost to shame as Woman:* The observation is clearly offered as an illustrative quotation, and the sentiment is certainly Euripidean. But the extant tragic line nearest it in expression is Sophokles *Elektra* 622.

32. *A Commissioner of Public Safety:* That is, *a proboulos,* one of the ten extraordinary Athenian officials appointed in 413 after the Sicilian catastrophe as a check on legislative excesses. Chiefly responsible for drafting the agenda of Senate and Assembly, the commissioners were drawn from men over forty years of age. The two whose names we know were well along: Hagnon was over sixty, Sophokles (if the poet is meant, a matter not absolutely settled) eighty-two. But these instances scarcely prove Wilamowitz' contention that decrepitude was a necessary qualification for the office; and Aristophanes' Commissioner, for all his choleric conservatism, is marked by vigor and intellectual curiosity.

36. *goddess of the dew:* That is, Pandrosos, one of the daughters of Athens' legendary King Kekrops. A tutelary divinity in her own right, she had a shrine in the Erechtheion—and was never identified with Artemis. Having said this, I follow in the translation an unprovable theory of Rogers': that *pandrosos* "all-bedewing" just might be an epithet of the moon-goddess, classical antiquity's best-attested virgin, who is otherwise invoked here in three out of four instances.

36. *ISMENIA:* As stated in the Introduction (p. 5), I here assign two lines in Attic Greek (447-48) to a Theban hostage, for no better reason than symmetry.

39. *the Friends of Oligarchy:* This expansion makes more explicit a reference to the political clubs, or *synōmosiai,* who caucussed and combined their votes to gain verdicts and offices, thus paving the road for the oligarchic upheaval in May of 411.

41. *Yᵉ menne must see to yᵉ warre: Iliad* 6.492 (Hektor to Andromache).

42. *"What Athens needs is a Man":* Traditionally interpreted (perhaps with too much enthusiasm) as a reference to the longing of the Athenian commonality for the return of glory-and-shame Alkibiades, who obliged the following summer.

43. *Pacifiers:* In the Greek, *Lysimachas* "Battle-settlers," a pun on the name of the heroine; also, if D. M. Lewis is right, a reference to her real-life model Lysimache—in 411, priestess of Athene.

45. *to snag important posts:* Most of this rather torturous allegory is self-explanatory, but the "clumps" are the political clubs, or "Friends of Oligarchy," mentioned earlier. See above, note to p. 39.

46. *To the audience:* Or, possibly, to the Chorus of Men. I do not accept Van Leeuwen's emendation here (598), but I do follow him in taking the line to be an interrupted exhortation to all available and qualified males.

46. *with her spindle:* Here and earlier, the women are certainly armed, but with what? The pronouns supplied by the Greek are tantalizingly

specific in gender, but in nothing else; solutions usually bring out the worst in interpreters. I have tried to assign appropriate weapons early, and continue them to this denouement—but visualizers (or producers, if any there be) are at liberty, as elsewhere, to use their imaginations. One caveat: the Greek will not bear a direct repetition of the bath given earlier to the Old Men by the Old Women.

page 47. *my payroll:* The *triobolon,* the three-obol per diem wage for jury duty, which often constituted the only income of elderly men. It would naturally be stored inside the Citadel in the Treasury.

47. *WOMEN ticking off troops:* Emending πολίτας at 626 to ὁπλίτας.

47. *Harmodios, Aristogeiton, and Me:* The reference, to a famous statuary group by the sculptor Kritios in the Athenian Agora, picks up an earlier quotation from a popular *skolion,* or drinking-song, on the assassination of the tyrant Hipparchos: "I'll carry my sword concealed in a myrtle bough. . . ." The translation expands on the idea, but hides the quotation in the familiar "sword in olive branch."

48. *this proud progression:* Since this passage is frequently cited as primary evidence for the *cursus honorum* of a high-born young girl in fifth-century Athens, here are the steps set forth a bit more explicitly: (1) *arrêphoros* ("relic-bearer") to Athene, one of four little girls who carried the Goddess' sacred objects in Her semi-annual festival of the *Arréphoria;* (2) *aletris* ("mill-girl") to the Founding Mother (doubtless Athene), one of the girls who ground the meal to be made into sacrificial cakes; (3) *arktos* ("she-bear") at the *Brauronia,* a festival of Artemis held every fifth year at Brauron in Attika, centering on a myth which told of the killing of a tame bear sacred to that goddess; and (4) *kanêphoros* ("basket-bearer"), the maiden who bore the sacrificial cake and led the procession at Athens' most important festivals, such as the City Dionysia and the Great Panathenaia.

48. *the Mutual Funds from the Persian War:* This money originally made up the treasury of the Delian League, an alliance of Greek states against Persia formed by the Athenian Aristeides in 477; following its transfer, for safety's sake, from the island of Delos to Athens in 454, it became for all practical purposes Athenian property, supported by tribute from the Allies. Athens' heavy expenses in Sicily, followed by the Allies' nonpayment and defection, made this question all too pointed in early 411.

49. *to the Heights:* To Leipsydrion, in the mountains north of Athens, where the besieged Alkmaionid exiles held out for a time against the forces of the tyrant Hippias. Since this siege, ever after symbolic of the Noble Lost Cause, took place in 513, commentators find it necessary to point out that the Chorus of Men couldn't *really* have fought in a battle 102 years before; that they are pretending, or speaking by extension for the Athenian Fighting Spirit, or whatever. Seemingly, this goes without saying; actually, it is dead wrong. Dramaturgy has little to do with geriatrics; Aristophanes needed a Chorus of Men old enough

to be hidebound, decrepit, so old that they would first see the Women's Revolt, not in terms of sex, but of politics—the recrudescence of a personally experienced tyranny. He was cheerfully prepared to have them average 120 years of age, if anyone cared to count. The critical attitude gives one pause: A modern American playwright who composed a fantastic comedy, set in the present, featuring a Chorus of GAR members—would he be greeted with a flourish of actuarial tables?

page 51. *Pan's grotto:* A cave on the Akropolis containing a shrine to the god, outside the Citadel wall, which it adjoined on the northwest.

54. *That snake's a fabrication:* By inserting this speech (and the reply to it) I do not wish to make Lysistrata a religious skeptic, but to point out the joke. No one had ever seen the snake; even its most famous action, that of assisting Themistokles to persuade the Athenians to abandon the city before the battle of Salamis, had been accomplished by its nonappearance.

59. *Kinesias:* A perfectly good Greek name, but in this context it evokes a pun on a common sexual application of the verb *kinein* "move."

66. *Only the table gets laid:* In the Greek, Kinesias compares his phallos to "Herakles at table"—a stock comedy bit wherein the glutton hero, raving with hunger, is systematically diddled of his dinner by his hosts.

69. *The Commissioner:* I maintain the Commissioner as Athens' representative in this scene (980-1013), not primarily because of the testimony of the manuscripts (shaky support at best), but from the logic and structure of the speeches themselves. Coulon assigns them to a *Prytanis,* or member of the Executive Board. In this he follows a whim of Wilamowitz, who took a hesitant suggestion by Van Leeuwen and exalted it into a new principal character in the play—one of the unhappiest changes ever made in an Aristophanic text. The caution of Van Leeuwen, who usually knew no fear as an editor, should have given anyone pause.

70. *a Spartan epistle:* Correctly, a *skytalê,* a tapered rod which was Sparta's contribution to cryptography. A strip of leather was wound about the rod, inscribed with the desired message, and unwound for transmission. A messenger then delivered the strip to the qualified recipient, who deciphered it by winding it around a rod uniform in size and shape with the first. Any interceptor found a meaningless string of letters.

71. *The most unnerving work of nature:* The ensuing reconciliation scene, with its surrogate sexuality, is one of the most curious in Aristophanes. It is not lyric; yet both its diction, oddly diffuse and redundant, and its meter, a paeonic variation on a common trochaic dialogue measure which paradoxically makes it much more regular, seem to call for extensive choreography. I have tried to hedge my bet by stilting the English and employing an irregular scheme depending heavily on off-rhymes.

73. *CHORUS OF MEN:* Coulon, with most other modern editors, assigns the two strophes here (1043-57; 1058-71), plus the two which follow

the subsequent scene (1189-1202; 1203-15), to the entire Chorus, which thereby demonstrates its new-found unity. This seems possible, but unarticulated; even in this play, antistrophic responsion does not necessarily indicate opposition. By paying attention to the matter of this Indian-giving, I have tried to indicate the appropriate diversity within unity: here, first Men (money), then Women (cooking); following Lysistrata's address, first Women (dress and ornament), then Men (grain). In any case, the manuscript indications, giving the first two strophes to the Women and the last two to the Men, appear impossible.

page 75.   *Kinesias:* So I assign the leadership of the Athenians in this scene. Coulon follows Wilamowitz in allotting it to the latter's beloved "Prytanis." The manuscripts commit themselves no further than "Athenians," which is at least safe. It is definitely not the Commissioner.

75.   *that self-appointed Purity League:* See Glossary, s.v. "Hermes."

79.   *the Tyrant's days:* The reign of Hippias, expelled by the Athenians in 510 with the aid of Kleomenes and his Spartans, who defeated the tyrant's Thessalian allies.

80.   *let's try Thessaly:* Puns on proper names, particularly geographical ones, rarely transfer well, and the following bits of sexual cartography will show. "Easy Mountain": an impossible pun on Mt. Oita, replacing the Greek's *Echinous,* a town in Thessaly whose name recalls *echinos* "hedgehog"—slang for the female genitalia. "Maniac Gulf": for Maliac Gulf, with less dimension that the Greek's *Mêlia kolpon,* which puns both on bosom and pudendum. The "legs of Megara" are the walls that connected that city with her seaport, Nisaia.

82.   *to the door of the Akropolis:* This stage direction, and what follows it, attempt to make sense of a desperate situation in the manuscripts, whose chief accomplishment is to differentiate between Athenian and Spartan. In the passage 1216-46, I assign to the Commissioner those lines given by Coulon to the "Prytanis," and to Kinesias those he assigns to "an Athenian," with the following exceptions: the Koryphaios of Men receives 1216a ("Prytanis," Coulon) and 1221 ("Athenian," Coulon); the Commissioner receives 1226 ("Athenian," Coulon).

83.   *in Spartan:* This rendering of 1225 in dialect, and the reading of 1226 as an ironical question, is prompted by a notion of Wilamowitz', to whom an uncommon verb form seemed clear enough evidence of Spartan to warrant a native informant on stage 18 lines early. I am not sure of the validity of his perception, but it allows other solutions, such as the present one: Kinesias is awash with wine and international amity, and the Commissioner is amused.

85.   *LYSISTRATA:* Coulon, following Wilamowitz' ungallant suggestion, takes this speech from Lysistrata (1273-78) and gives it, plus the dubious line following the choral song (1295), to the "Prytanis"—thus crowning the play and turning a superfluous man into an unnecessary hero.

Glossary

ACHARNAI: Largest of the rural demes of Attika, located about seven miles north of the city of Athens.

ADONIS: Mythical youth of marvelous beauty, beloved of Aphrodite, early cut off by a boar. His death was regularly bewailed by women of Greece and the East at summer festivals.

AISCHYLOS, AESCHYLUS: The great Athenian tragedian (525-456 B.C.).

AJAX, AIAS: Greek hero of the Trojan War, son of Telamon of Salamis.

AKROPOLIS: The citadel of Athens.

AMAZONS: The mythical race of warrior-women, said to have invaded Attika in heroic times to avenge the theft of their queen's sister, Antiope, by Theseus of Athens.

AMYKLAI: A Lakedaimonian town, traditional birthplace of Kastor (q.v.) and Pollux, site of a temple to Apollo.

APHRODITE: Goddess of beauty and sexual love.

ARISTOGEITON: Athenian hero who, with Harmodios, assassinated the tyrant Hipparchos in 514 and was put to death. With the expulsion of Hipparchos' brother Hippias four years later, the tyranny of the Peisistratids came to an end. Statues to Harmodios and Aristogeiton were erected in the Athenian Agora.

ARTEMIS: Goddess of the hunt and moon, sister of Apollo.

ARTEMISIA: Queen of Halikarnassos, who, as an ally of the Persian King Xerxes in his invasion of Greece, fought with particular distinction at the sea battle of Salamis in 480.

ARTEMISION: Site on the northern coast of Euboia, off which the Athenians defeated the Persians in a sea battle in 480.

ATHENE, ATHENA: Goddess of wisdom and war; patroness of Athens, and thus particularly associated with the Akropolis (q.v.).

BACCHOS: Dionysos, the god of vineyards, wine, and dramatic poetry, celebrated at Athens in a series of festivals, among them the Lenaia (January–February) and the City Dionysia (March–April).

BOIOTIA: A plentifully supplied state directly northeast of Attika, allied with Sparta during the Peloponnesian War.

CHARON: A minor deity in charge of ferrying the souls of the dead to Hades.

DEMETER: The Earth-Mother; goddess of grain, agriculture, and the harvest.

DEMOSTRATOS: A choleric Athenian demagogue, first to propose the disastrous Sicilian Expedition of 415-413.

EROS: God of sensual love, son of Aphrodite.

EURIPIDES: Athenian tragedian (480-406 B.C.), whose plays and private life furnished Aristophanes with endless material for ridicule. Euripides' determinedly ungallant representation of women (Phaidra in *Hippolytos,* for instance), alluded to in *Lysistrata,* becomes the basis for Aristophanes' next play, the *Thesmophoriazusae.*

EUROTAS: A river in Laconia, on which is located the city of Sparta.

HARMODIOS: Athenian hero; assassin, with Aristogeiton (q.v.), of the tyrant Hipparchos.

HEKATE: Goddess of the moon, night, childbirth, and the underworld.

HELEN: Daughter of Leda and Tyndaros, wife of Menelaos of Sparta. Her abduction by Paris of Troy furnished a *casus belli* for the Trojan War.

HERMES: God of messengers and thieves; in Athens in every doorway stood a statue of Hermes (i.e., a *herm,* usually a bust of the god surmounting an ithyphallic pillar), protector of the door and guardian against thieves—it takes one to know one. The wholesale mutilation of these statues by persons unknown, just before the sailing of the Sicilian expedition in 415, led to the recall of Alkibiades—and thus, perhaps, to the loss of the expedition and ultimately of the war.

HIPPONAX: A satirical iambic poet of Ephesos (fl. 540 B.C.), noted for his limping meter and his touchy temper.

KARYSTIAN: From Karystos, a town in Euboia allied to Athens, whose male inhabitants enjoyed a seemingly deserved reputation for lechery.

KASTOR: Divinity, son of Leda and Tyndaros, or of Leda and Zeus; twin of Polydeukes (Pollux), with whom he constitutes the Dioskouroi. These twin gods were particularly honored by their native state of Sparta.

KIMON: One of Athens' greatest generals (died 449 B.C.); in the years following the Persian Wars, principal architect of the Athenian Empire—an activity abruptly interrupted by his ostracism in 461.

KLEISTHENES: A notorious homosexual; on that account, one of Aristophanes' favorite targets for at least twenty years.

KLEOMENES: Sixth-century king of Sparta, whose two Athenian expeditions had rather different results: The first, in 510, materially assisted in the expulsion of the tyrant Hippias; the second, in 508, failed to establish the power of the aristocratic party led by Isagoras.

KORINTH: Greek city allied to Sparta during the Peloponnesian War; situated on the strategic Isthmus of Korinth.

KYPROS: A large Greek island in the eastern Mediterranean, especially associated with the goddess Aphrodite, said to have stepped ashore there after her birth from the sea-foam.

LAKONIA: The southernmost state on the Greek mainland, Athens' principal opponent in the Peloponnesian War. Its capital city is Sparta.

LENAIA: An Athenian Dionysiac festival, celebrated in January–February.

LEONIDAS: Spartan king and general, who led his 300 troops against Xerxes' Persian army at Thermopylae in Thessaly (480).

MARATHON: A plain in eastern Attika; site of the famous battle (490 B.C.) in which the Athenian forces under Miltiades crushingly defeated the first Persian invasion of Hellas.

MEGARA: The Greek state immediately to the west of Attika; also, its capital city.

MELANION: A mighty hunter, evidently proverbial for his chastity. Probably not to be identified with Meilanion (Milanion), victorious suitor of the huntress Atalante.

MENELAOS: Legendary king of Sparta; husband of Helen (q.v.).

MESSENIA: The western half of Lakedaimon in the Peloponnese; in spite of revolutions, held by Sparta from ca. 730 B.C. until her defeat by Thebes at Leuktra in 371 B.C.

MIKON: A famous Athenian painter of murals, who flourished between the Persian and Peloponnesian Wars.

MILESIAN: From Miletos, a city in Karia in Asia Minor, which had broken off its alliance with Athens in mid-412, following the Sicilian disaster.

MYRONIDES: Athenian general in the period between the Wars; his best-known victory was over the Boiotians at Oinophyta (456).

PAN: Rural Arkadian god of the flocks and woodlands; his cult at Athens was instituted by way of thanks for his help to the Athenians at the battle of Marathon.

PEISANDROS: Engineer of the oligarchic revolt which overthrew the Athenian constitution in May 411 and set up the Council of Four Hundred.

PERIKLEIDAS: The ambassador sent by Sparta to beg Athenian aid in putting down the Messenian revolt of 464.

PHORMION: Athenian admiral, noted for his victory over the Korinthians at Naupaktos in 429.

POSEIDON: Brother of Zeus and god of the sea. As god of the sea, he girdles the earth and has it in his power, as Poseidon the Earthshaker, to cause earthquakes. In still another manifestation, he is Poseidon Hippios, patron god of horses and horsemen.

PYLOS: Town of the southwestern coast of Messenia whose capture by Athens, along with the neighboring island of Sphakteria, in 425-24, became a *cause célèbre* of the Peloponnesian War, and remained a thorn in Sparta's side until they retook it in 409.

SALAMIS: An island in the Saronic Gulf, between Megara and Attika. Subject to Athens, it is divided from the shore by a narrow strait, site of the famous sea battle of 480 which saw the defeat of Xerxes' Persians by Themistokles' Athenians.

SAMOS: A large Aegean island lying off the coast of Ionia. At the beginning of 411, the effective headquarters of the Athenian forces, who had just aided a democratic revolution there. Other Athenians, especially Peisandros, were already fomenting an oligarchic counter-revolution.

SICILY: Scene of Athens' most disastrous undertaking during the war, the Sicilian Expedition of 415-413, which ended in the annihilation of the Athenian forces.

SKYTHIANS: Barbarians who lived in the region northeast of Thrace. Skythian archers were imported to Athens for use as police.

SPARTA: Capital city of Lakonia, principal opponent of Athens during the Peloponnesian War.

TAŸGETOS: A high mountain in central Lakedaimon that separates Lakonia from Messenia.

TELAMON: Legendary king of Salamis; father of Aias.

THASIAN: From Thasos, a volcanic island in the northern Aegean, celebrated for the dark, fragrant wine produced by its vineyards.

THEBES: The principal city of Boiotia; during the Peloponnesian War an ally of Sparta.

THEOGENES: An Athenian braggart, member of the war party.

THESSALY: A large district in northern Greece.

THRACE: The eastern half of the Balkan peninsula.

TIMON: The famous Athenian misanthrope, a contemporary of Aristophanes; a legend during his own lifetime.

ZAKYNTHOS: A large island in the Ionian Sea, south of Kephallenia and west of Elis; during the Peloponnesian War, an ally of Athens.

ZEUS: Chief god of the Olympian pantheon: son of Kronos, brother of Poseidon, father of Athene. As supreme ruler of the world, he is armed with thunder and lightning and creates storms and tempests.

The Acharnians

Translated by Douglass Parker
with sketches by Geraldine Sakall

CONTENTS

SAGITTARIO

ΕΥΡΙΠΙΔΑΡΙΣΤΟΦΑΝΙΖΟΝΤΙ

VERBERATORI SUO

VAPULARIS INTERPRES

D. D. V. S. L. L. M.

Introduction

The Play

The Acharnians was first produced at Athens early in 425 B.C.—the sixth year of the Peloponnesian War. About it we may make two initial statements:

    1) It is Aristophanes' earliest extant play.

    2) Its chief message is an argument for Peace.

These are undisputed facts, and it is perhaps curious that their fusion should create a hurdle to critical understanding of the play. But hurdle there is. By (1), literary history, which still probes with the clammy finger of nineteenth-century idealistic materialism, is compelled to find a certain primitiveness here, so that the poet's art will show an ascending organic development to the *Birds* and, later, the *Frogs*. In (2) the solution to this problem is found. Though the *Acharnians* is, it is suggested, too excellent in its parts for wholesale censure, it can still be relegated to the second rank on grounds of structure, by a strain of reasoning that runs somewhat as follows: "The play is about Peace. But the protagonist achieves Peace by the middle of the play—which therefore outruns its theme and is inferior to *The Frogs* or even the *Lysistrata*, which encompass their messages with nothing left over."

Curious reasoning, but not intrinsically impossible. Any cursory look at our play would appear to bear it out. Thus, the Chorus's address to the audience, the Parabasis, splits the play. In the first half, the old farmer Dikaiopolis ("Just-City") engages in a successful uphill fight to attain Peace; in the second, he proceeds to reap its fruits. The first half contains the argument, particularly the deservedly famous speech of Dikaiopolis to the audience, which justifies the Spartans; the second is made up of a series of farcical scenes, completely hedonistic in content with little or no political reference at all. A humpbacked product, many conclude; brilliant but artistically faulty pamphleteering, where the end does not follow from the beginning.

Logically, this is not indefensible. Empirically, it is an impossible judgment, violating any reasoned experience of the play, and utterly failing to explain certain foreign elements which swell even the first half of the play. Why, for instance, the visit to Euripides, the beggar's clothes, the relentless parody? What has this sort of aesthetic statement to do with War *or* Peace? And *is* the second part of the play merely farcical scenes in a random order?

Our answers begin to appear in the opening soliloquy, a hedonistic calculus which establishes the fundamental polarity of the play: Pleasure—Pain. The joys and sorrows totted up by Dikaiopolis in the first sixteen lines are purely aesthetic and can in no way be laid to the account of War or Peace. After this initial statement follow the pleasures and pains of the flesh, and for these Peace and War are responsible: the expansiveness of the country town against the stinginess of the enforced home, Athens proper. The presentation of the Peace as wine (via a latent pun in the Greek *spondai*—"libations" and hence "truce") welds cause and effect together, playing off the repeated complaint about war, which "cut down the vines." And the visit to Euripides, the acquiring of the rags—these ally the bad art bemoaned at the play's beginning, the flapping fustian, with the scrannel misery, war-born, at which our hero Dikaiopolis rebels. And, in Lamachos, the same rodomontade unites with jingoistic militarism, and hence with war itself.

In these terms the play is set, and in these terms it develops after the Parabasis. We do not here have unconnected scenes in no particular order, but a steady rise of Dikaiopolis on the scale of pleasure. Overt politics taken care of, we now see Dikaiopolis proceed from an initial success over the dirt-poor Megarian to a greater one over the prosperous Theban, after which he can demonstrate briefly his superiority to the average Athenian, rich or poor, rural or urban, and then plunge into the penultimate scene with Lamachos—the armoring scene—where Peace, plenty, and comedy lock in deadly stichomythia with War, poverty, and tragic gush. And, in the last scene, tragic hero, reduced to ridiculous wretchedness by war, confronts comic hero, exalted by drinking the very wine which is Peace, and the victory of Dikaiopolis is complete. Peace has defeated War, pleasure has put down pain, good art has overcome bad.

The reason for the thoroughgoing parody of Euripides' *Telephos,* a play produced in 438, thirteen years before the *Acharnians,* at length becomes plain. The King of Mysia who led the Greeks to war is metamorphosed into the beggar who, by example, points the way to peace, and our comedy is a tragic reversal—or, rather, a reversal of tragedy. Not a lofty character brought low, but a lowly, miserable old man raised to the peak of pleasure and success. Throughout it all, the Chorus of Acharnians remains static in fortune (though changing in attitude)—a yardstick against which to measure the progress of Dikaiopolis. At their first entrance, they are old as he is old, wretched as he is wretched. Through the latter half of the play, they lust continually for the food, wine, and sex which he achieves—and, such is the fate of controls, they receive none. But Dikaiopolis, once aged, is now rejuvenated; younger, if performance means anything, than the prematurely decrepit Lamachos.

Certainly the *Acharnians* is about Peace, and *for* Peace. And we may forever wonder at the make-up of a citizenry that would not only allow the performance of such a play, in the depths of a life-and-death war, at a public festival (the Lenaia), but would also award it first prize in the comic competition. But we must not let this lead us into the critical syndrome which equates "message" with "plot" automatically. The *Acharnians* is a unity—a highly skillful unity—of intrinsically disparate themes around a central focus, the Pleasure-Pain antinomy. And Peace, while the most important part of this unity, is still a part. Aristophanes was a playwright first, and this is a play.

Translation

The language of this translation is American English; its aim is comprehensibility as poetry, drama, and humor to a putative educated Greekless *hearer*—though that such will exist is, admittedly, a fairly feckless hope. To this end, I have expanded where necessary and important, particularly in the core of the play, the *agōn*—Dikaiopolis' defense to the audience and his subsequent confrontation by Lamachos—where it seems vital to me that every shift of thought be understood. That this swells an already long speech to prodigious size, I do not deny; I can only plead that poetry, drama, and humor, individually and collectively, have no greater enemy than the footnote. Thus, areas of metaphor have been changed on occasion, or expanded, or supplemented, or sometimes suppressed entirely. The fact of a joke in the original has been considered as of more importance in translation than the particulars of that joke. Names which involve puns (as they do a good half of the time in Aristophanes) have sometimes been translated, as those of the individual Acharnians; sometimes left unchanged, as Dikaiopolis; sometimes changed completely, as in the case of the Persian envoy, whose name in Greek, *Pseudartabas*—"False (Persian) Measure"—appears here as *Shambyses* to convey the falseness and Persianness.

One difficulty in this particular comedy deserves mention. The action of the *Acharnians* is articulated throughout by a clash between Euripidean *Schwärmerei* and what, for the purposes of the play, we are to regard as normal speech. In default of any contemporary tragic diction that can be parodied—except by making it flatter, which is antithetical to Aristophanes' practice—I have had recourse to the same ranting fustian which, in one guise or another, has marked highfalutin windiness in English for at least 350 years. Further, since even the "normal speech" is declamatory rhetoric of a texture surpassed in English only by Ben Jonson, I have not attempted to render any part of the play into the flattest possible English, which has become the fashion. But English rhetoric needs more space to work in than Greek, and the result has inevitably been more expansion. I have often, therefore, lost the conciseness of this most concise play of Aristophanes. Unhappily—but I would rather be understood.

Finally, I have had in mind, throughout this translation, not the ancient Theater of Dionysos in Athens, but the normal present-day proscenium stage. This is not to say that I regard it as an improvement, but as a fact—a fact whose attempted reform in a translation of a difficult Greek comedy can only obscure more important things.

In short, in changing a myriad of details to gain the impression of the whole without recourse to footnote upon footnote, I have been falsely true. Which is not the same thing, I trust, as being truly false.

Text

The text is basically that of Victor Coulon in the Budé series (first published 1923), supplemented by those of Van Leeuwen (1901), Rogers (1910), Elliott (1914), and Cantarella (1953). "Supplemented" is no word to use for that fantastically enjoyable amalgam of useful knowledge and wild rhetoric, the edition (with copious notes and translation into glossematic Shakespearian) of W. J. M. Starkie (1909). Some important deviations are commented on in the notes. The division of speeches between the two Koryphaioi is due, in the main, to the work of John Williams White, whose long-ago study "An Unrecognized Actor in Greek Comedy" (*Harvard Studies in Classical Philology* 17 (1906), pp. 159 ff.) was utilized fully only by Starkie. More modern editors seem, at times, to live in fear of helping the reader.

Acknowledgments

I should like to express my gratitude to the University of California for the faculty grants which made possible the typing of several stages of the versions of both the *Acharnians* and the *Wasps,* and to a number of my colleagues, primarily Donald Johns, William Sharp, and Marshall Van Deusen, for supplying my rantings with a receptive audience and acute criticism. I am also indebted to two of my former students, Joseph Winkler and Theodore Gulesarian, for forever asking "Why?" and to Donna Lippert for complete complaisance and competence in the face of rather curious demands placed on a typist. The sum of my wife's contributions is too staggering to be enumerated (as any woman whose husband has tried to become an Athenian comic poet will know), and my gratitude is in proportion. The onlie begetter of this work, who added to the normal editorial functions that of licking his contributor into shape as a mother bear does her cub, is remembered in the dedication.

DOUGLASS PARKER

Characters of the Play

DIKAIOPOLIS, *an elderly Athenian*

A HERALD

OLYMPOS, *a peripatetic divine*

AN AMBASSADOR

SHAMBYSES

THEOROS

FIRST KORYPHAIOS

SECOND KORYPHAIOS

CHORUS *of aged charcoal-burners from Acharnai*

DAUGHTER *of Dikaiopolis*

WIFE *of Dikaiopolis*

KEPHISOPHON, *servant and secretary to Euripides*

EURIPIDES, *a tragedian*

LAMACHOS, *a military man*

A MEGARIAN

TWO LITTLE GIRLS, *daughters of the Megarian*

AN INFORMER

A THEBAN

NIKARCHOS, *an informer*

LAMACHOS' SERVANT

A FARMER

A BEST MAN

A MAID OF HONOR

A MESSENGER

MEMBERS OF THE ASSEMBLY	ODOMANTIANS	AMBASSADORS
EUNUCHS	SLAVES	WHORES

7

SCENE: *A street in Athens, representing, in the Prologue, the Pnyx—the meeting place of the Athenian Assembly. In the background are three houses, which belong, from left to right, to Dikaiopolis, Euripides, and Lamachos. Dikaiopolis, a disconsolate, ragged old farmer who has been forced into Athens to do sentry duty, is discovered alone before the Pnyx.*

     DIKAIOPOLIS

Soliloquizing.

     I have measured out my life in peptic ulcers.
     Pleasures, sparse.
              Quite sparse.

Counting on his fingers.

                   Precisely four.
     But Sufferings—numberless:
                 my life is Destiny's Dump.
     Come right down to it, what Pleasure have I known that truly
     deserved the title of Unalloyed Joy?
                  The first
     was that warm, satisfied, happy glow in my stomach
     when I saw Kleon fairly caught in that comedy
     by Aristophanes, compelled to belch up those five talents.*
     That was a tonic. The Knights won my inexpressible
     love for managing that. What a delicious day
     for Hellas!
             But that blessing was blotted out, of course,
     by the torment of a terrible tragedy. Tingling in anticipation
     of an Aischylos revival, aching and gaping in the audience,
     I heard the announcement: *"THEOGNIS* WILL PRESENT HIS
        PLAY."
     Theognis? It felt more like Thrombosis, I tell you.
     But I did have another Pleasure—Pleasure Two:
     In the musical competition, I smiled to hear Dexitheos
     sweetly drown out those jangling modern discords
     with an old-time tune.
               Not that *that* lasted, either.
     (Doesn't anyone play *music* any more? This year
     it was that foul-lipped flutist Chairis, sneaking in
     with all those new-fangled trills. He murdered the hymn
     and me. Death and a dislocated neck—
                   I ducked.)

Giving way completely to irritation.

     But never, ever, since I began to wash,
     have I been so bitten in my brows by soap as now,
     when there's a stated meeting of the Assembly called
     for dawn, and here's the Pnyx—completely empty!

Everybody's down at the Agora, gabbing, cackling,
running away from the Masters-at-Arms. Nobody's
going to rope *them* into their civic duty. No, sir!
The Executive Board* hasn't come!

                              Oh, it will—
late, shoving and jostling—you know how—
streaming down in a bunch to get the first bench;
but they don't give a damn for peace and how to get it.
Oh, Athens, Athens!
So I come to Assembly—as usual, first—and *sit*.
But what's to do when you're all alone?

                              Well,
Thinking and ticking his activities off on his fingers.
     I sigh,
          I yawn,
               I stretch . . .

                    sometimes I fart.
     I try to think of things to do . . .
                              I write . . .
     I pluck out my gray hairs . . .
                    I balance my books . . .

Becoming conscious of his finger-counting and thus his unhappiness,
he lapses briefly into declamation:
     I fix my eyes upon my fields and lust for Peace.
     I loathe the stingy, greedy city. I long
     for my own ungrudging countryside, my generous village,
     my openhearted home sweet home. *It* never barked,
     "Buy coal! Buy oil! Buy vinegar!" Gratis it gave me
     everything, unstintingly supplied my wants, and that blasted
     city byword "BUY"—
                    Goodbye to that!
     So here I am. By god, I'm ready to boo,
     to interrupt, to heckle every speaker who dares
     to say a word on any subject but Peace.
Commotion off-stage.
     Well, look! Here's the Executive Board—and it's noon.
     Didn't I tell you? Just what I was saying:
     Every last one of them pushing to sit up front.
Enter the citizens pell-mell, directed by a rather stuffy,
stentorian Herald. Olympos, a tattered, ascetic-looking*
creature, approaches cautiously.

     HERALD
     MOVE UP TOWARD THE FRONT! MOVE UP INSIDE
          PURIFIED GROUND!

OLYMPOS
Did anyone speak yet?

HERALD

                Who wishes to address us?

OLYMPOS

                                      Me.

HERALD
Who are you?

OLYMPOS

          Me? Olympos.

HERALD

                You're a god?

OLYMPOS

                          That's it,
an Olympian god. You see, Triptolemos and Demeter
conceived Olympos the first; he begat Keleos
who conceived a child by my grandmother Phainarete
and begat Lykinos, my father, and he begat me.*
Q.E.D., I am immortal, and the logical choice
to conclude a Peace with Sparta—in fact, expressly
commissioned by Heaven. But the Executive Board
refuses to pay my expenses. Can you imagine?
The gall of them—keeping a *god* on short rations.

HERALD
POLICE!

OLYMPOS
As two Skythian bowmen drag him off, kicking and screaming.
                But I'm a *god,* I tell you, a *god!*
My great-great-grandfather was a god, my great-great-grandmother
was a goddess, my mother and father, even my uncles : . .

DIKAIOPOLIS
To the Executive Board.
          Gentlemen, this is treason against the Assembly!
You can't arrest a man for opposing War
and promoting Peace!

HERALD

               You, there! Sit down! Quiet!

DIKAIOPOLIS
Apollo, no, unless you listen to me now
and bring in a bill for Peace! Open debate!

HERALD

Disregarding him and looking off-stage.

THE AMBASSADORS FROM THE GREAT KING OF PERSIA!*

DIKAIOPOLIS

The Great King, yet!

I'm sick of all these embassies,
and Persian popinjays, and Asiatic hocus-pocus—

HERALD

SILENCE!

*Enter the Athenian ambassadors returned from Persia, dressed in
garish, outlandish misrepresentations of Persian haute couture.*

DIKAIOPOLIS

Oh, no! Holy Ekbatana, what a get-up!

The first ambassador advances and addresses the assembly.

AMBASSADOR

You dispatched us to visit the Great King's court
at a *per diem* salary of two drachmas a man—precisely
eleven years ago today.

DIKAIOPOLIS

Now I *am* sick—
eleven years of drachmas down the drain!

AMBASSADOR

Choked with emotion.

Let me tell you, it was a hard and bitter life
we led those long eleven years!

Ah,

that soul-sapping saunter across the plateaus, that endless
shade, deliciously beating down from the awnings,
that enforced recumbency in luxurious litters! We
were unmanned!

DIKAIOPOLIS

Everything here was manned, of course—
by *me*.

Ah, that ankle-snapping sentry-saunter
along the endless, littered City Walls!

AMBASSADOR

Nearly in tears.

And those pitiless Persian hosts! They compelled us to drink
sweet wine, wine without water, from gold and crystal
goblets—they actually made us drink it *neat!*

DIKAIOPOLIS

Oh, you poor addled Athenians! Don't you see
they're diddling you?

AMBASSADOR

Apologetically.

These Persian fellows, now—
they're not civilized, you know. True men, to them,
are those who excel in the pleasures of the festive board.

DIKAIOPOLIS

A status we reserve for adepts in buggery.

AMBASSADOR

After three years, we came to the Great King's court.
But there'd been a purge, and he'd evacuated,
for eight months' privy business in the Crapathians.*
He took his whole army to shit—Expense meant nothing.

DIKAIOPOLIS

I know, he's got piles. Anyone else would be wiped out
inside of a month. At most.

AMBASSADOR

—But when he returned,
He played the host as only the Great King can.
Ah, Magnificence! He served us up whole oxen
fricasseed in pots!

DIKAIOPOLIS

And heifer pie, I suppose.
—Fake! Humbug!

AMBASSADOR

—He set one bird before us
three times the size of Kleonymos. It was a *roc,*
they said.

DIKAIOPOLIS

Roc? *Rook* would be more like it.
You and your two drachmas a day!

AMBASSADOR

—And now,
we have returned to Athens with Shambyses,
councillor and confidante of the King himself,
one of those upon whose selves and services
the Grand Monarch so vitally depends, that they
are called the Very Eyes of the Great King himself.
I present, gentlemen, Shambyses, the Great King's Eye.

DIKAIOPOLIS
I devoutly wish that a raven would peck yours out—
the Ambassador's Eye.

HERALD

SHAMBYSES, THE GREAT KING'S EYE!

*Enter the Eye of the King, Shambyses. He wears Persian clothes
and a mask which depicts an enormous eye above and a beard below.
In spite of this—or perhaps because of it—he seems to have
some difficulty in seeing: he keeps moving his head from
side to side, walks slowly and unsteadily, and is escorted and
supported by two attendants dressed as eunuchs.*

DIKAIOPOLIS
Holy Herakles!

*Making a comparison between Shambyses' eye and the eyes normally
painted on the sides of Greek ships.*

By god, fellow, you certainly look shipshape.

*Shambyses, missing the lead of his eunuchs, gets tangled in his
cloak and falls.*

Doubling the cape, eh?

*The eunuchs carefully point the bogus Persian toward the
Executive Board.*

Well, safe harbor at last!

*Shambyses, dubious, stumbles, and is only saved by clutching
the Ambassador.*

That's it, tie up to the dock.

Dikaiopolis looks closely at the beard below the eye and flips it.

Your porthole's open.

AMBASSADOR
Very well, Shambyses. Inform us what the King
commissioned you to tell the Athenians. Proceed.

SHAMBYSES
Loudly and majestically.

ARTASHMEDLAP XARXES TWOGGLE SATRAP!

Dead silence.

AMBASSADOR
Somewhat nervously, to Dikaiopolis.

Do you understand what he's saying?

DIKAIOPOLIS

I'm no soothsayer.

AMBASSADOR

Relieved.

> Well. He says the King will send us gold.
> —Come on, now, speak up clearly about the *gold.*

SHAMBYSES

> WOAN GETTUM NO GOLDUM, GAPASSITY IONISH!

DIKAIOPOLIS

> That was certainly clear! We've been had again.

AMBASSADOR

> Well, what's he saying?

DIKAIOPOLIS

> What's he saying? He calls
> the Ionians gap-assed idiots if they expect
> to get any gold from Persia.

AMBASSADOR

Desperately.

> No! He's talking
> about the CAPACITY of all those bullion boxes!

DIKAIOPOLIS

> Bullion, balls!
> You cheap imposter! It's over!
> Get out of here! I'll grill this fellow myself.

*The Ambassador retires in evident confusion. Dikaiopolis plants
himself squarely in front of Shambyses and waggles his fist in
the face of the King's Eye.*

> Now look, you. A clear answer, with this in your face,
> or the Great King of Persia will have a bloodshot Eye:
> *Does* the Great King intend to send us gold?

Shambyses shakes his head. The two eunuchs jerk their heads back.

> We're being bamboozled by our ambassadors, then?

*Shambyses gives a single nod. The two eunuchs waggle their heads
up and down.*

> Look! These eunuchs nodded their heads in the Greek way.
> These aren't Persians—This is local talent.

Peering closely at the first eunuch.

> Eunuchs, eh? Better say *uniques.* I know *him.*
> It's limp-wrist Kleisthenes, the All-Athenian Boy!*

To the first eunuch, disgustedly.

> Do you even invert disguises! You took the advice
> of your rash and ready rump and shaved the wrong end!
> Eunuchs and beards are a contradiction in terms! Understand?

16

To the second eunuch.

>   And who's this? Straton, maybe?

Complete confusion.

HERALD

>   Silence! Sit down!
> THE COUNCIL SUMMONS THE GREAT KING'S EYE TO DINE
> IN THE EXECUTIVE HALL.

*The procession—ambassadors, Shambyses, eunuchs—collects
itself and exits.*

DIKAIOPOLIS

To the audience.

>   By god, all this is enough
> to make a man choke! And then they squeeze me out here
> to cool my heels, to boot. But I've never seen
> the door that managed to shut *them* out from a dinner!
> Enough of this—the time has come for action,
> grand and awful.

>   Where's Olympos?

OLYMPOS

Skulking back, considerably the worse for wear.

>   Present!

DIKAIOPOLIS

> Here are eight drachmas. Take them and make a truce
> with the Spartans in *my* name. A private treaty,
> for me and my wife and children.

To the Assembly.

>   As for you,
> send out all the embassies you want!
> Stand there forever with your mouths hanging open!

Exit Olympos on the dead run.

HERALD

> THEOROS, OUR AMBASSADOR TO THE COURT OF SITALKES!*

THEOROS

Effeminate and mincing.

> Here I *am!*

DIKAIOPOLIS

>   The carpet's out for another swindler.

THEOROS

> We wouldn't have stayed in Thrace for *such* a time . . .

DIKAIOPOLIS

> I know: if you hadn't been drawing *such* a wage.

THEOROS
—if it hadn't snowed all over Thrace and simply made
the rivers *freeze*—

DIKAIOPOLIS
                         —just about the time
Theognis was cooling off his audience here
with one of those frigid tragedies of his.

THEOROS
I passed the days in drinking with Sitalkes;
and you know, my dear, he's Philathenian to a *fault*—
simply *mad* about us all, so much enamored
that he scrawls on his walls, "The Athenians are *lovely!*"
His son—we made him a citizen—was, oooh, *wild*
to skin our Athenian sausages. He got down on his *knees*
and actually *begged* his father to send his adopted
country some aid and succor! Sitalkes swore
to help, to send us *such* an army we'd shout,
"Oooh, what a swarm of *locusts* is coming this way!"

DIKAIOPOLIS
I'm damned if I believe a single thing
you've said—except that bit about the locusts.

THEOROS
And now he's sent us the most *warlike* race in Thrace!

DIKAIOPOLIS
Oh-oh! I begin to see the light.

HERALD
                    YOU THRACIANS,
WHO CAME WITH THEOROS, FRONT AND CENTER!

*Enter a detachment of Odomantians, notable for a hugeness of body,
a savage vacuity of expression, and an alarming length of violently
red-tipped phallus.*

DIKAIOPOLIS
                                        What's *this?*

THEOROS
THE ARMY OF THE ODOMANTIANS!

DIKAIOPOLIS
                              Odomantians?
Examining the troops more closely.
                              What happened here?

Who docked the Odomantian cock?

THEOROS
> You pay these men
two drachmas each per day, and they'll ram and jam
Boiotia right into the *ground!*

DIKAIOPOLIS
> Two drachmas a day?
For these walking appetites? They don't even come with foreskins!
And for *this* you'd turn your backs on our own Navy?

*During this exchange, some of the Odomantians have managed to
pilfer Dikaiopolis' garlic—the sole remains of his solitary
breakfast—divide it with their fellows, and begin eating it,
noisily. Dikaiopolis suddenly realizes his loss.*

Help! I'm ruined! I'm plundered! An Odomantian raid!
Drop that garlic!

THEOROS
> *Naughty!* I wouldn't go near:
they're garlic-primed, like gamecocks—and, oooh, are they *game!*

DIKAIOPOLIS
To the Executive Board.

Gentlemen, are you going to stay in your seats
and do nothing, while I'm being robbed and maltreated
by a bunch of barbarians, here in the very heart
of Athens? I'm a citizen, remember?
> Well?

*If the members of the Executive Board do remember, they give no
indication of it: there is no reply. First abashed, then annoyed,
Dikaiopolis tries a different tack. He sticks out his palm,
looks at it, looks at the sky, and announces:*

I move the Assembly adjourn, and table discussion
of the Thracians' wages.
> It's a nondebatable motion—
Divine Intervention. Briefly, I've just received
a sign from Heaven—I felt a drop of rain.

This seems agreeable all around.

HERALD

LET THE THRACIANS RETIRE, TO RETURN DAY AFTER
TOMORROW. THE ASSEMBLY IS HEREBY DECLARED
ADJOURNED.

*General exit, in haste, by the Herald, the Executive Board, the
members of the Assembly, Theoros, and the Odomantians—in short,
by everybody but Dikaiopolis, who stands in center stage, looking
disconsolately about him.*

DIKAIOPOLIS
That's legislation for you:
I lost my lunch.

Looking off.

Look, here's Olympos back from Sparta already.
Welcome, Olympos!

OLYMPOS

*Entering on the dead run again, bearing three leather bottles.
Throughout this scene, he is very nervous, continually looking
back over his shoulder.*

No "welcomes" until I can stop.
Mind if I run? I have to keep fleeing to flee
those Acharnians.
Every bit helps, you know.

DIKAIOPOLIS

What's up?

OLYMPOS
Well, I was en route with the treaties, and someone
smelled them out—
true Acharnian elders, they were:
the real thing, hearts of oak, ribs of rock,
the authentic, genuine old maple-hearts
of Marathon. They set up a shout:
"You cesspool!
You dare bring a truce when our vines have been cut down?"
Then they gathered up rocks in their cloaks. I tried
to get away, but they kept following me
and shouting.

DIKAIOPOLIS
Let them shout. Have you got the treaty?

OLYMPOS
Producing his wine bottles.

But certainly. I have three samples right here.

Proffering the smallest bottle.

Here's the five-year vintage Peace. Taste it.

DIKAIOPOLIS
Uncorking and sniffing.
Pew!

OLYMPOS
What's wrong?

DIKAIOPOLIS

> There's caulk in it. It smells
of pitch and shipyards.

OLYMPOS

Proffering a somewhat larger bottle.

> All right, here—try this.
The ten-year vintage Peace. Take a taste.

DIKAIOPOLIS

Uncorking, sniffing, and making a wry face.

> Ugh. This has
the stink of top-level conferences. It's turned sour,
just like our Allies.

OLYMPOS

Holding out a huge bottle.

> Very well, try this:
a thirty-year vintage Peace on land and sea.

DIKAIOPOLIS

*Uncorking and sniffing, then sniffing again incredulously,
then tasting, then tasting again and breaking into a broad smile.*

Festival of Bacchos! The true bouquet of bliss!
This has the aroma of nectar, the whiff of ambrosia,
I taste the end of forced marches and short rations,
and in my mouth the wine sets up a chant:
Goodbye to Regimentation!
> This is mine!
For drink and sacrifice, this is the wine I choose!
And for the Acharnians—a long farewell from me.
My war is over, my distress is done!
I'll celebrate the Feast of Dionysos,
God of Wine,

Holding up the bottle.

> and now the God of Peace.

OLYMPOS

And, as for me, I'll run away from the Acharnians.

*Both exit, Olympos off-stage as fast as he can, Dikaiopolis
slowly and luxuriously into his house.*

After a short pause, the Chorus enters, wheezing and puffing in
slow and painful pursuit, led by the First and Second Koryphaioi.
They are dressed in long, ragged cloaks, and represent aged charcoal-burners
from the Athenian deme of Acharnai. The scene is understood
to have shifted from the Pnyx to the environs of Dikaiopolis'
house, outside the walls of Athens.

FIRST KORYPHAIOS

This way, men! Over here! Follow him—track him down!
Sound out everybody you meet! Trapping the traitor
is a Civic Duty—

Athens Expects, and all that.

To the audience.

—Pardon,

but is there anyone in the house who can possibly give us
some information? Did a man run through here recently, holding
(excuse the word) a TRUCE? And if so, which way did he go?

FIRST SEMICHORUS

Woe—he has vanished! Woe—he has fled!
Woe for my own decrepitude!
Woe for my youth, for the thews which knew
to shrug a burden and run to a draw
PHAŸLLOS the fleet.* If Then were Now,
this scum with the treaty wouldn't escape
and swirl with scornful ease from my grip:

If Now were Then,
I'd run him down!

SECOND KORYPHAIOS

But it's Now, not Then. Be realistic, men—just look at us:
I've pulled up lame already; old Lakrateides' legs
are practically ossified. But still, let's not give up the chase!
It's a Question of Honor: We may be doddering, decrepit, ramshackle—
But we're ACHARNIANS first, by god! If he gets away, it's Disgrace—
our proud name ground in the dust by the heel of a light-foot Traitor!

SECOND SEMICHORUS

Damn him, O Zeus and Gods on high!
Damn his truce! But especially
damn the SPARTANS forevermore!
They left my fields dead and sere,
they razed my grapes—and they'll reap WAR!
I'll stick and stake them! I'll thrust and pierce
right up to the stock—and never cease
till the last one refrains
from trampling my vines!

FIRST KORYPHAIOS

First things first. Later, the War; Now, the Traitor.
Stalk him, dog him, ferret him out! Ransack the world!
And leave no stone unturned—he might have crawled underneath.
If not, take the stone along and throw it when we find him.

DIKAIOPOLIS
From within his house.
LET EVERYONE KEEP HOLY SILENCE!

SECOND KORYPHAIOS

Be still, everybody! Didn't you hear that call for silence?
This is the fellow we're looking for!—Look, out of the way!
I think our man is coming outside here to sacrifice.

*The Chorus retires to the right. Dikaiopolis emerges from his house,
carrying a pot. He is followed by his daughter, who carries a basket
containing the offerings; his wife; and two slaves, who bear
a huge phallus on a pole.*

DIKAIOPOLIS
LET EVERYONE KEEP HOLY SILENCE!
He surveys his group.
The basket bearer should move up front just a bit.
His daughter moves slightly forward.
And Xanthias ought to set up the Phallus.
Xanthias and the other slave wrestle the phallus into an erect position.
—Daughter,
put down the basket, and we'll begin the rite.

DAUGHTER

Mother, hand me the ladle. It's time to pour
the sauce over the cake.
She does so. Dikaiopolis gives his entourage a last inspection.

DIKAIOPOLIS
Excellent!
He prays.

O Lord Dionysos,
Let this procession and this solemn sacrifice we make
find favor in your eyes. May I and all my household
conduct once more the country festival by which
we honor you as God of Growth and Increase.
Once again let us celebrate the Country Dionysia.*
Grant, O Lord, your blessings now on me,
freed from the army's service and returned to yours.
And let this Peace of Thirty Years endure,
and bring us health, wealth, and true happiness.
Amen.

*He turns to his daughter. He is obviously somewhat distressed
by her ragged, not-too-clean clothing (a condition which she
shares with the rest of the family; Peace has come to Dikaiopolis,
but Prosperity has not) and her gawky adolescence. He conceals
the distress from her, but not from the audience.*

> Daughter dear, you have an important role
> in a most holy rite: you're bearing the basket for Bacchos.
> So be correct and proper. Look demure. Dainty. Sweet.

The daughter tries. He shudders, and speaks in a disgusted aside.

Did I say sweet? Sweet as vinegar!
> That's perfect, darling.

It'll be a lucky man who marries you, it will!
You'll breed him a lovely tribe—polecats, probably—
just like their mother—farting away in the wee hours.
The dawn comes up like thunder, so does she.
Move on, dear, but careful—someone in that crowd

He gestures at the empty stage.

might sneak up in the confusion and nibble off
all these jewels.

He points to the audience.

Watch out for *that* mob, too.

To the slaves, who have set the phallus down.

Xanthias, you know what this is? It's a phallic procession.
This is the Phallus, the Symbol of Phales, the god.

He indicates his daughter.

And *that* is the basket bearer, the Ritual Virgin.
Now, the two of you get in behind that Virgin
and erect that Symbol—and keep it erect.

Don't droop!
I'll bring up the rear and sing the Phallic Hymn.

To his wife.

Get a good seat, dear—watch from the roof.

His wife disappears into the house, to reappear a moment later on the roof.

For-*ward!*

The procession makes a slow circuit of the stage, in time with Dikaiopolis'
singing of the hymn to the personified phallus, Phales.

O Phales, Bacchos' fellow, friend,
carouser, king of guests,
night-wanderer, adulterer—
Holy one, O Pederast!
O Phales, Phales, favor our feast.

I greet you after six years, Lord.
Gone beyond recall
are war neuroses and Lamachóses;
my shield hangs on the wall.
O Phales, Phales, favor our feast.

My night patrols are sweeter now:
I guard against the raids
and forays on my firewood, led
by sexy serving-maids.

When one comes jouncing down the hill
with faggots in her hand,
the Larceny is petty—but
the Penalty is grand!

I mount a sudden flank attack,
and take her by surprise,
I enfilade her vineyard, then
de-grape her, Spartanwise!
O Phales, Phales, favor our feast.

O Phales, enter in to us,
and join us in our songs!
Come share our drink, and spread our joy!
Stay up to hail the dawn!

And when the rout is over, Lord,
and all the songs are sung,
a cup of Peace to clear the head—
and only the shield stays hung!
O Phales, Phales, favor our feast.

*The Chorus bursts from concealment and rushes upon the procession.
The daughter and the slaves escape into the house, and the wife
disappears inside from the roof, leaving Dikaiopolis, hugging his pot,
to confront a shower of stones, not too accurately thrown,
from the angry Acharnians.*

FIRST KORYPHAIOS
That's the man! That's the man! Slash him! Smash him!

SECOND KORYPHAIOS
That's the scoundrel. That's the traitor! Rush him! Crush him!

DIKAIOPOLIS
Holy Herakles, what's this? Look out, you'll smash the pot!

FIRST KORYPHAIOS
You're the one we'll crush to death, you rotten renegade!

DIKAIOPOLIS
Unperturbed.
Would you mind disclosing the nature of the charge, reverend
Acharians?

FIRST KORYPHAIOS
What a question! You've got no shame—and you'll get no pity!

You betrayed the City—YOU MADE A TRUCE ON YOUR OWN!
  And still
you have the gall to look Athenians like us in the eye!

DIKAIOPOLIS
I admit it. I made a truce—but I had reasons. Listen.
FIRST KORYPHAIOS
Listen to *you?* You listen to *me:* We're entombing you *now!*

DIKAIOPOLIS
Not before you hear me, friends. Please let me speak.

FIRST SEMICHORUS
Gyrating menacingly.

> We refuse! We'd sooner hear Kleon—
> till now, the height of our hates.
> And *him* we plan to flay and tan
> and make into shoes for the Knights!

FIRST KORYPHAIOS
Nothing can change the facts. You made a Truce with the SPARTANS!
We don't want orations—we don't want harangues—WE WANT
  VENGEANCE!

DIKAIOPOLIS
Your singleness of purpose is praiseworthy, Sirs—but scarcely relevant.
Don't stumble over the Spartans—they're peripheral. The question
is the Peace. Hear me, and decide: did I do a Good Thing?

SECOND KORYPHAIOS
GOOD THING? A Truce with SPARTANS? How can you trust
  them? They swear
by adulterated altars, diluted libations, and hollow handshakes!
GOOD THING!

DIKAIOPOLIS
          This is madness, friends. I know the Spartans, too,
and the fact remains that they're not to blame for all our troubles.

FIRST KORYPHAIOS
NOT ALL! You've compounded your treason; this is Patent Betrayal!
  NO QUARTER!

DIKAIOPOLIS
I repeat: *The Spartans are not to blame for all our troubles.*
Why, I, as I stand before you now, could point out a sizable
number of complaints that the Spartans have against us, complaints
that are well-authenticated and, more important, perfectly reasonable.

SECOND KORYPHAIOS

Staggering, hand to chest.

> Sorry, men—my heart can't stand shock the way it used to.
> I never heard the like!—You mean you'll defend the ENEMY? HERE?
> TO US?

DIKAIOPOLIS

> Since you put it that way, yes.

With a wave at the audience.

> And such is the power of Truth
> on the sovereign people of Athens, that I feel little or no
> hesitation at offering to address this crowd like What's-his-name
> in Euripides' play.

SECOND KORYPHAIOS

> What play?

DIKAIOPOLIS

> I forget. But the name doesn't matter.
> It's the *mise en scène,* the stark, tragic alternatives:
> Victory
> or Death—in this case, Persuasion or Decapitation. I'll speak with my
> head . . .

SECOND KORYPHAIOS

Eagerly.

> On the Block?

DIKAIOPOLIS

> No, this is still a Comedy—with my head on the
> Breadboard.*

FIRST KORYPHAIOS

Resolute as ever, to the Chorus.

> Townsmen, neighbors, up and at him! Fling those stones!
> Outfit this turncoat properly—dress him in Spartan colors:
> rich, shiny, sticky, gooey, bloody RED!

DIKAIOPOLIS

As the Chorus, with wild shouts, advances again.

> What have we here—another flare-up? I swear, you men
> have clinkers for hearts. Occupational hazard, I imagine.

The brandishings become more violent.

> Hmmm.
> I take it, members of the Ancient & Noble Order of the Sons
> of Acharnai, that, deep down, you don't prefer to hear my speech?

FIRST KORYPHAIOS

> Never!

DIKAIOPOLIS
Is this final?

FIRST KORYPHAIOS
NEVER!—I mean, yes—it's final.

DIKAIOPOLIS
That's really too bad.

SECOND KORYPHAIOS
We'll die before we listen to you!

DIKAIOPOLIS
I suppose you might. But don't on my account, Brothers of the
Benevolent
& Protective Association of Aged Acharnian Heroes.

FIRST KORYPHAIOS
TRAITOR,
YOU DIE!

He raises a rock. The Chorus follows suit.

DIKAIOPOLIS
Now, look here, Gentlemen, this has gone far enough!
This brawling and backbiting is simply too much, and I hereby serve
notice
that I intend to bite back. "Die," you say, do you?
Well, it's Death for Death—REPRISALS, Gentlemen!
I hold as
hostages
your most adored, your dearest friends and relatives—the which
I now shall flay and disembowel before your horrified gaze.

He turns on his heel and enters his house.

SECOND KORYPHAIOS
Men of Acharnai, neighbors, what could he mean? Do you think
he has one of our children penned up inside his house?

FIRST KORYPHAIOS
Impossible!

SECOND KORYPHAIOS
That may be so, but where do you suppose he gets
his confidence?

*Dikaiopolis returns and stands before his door. In his left hand
is a large scuttle full of charcoal; in his right, a huge carving knife.
The Chorus recoils in horror.*

DIKAIOPOLIS
Very well, Sirs—stone if you must. But a word of warning:

One pebble in my direction, and I'll destroy this scuttle
and its defenseless contents.

Any charcoal-lovers* present?

He raises the knife.

By god,

I'll find out soon enough.

CHORUS

—No! No! Not that!

—I can't bear to look!

—I'll die!

—That scuttle's a schoolmate!

A neighbor!
—An old and valued family friend!

—No, please! I beg you!

—I implore you, whatever you do, DON'T!

—NO!
—NO!

DIKAIOPOLIS
Gentlemen, your little friends are doomed. Those howls and pleas
are futile—I refuse to listen.

SECOND KORYPHAIOS

Can't you reconsider, Sir?

Does Friendship, tried in the furnace, mean nothing at all to you?

FIRST KORYPHAIOS
Can't you see that even a lump of carbon has feelings?

DIKAIOPOLIS
Why should I listen to you? Did you listen to me?

SECOND KORYPHAIOS

Then speak!

Give us ALL the particulars, here and now!

FIRST KORYPHAIOS

There's nothing

we crave to hear so much as a good pro-Spartan speech!

SECOND KORYPHAIOS
It may mean nausea, cramps, and heartbreak—but I won't betray that
scuttle.

DIKAIOPOLIS
All right—but show good faith. Shake the rocks out of your cloaks.

The members of the Chorus shake their cloaks violently.
A clatter of rocks to the ground.

SECOND KORYPHAIOS

There they are, Sir. And now, Fair Play. Put that sword away.

DIKAIOPOLIS

I still have my doubts. Not that I don't trust you, of course,
but one or two rocks might still be lurking in your folds.

SECOND SEMICHORUS
Gyrating desperately, flapping their cloaks.

> We've shaken them out—not a pebble!
> We are, Sir, de-lapidated.
> So keep your word, and put up your sword,
> and commence your defense, as stated.

Retaining the scuttle, Dikaiopolis puts the carving knife down.
A sigh of relief from the Chorus.

DIKAIOPOLIS

Saved—from disaster scarcely a stone's throw distant,
Gentlemen. No thanks to you. You were ready to rock me
with your war cry, and thus ensure the death of Your Own—
these poor coals from Parnes, mute martyrs
to their comrades' monomania.
Gaze at this pitiful scuttle,
still quivering and distraught! At your attack, black fear
clutched at its vitals—and squeezed. Squidlike, it squirted
an entire peck of coal dust over me—its Savior.
Gentlemen, I ask you: *Aren't you ashamed of yourselves?*
Look at you: Men?
MUST! Venerable verjuice—
raw wine in rotted bottles, stopped forever
against the infusion of Opposing Views, Fair Play,
or Common Sense.
Case in point—the Present.
You burst your seams, and spray your howls and stones,
while here I stand, willing to expose my every
last pro-Spartan argument from the Breadboard. Did *I*
give in to passion, or madness, or pique? And yet
I swear I love my life no less than you.

FIRST SEMICHORUS

> We must protest your reticence:
> We're aching for your eloquence,
> and beg you, in all deference,
> to put aside your diffidence
> and bring your Breadboard out—
> AND SPEAK, YOU LOUT!

FIRST KORYPHAIOS
Observe the rules you made—remember? Persuasion
or Decapitation? Now set up that Board of Inquiry and commence.

*Carrying the scuttle, Dikaiopolis enters his house, to emerge in
a moment staggering under the weight of a huge breadboard. This
he places prominently before the house.*

DIKAIOPOLIS
Proceed with your inspection, Gentlemen. I trust that everything
will meet your specifications. Over here, the Breadboard.
—And here, unaccustomed as I am . . .
                                        You have reservations?
Rest assured, Gentlemen, that I have none. Observe:
nothing up my sleeve, no concealed shields, breastplates,
bucklers, cuirasses—or mental blocks. My defense
of Sparta will not be buttressed with qualifications, or hedged
about with Significant Omissions. I shall speak the truth
as I see it, unarmed and steady as a rock . . .
                                        in fact,
Petrified. Know Your Enemy, they say. Well,
I Know My Audience (which, in this case, is the same thing),
and Knowledge is Terror. Look at them:
                                    First, the Farmers,
up from the country for the day. A happy breed—
too happy. Wafted into mindless bliss by any
flag-waving, any patriotic puff from a charlatan,
and to hell with the facts—their country, right or wrong—
true Slaves of the Laud. Their price is praise. They're bought
and sold by demagogues, and never know it.

Pointing at another section of the audience.

                                    Next, mark
the Gaffers—crabbed old men who gum their gruel
and long but to bite again—and, possessed of nothing
sharp but their convictions, enroll as jurors
and convict, over and over, in merciless mastication.

Pointing at another section of the audience very specifically.

And Kleon.*
                Him I know from—shall we say?—
personal experience. Last year's comedy provoked him.
To say the least. He dragged me into the Senate House,
sued me, and opened the sluicegates. Slander and lies
gushed from his tongue in torrents, and down the arroyo
of his mind there roared a flash flood of abuse. To purge me,

he purged himself—and in the offal, filth, and fetor
of his verbal diarrhea, I nearly smothered, mortally
immerded.

To himself.

But wait. They're all Athenians, and every
Athenian responds nobly to the Appeal to Poverty.
That's IT! I'll dress in wretched rags, in pitiful
patches—the picture of a beggar!

—May I have your permission,
Gentlemen, to retire for a moment and change my costume?

SECOND SEMICHORUS

We feel this oversubtlety
must indicate anxiety.
Thus we, in all humility,
suggest invisibility,
or some such folderol—

BUT HURRY—DON'T STALL!

SECOND KORYPHAIOS

Go change. And be as clever as you like. But remember:
There is no delay allowed in this debate!

The Chorus retires to the right, leaving Dikaiopolis alone.

DIKAIOPOLIS

Now, if ever, must I assume a Hero's
Soul . . . But where to get hold of one? And where
to find those rags, for that matter? Let's see . . .

Of course!

There's only one source of supply:

EURIPIDES!

It's obvious—

he produces the rattiest heroes in town.
He strides purposefully to Euripides' house, center, and
bangs on the door.

Porter!

KEPHISOPHON*
Opening the door and peering out lugubriously.

Whence is that knocking?

DIKAIOPOLIS

Hello. Is Euripides in?

KEPHISOPHON

Within, he is without—if you have the wit
to conceive me.

DIKAIOPOLIS

I can't even understand you. You say
he's *in* and *not* in?

KEPHISOPHON

Precisely, Reverend Sir.
It's a paradox—the exegesis is really quite elementary:
His mind is *out*side, culling floscules of fustian,
bouquets of lays and poesies—while he himself
is *in*side, feet up, composing a tragedy in well-wrought
earnest. He has, in short, achieved Dissociation
of Sensibility.

DIKAIOPOLIS

Ah, Euripides, happiest of dramatists!
Did ever such a subtle servant exist in nature?
What other playwright has philosophers for slaves?

—Very well,
summon him out.

KEPHISOPHON

But that's impossible!

DIKAIOPOLIS

Notwithstanding,
summon him anyway.

Kephisophon retreats inside with a sniff and slams the door.

No matter. You won't get rid of me—
I'll batter the door. Down, if I have to.

He bangs on the door, shouting.

EURIPIDES!

No answer.

YOO-HOO, EURIPIDES!

No answer. He stops knocking.

No use. How *do* you call
a tragedian to the door?
Of course!

Tragically.

If e'er you hearkened
to mortal in torment, Euripides, hearken now,
I pray you, to me, Dikaiopolis—blasted from birth.

He taps lightly. The double doors spring open at his touch, exposing
Euripides' study, which rather resembles a junk shop. The floor
is littered with oddments, mostly receptacles in various stages of
disrepair, while all about the walls is hung and piled a profusion
of impossibly ragged cloaks and hats. Euripides himself is reclining,
facing the audience, on a couch which resembles a chaise longue.
He is meditating vacuously, tablet and stylus in hand. Kephisophon
stands at the head of couch with tablet and stylus, imitating his
master in every particular. Both look up, annoyed, at the interruption.

EURIPIDES
Hence, pest! I'm busy.

DIKAIOPOLIS
                    Have the stagehands wheel
your set out here.

EURIPIDES
            But that's impossible!

DIKAIOPOLIS
                        Notwithstanding,
have them do it anyway.

EURIPIDES
                Very well. They may wheel
me out—
Glancing from the couch to the floor, a distance of about two feet.
            but I have no time to waste in descending.

The set is wheeled forward to the center of the stage.
Dikaiopolis stands by it.

DIKAIOPOLIS
EURIPIDES!

EURIPIDES
                    Why this vociferous apostrophe?

DIKAIOPOLIS
                                        Normally,
they tell me, people write with their feet on the ground.
But yours don't touch it.
                    —No wonder your heroes are cripples!
And why in the world are you dressed in those miserable, filthy
tragic rags?
                    No wonder your heroes are beggars!

To himself.

Heroes? Beggars? I almost forgot.

To Euripides.

                              In my need,
I implore you by your knees.

He kneels by the couch and tries to clasp the tragedian around
his legs, an undertaking quite distasteful to Euripides, who
keeps struggling to disentangle himself.

                              O Knees of Euripides,
vouchsafe me a tatter or two from that threadbare tragedy
of yours. You see, I have to make a lengthy formal
defense to the Chorus, and I absolutely must persuade them:
I either turn their heads, or lose my own.

EURIPIDES
You wish rags, eh?

DIKAIOPOLIS
                    Yes, rags.

EURIPIDES
                         Have you a preference?

He gestures at the accumulation of ragged clothes.

DIKAIOPOLIS
                                        Er—yes . . .

EURIPIDES
Specifically, then, which rags?—Confused, eh?

Pointing to a set of rags. At each successive name, he indicates another.

Do these
strike a chord? My best. Monuments to misery.
Oineus wore them—you remember the play, of course.

DIKAIOPOLIS
No, not Oineus. It was someone even more miserable.

EURIPIDES
Poor, blind Phoinix, perchance?

DIKAIOPOLIS

No, not Phoinix.
It was someone else. Even shabbier than Phoinix.

EURIPIDES
Than Phoinix?—What fouler, more unlovely tatters
could there be?—Perhaps the scraps of Philoktetes the beggar?

DIKAIOPOLIS
No, not him. This Hero beggared all description.

EURIPIDES
Then you must mean this—the loathesome, bedrabbled burlap
worn by Bellerophon the cripple.

DIKAIOPOLIS

No, not Bellerophon.
—First, my Hero was a combination of all those others—
not blind, though. But he *was* a beggar, a cripple, and a windbag:
The Perfect Orator.—Does that help?

EURIPIDES

Proceed.

DIKAIOPOLIS

Let me think.
It's been almost fifteen years . . .

Oh, yes—he wasn't
really a beggar.

EURIPIDES
They never are.

DIKAIOPOLIS

But he dressed
as a beggar in order to make a speech—like me.
He had to convince some Greeks that he wasn't a traitor.
To do this, he had to prove that some war was pointless—
that its cause was some woman or other who wasn't worth it.

EURIPIDES
They never are.

      —But hold on a minute! Was this
the Trojan War? And Helen?

DIKAIOPOLIS

      That's right—And he spoke
with his head on a Block—like me—and won over the King.

EURIPIDES
Agamemnon?

DIKAIOPOLIS

      Yes, that was the King—And just when he had
the Greeks convinced, in came a soldier . . .

EURIPIDES

      Achilles?

DIKAIOPOLIS
Yes. And . . .

EURIPIDES

      I know! It's . . .

DIKAIOPOLIS

      This soldier upset everything.
He threatened to kill . . .

EURIPIDES

      But I . . .

DIKAIOPOLIS

      . . . the Beggar—who was really
a King!

EURIPIDES

      It's *The Tragicall* . . .

DIKAIOPOLIS

      But what I forget . . .

EURIPIDES

      . . . *Historie* . . .

DIKAIOPOLIS
. . . is how it turned out.

EURIPIDES

      . . . *of Telephos, King of Mysia!*

DIKAIOPOLIS
Telephos! Yes! Oh, to swaddle myself in Telephos'
vile vestments! I supplicate you, Euripides: Please
confer upon me that mighty Hero's clout!

EURIPIDES

I'd love to.
   So be it.

      —Kephisophon, tender him the tatters
of Telephos. You'll find them over there, sandwiched in
between Ino's rags and Thyestes' patchwork.

*Kephisophon digs out a particularly loathesome cloak. Euripides
turns to Dikaiopolis.*

           Behold!
O happy man, since even now the object
of all your desire shudders expectant for your grasp!
Take, and, taking, love these shoddy shreds!

DIKAIOPOLIS

Taking the cloak, lifting it up, and peering through the numerous holes.

O Zeus, whose holy gaze does pierce and penetrate
through all our mortal raiment to the shuddering clay
beneath, grant that I may now be garbed
most grievously, in the world's most woebegone weeds.

He puts the cloak on, then holds it wide before Euripides.

  Euripides, the breadth of your generosity is justly vaunted—

Shaking the perforated folds of the cloak.

not to say vented—and such beneficence, I am sure,
would never knowingly be left unfinished. I beg you,
cap this kindness, Sir: Bestow upon me
the appropriate, matching props—but, most of all,

Pointing.

that little Mysian bonnet to shroud my head.

Striking a tragic attitude.

  This very day must I a mendicant mime,
  must be the thing I am, yet seem another.
The audience, of course, is sure to know who I am—
but the Chorus must stand there stupefied, a flock of fools
for me to twit and twiddle with tragic ironies.

EURIPIDES

I accede.

*He motions to Kephisophon, who procures the bonnet and gives it
to Dikaiopolis. This sequence of events is repeated with subsequent items,
the basket excepted.*

  I do endorse and approbate, Sir,
  your torturous, twisted plots, the protean offspring
  of a mind thick-packed with thin-drawn strands of craft.

DIKAIOPOLIS

Putting the bonnet on, then taking it off in a sweeping bow.

Fortune attend you, Sir,—and, as for Telephos,
may that which I intend attend him:

In a loud mock-aside.

                     Fairer
Fortune, for Telephos is I, and I am Telephos.
—Say, that's not bad! Do the quotes come along with the cloak?
—However, Sir, my need is still a great one:
My guise literally cries for a beggar's staff.

EURIPIDES

Take it.

       And now, Sir, hie thee hence, from out
this vaulted marble pile.

DIKAIOPOLIS

To himself, loudly.

                 Alas, my Soul,*
dost see how I am scorned and thrust away
though yet in grating need of tragic trash?
Come, be importunate, Soul: Increase your appeals!
Expand your prayers! Broaden your orisons!

                           —Euripides,
please fetch from your treasures a trifle for an indigent beggar?—
A tiny, battered, burned, and broken basket?

EURIPIDES

What need hath wrought within thy soul this wish
for wicker, wretch?

DIKAIOPOLIS

            Who *needs* it? I just *want* it.

EURIPIDES

Snatching the basket from Kephisophon and throwing it at Dikaiopolis.

Look, you bother me. Now, dammit, GET OUT!

DIKAIOPOLIS

                       Alas!
Fortune attend thee, and mayst thou grow in grace
as well as e'er thy mother did— in groceries*

EURIPIDES

Dammit, LEAVE ME ALONE!

DIKAIOPOLIS

                   Just one more thing?—
A lopsided, misfired mug that's chipped on the lip?

EURIPIDES

Take it to perdition, damn you!

And be apprised
that you do sorely vex and gall our halls!

DIKAIOPOLIS

Have you ever sat through one of your own tragedies?
Talk about pure, unadulterated pestilence!
—Euripides,
sweet, *generous* Friend to All, I make this solitary
request, just this:

A teeny pot, a pottie,
please, and a sponge to go with it?

EURIPIDES

Sponge is right!
Do you want to wipe me out?

DIKAIOPOLIS

No, *me*—We beggars
are cleanly where it doesn't show, you know.

EURIPIDES

But this
is horrible—you're stealing my whole tragedy!
—All right,
take it, and, for god's sake, LEAVE!

DIKAIOPOLIS

I *am* leaving—
but whither? I lack the *sine qua non*—without it,
Dikaiopolis is dead!
—Euripides, prince of philanthropists,
grant this boon and I shall quit you forever:
Place in the basket a handful of withered leaves
to make my wretched breakfast, lest I die.

EURIPIDES

Die? You'll be the death of *me:* You've beggared
my repertory, looted my dramaturgy—MY PLAYS ARE GONE!

DIKAIOPOLIS

And so am I. I beg no more. I go.
I am become a noisome nuisance in the nostrils
of royal men, unknowing that lords do loathe me.

He turns, takes a step, then turns back.

Oh, NO! Oh, LOST!

I have forgot the hingepin
of my hope, the plinth of all my expectation!
—Euripides, epitome of magnanimity, seraph of sweet
charity, Good Guy *sans peur et sans reproche*—
may I be dissolved beyond redemption, if ever
I make petition more, beyond this lonely,
onliest request: *Give me thy mother's legacy:*
A pound and a half of wilted water cress?

EURIPIDES
Livid, to Kephisophon.
This man mouths insolence! Ho, occlude the portcullis!
Kephisophon pushing, the set is drawn back to its original position.
The doors shut with a crash, and Dikaiopolis is left alone.

DIKAIOPOLIS
O rash! O hasty! O most ungenerous! O crass!
—Ah, Soul, we must fare away without the cress.
Soul of my Soul, do you know what shortly awaits you?
The dread debate which you must make on behalf
of SPARTA?
                              —O my Soul, I'm glad I'm not *you!*
He draws an imaginary line in front of him with the beggar's staff.
Behold the starting line. And now, Get Ready—
Get Set—and GO, my swiftly coursing Soul!
He takes three or four brisk steps, then stops, slumping.
What's this? You *stop?* You swallow Euripides whole
and STOP?
                         O brave! Up, up, my enduring Heart!
Patience! Fortitude! Speed to the goal, O Soul!
He points to the Breadboard before his door.
Take up your stand, and speak, and speak the truth,
and then, unflinchingly, present your head to the dreadful
Breadboard.
                    Courage! Show some backbone, Heart!
Forward . . . MARCH!—Attaboy, O my Soul!
*He sets off manfully for the Breadboard. Reaching it, he leans on it in
elaborate unconcern, to the great surprise of the returning Chorus.*

CHORUS
Singly, to Dikaiopolis.
            —What can you do?
                              —What can you say?
            —You're an alloy of iron and brass!
            —The stake is your head,
                              —you're only one man,

44

    —you're attacking Athens *en masse!*
      —Look, he doesn't shiver.
        —Not a quiver.
      —No shriek.
   —All right, you wanted it, Hero.
      —Now speak.

DIKAIOPOLIS
Gentlemen of the audience, I humbly ask your indulgence.
I am cognizant of my audacity: the mere appearance in a Comedy
of that tried-and-true *Tragic* staple, THE BEGGAR,
is sufficient to offend your sense of things-as-they-are.
But when said Beggar, in said Comedy, presumes to lecture
Athenian citizens on the welfare of their State,
outraged traditionalism is far too mild
a reaction to hope for.
                  And yet, my friends, bear with me.
Even Comedy is no stranger to justice, simple
morality, and truth; and though my ensuing remarks
may cause discomfort, irritation, and even pain,
they will undeniably be just, and moral, and true.

The further to ease your minds, I note in passing
that we are, so to speak, in closed session here.
A year ago, Kleon charged that I had slandered
the State in the presence of strangers, by presenting my play,
The Babylonians, at our Great Festival of Dionysos.
I do not admit the truth of this charge even now,
but I point out that it cannot apply to the present:
This is the Lenaia*—our personal, private feast—
Athenians Only; Foreigners Please Keep Out—
and neither troops nor tribute have yet arrived
from our Noble Allies. The whole great harvest of Empire
is winnowed, the chaff and straw are scattered abroad,
and only the citizens of Athens, the fine kernels
of grain, remain.
           —Not to forget, of course,
our Loyal Resident Aliens, whom, in completion
of a metaphor, I might term the nourishing bran.
My criticisms, then, are strictly *entre nous.*

Gentlemen, I am, have been, and always will be
a Spartan-hater. I loathe Spartans. I detest
Spartans. I abominate Spartans. In vengeance
for my darling vineyards, by the fell SPARTAN'S hand
untimely cropt—even as yours—I here

implore Poseidon the Earthshaker, god of Tainaros,
to shake, quake, shiver, and tumble their hovels
into rubble, to rain destruction on those damnable animals!

Changing tone completely.

But they're only human, and we're too hard on them, friends.
Why should we blame the Spartans for all our troubles?
Specifically, the War? The cause, if the truth were known,
was our own people—
                    Note, I do not say Athens.
Particularly note, Gentlemen, that I do *not* say
Athens.—
            It was our own men, a few corrupt men,
debased, mis-struck types, the bastard pinchbeck outpouring
of foreign mints, the all-too-common coins,
the Two-Bit Informers—the Co. of Kleon & Co.
It was they who denounced and reported as illegal the entry
of those little jackets they make over in Megara.
It was they who extended the rubric, PROHIBITED IMPORT,
to cover Megara's entire annual output.
It was they who glued their beady eyes to the Customs,
and, at first sight of a cucumber, a rabbit, a pig,
even a clove of garlic or a lump of salt,
bawled out, "MEGARIAN CONTRABAND!"—saw to confiscation,
and pocketed a fat percentage.
                            These matters were minimal,
purely domestic in their impact: Megara *did* have
other markets. Nevertheless, the stage
was set, and the required International Incident
followed shortly. Certain of the Youth of Athens—
Our Greatest Resource, Gentlemen, Our Hope for the Future—
got sloppy drunk at chug-a-lug, reeled over to Megara,
and carried off a Megarian whore.—
                            OUTRAGE!
DISGRACE! DISHONOR! And every Megarian hackle
went stiff with pride and vengeance. Reprisal was swift:
They abducted *two* whores from Aspasia's stable in Athens.
And the whirlwind of War burgeoned and burst on all Greece
simply to answer the question: WHO STOLE THE TARTS?
For Olympian Perikles, godlike in his wrath—and Aspasia's—
thundered and lightninged, wholly embrangling Hellas
with laws that read like nothing so much in the world
as drinking songs:

We hereby decree
that Megara be
placed under embargo.
Her cargo is consequently banned
from every market, from land,
from sea, and—
should the occasion arise—
from the skies.*

The Megarians, thus cut off from trade, replied
to our blockade by starving, slowly and painfully,
until they were reduced to applying to Sparta
for aid and assistance. They beseeched them, as fellow Dorians,
to press for a reversal of the Three-Prostitute-Statute.
No use. To all petitions and representations,
however reasonable, we returned one answer—

                                    NO.

And that's how, and when, and why the Spartans started
to rattle their sabers.

                      I sense an objection here.

Some one of you may say the offense, if offense it was,
was slight, and nothing to go to war about.
I can hear it now: "The Spartans' action was immoral!"
But what alternatives had they? Try the situation
on yourselves for size.

                      Put the case that some Spartan

sailed out in a rowboat to our most godforsaken island,
laid hold of the mangiest, scrawniest fleabag of a dog
in the place, and confiscated same.

                          What would *you* do?

Sit quietly at home?

                Not a chance.

                        You'd launch immediately

a fighting fleet of some three hundred ships
and fill the whole city with martial hullabaloo:
caterwauling soldiers shouting "Captain!"
the slosh of gilt on figureheads, the brays
for wages, market-racket, ration-ruckus,
wineskins, warwhoops, oarloops, pots for sale
and *smash!*—

                the crush for garlics, olives, onions,
chaplets,

        chops,

              flutists,

                    fist-fights,

                        black eyes.

While down at the docks it's bolts and jolts and spars
and oars, roars, planes, thongs, bongs,
and fifes,
       fracas,
          bos'ns,
             pipes,
                and tweets.
Put it all together, it spells CHAOS—
or War in Self-Defense, it's generally known.
And that, my friends, is precisely the way you'd act.
It's precisely the way the Spartans *did* act.
                    And if
you think anyone, even a Euripidean hero,
even Telephos, would behave in any other fashion,
you've no damn sense—
            which is not, of course, unlikely.

FIRST KORYPHAIOS
So? You sly, sneaky insinuator of sedition!
Your logic is looser than your morals. An informer or two
in town makes US guilty of aggression?—TREASON!

SECOND KORYPHAIOS
To the First Koryphaios.
Hold on; are you sure you heard him? That's not Treason!
He's right; he convinced ME! Every word of that speech
was Just! Also Moral! Not to forget True!

FIRST KORYPHAIOS
Justice be damned! Ditto Morality! Truth, too!
Anyway, who's HE to talk? Treason or not,
it's Insolence—which is worse! He won't get away with THAT!

*The First Semichorus makes for Dikaiopolis, but is stopped by the
Second, the members of which interpose themselves in the path
of the attack.*

SECOND KORYPHAIOS
Not so fast—what's your hurry? HANDS OFF!
For every finger you lay on him, you lose two!

*A brawl ensues between the two Semichoruses, in which the First
(the anti-Dikaiopolitans) gets considerably the worst of it.
They turn to the house of Lamachos, right, and call for help.*

FIRST SEMICHORUS

    Torn with travail,
    hemmed in, and harassed,
    we summon and hail
    that sterling militarist
    MAJOR LAMACHOS
    to rescue us.
    HELP! FRIEND LAMACHOS! HELP!

*Since no help seems forthcoming from Lamachos' house, and the
Second Semichorus is increasing its advantage, they turn desperately
to the audience.*

    We appeal to *you.*
    Would a General, if requested,
    or a Captain, *faute de mieux,*
    or even an Enlisted
    Man deliver us!
    They'll murder us!
    HELP! PLEASE, ANYBODY! HELP!

*There is a loud, gaudy fanfare. The fight stops, never to be resumed,
and the Semichoruses turn expectantly toward Lamachos' house,
where the door is opening. A pause. Then the fanfare is heard
again. A second pause, just slightly too long. Lamachos strides
through his door and stands before it, surveying the stage. He is in
full armor, wears a long cloak, and bears a considerable amount
of ordnance, including a shield with a huge Gorgon emblazoned
upon it, a sword, and two lances. These trappings are not realistic,
but visual parodies, violent exaggerations. Most noteworthy is the
helmet: various feathers are affixed to its cheekpieces, and it is capped
by, not one, but three huge, brilliantly dyed horsehair crests.*

*Lamachos, of course, is the original Miles Gloriosus, and possessed
of all the rodomontade, bluster, and boastful bloodthirstiness
that pertain to this type. But there is one important difference
between him and most of his successors in Western comedy, of
whom Falstaff is the best known:* Lamachos is a relatively young man,
and should be shown as such. *Both his trappings and his rhetoric
are much too large for him, and his command of them deserts him
frequently, as when he trips on his sword, or fails, for all his fustian,
to debate with Dikaiopolis. Dikaiopolis vs. Lamachos should be
visually recognizable as Age vs. Youth as well as Peace vs. War.
Lamachos need not be presented as a Boy Wonder, but he
should be the shortest man on stage.**

LAMACHOS

Who cried Havoc? Who waked the ghastly, grim-visaged
Gorgon from her shield?—I distinctly heard a shout
portending internecine struggle, slaughter, and decimation.
As a qualified patriot, I sped hotfoot to the fray.
—Well, where is it? Where am I to deploy
reinforcements? Where throw up my breastworks?
—You bloody fools—

WHAT HAVE YOU DONE WITH THE WAR?

DIKAIOPOLIS

O Lamachos! Hero of Crests and Purple Patches!*

FIRST KORYPHAIOS

That's the fellow, Major, right there! He just finished
slandering Athens! *In toto!* But especially US!

LAMACHOS

Treason?

Muttering as he crosses to Dikaiopolis.

Damned civilians.

*Stopping some distance from Dikaiopolis and peering at the
Euripidean outfit.*

A beggar, eh?

—You there, you scrubby vulgarian, have you the infernal
effrontery to—

DIKAIOPOLIS

Wheedlingly.

Major, *Sir,* a genuine hero
like *you* will certainly pardon a poor old beggarman
for tripping over his tongue once or twice. Please?

LAMACHOS

Don't shilly-shally, man. This treason: What did you say?

DIKAIOPOLIS

I forget—You see, these spells come over me.

LAMACHOS

Spells?

DIKAIOPOLIS

Vertigo. When I see armor, I'm frightened—
and when I'm frightened, I'm dizzy—and when I'm dizzy, my head
goes round and round and—

OOPS—there it goes!

LAMACHOS

What's this?

DIKAIOPOLIS

Pointing to the Gorgon on the shield.

That armor! Oblige an old beggar and hide that goblin?

LAMACHOS

Turning his shield around.

Very well.

DIKAIOPOLIS

No—upside down. Over here.

LAMACHOS

There it is.

DIKAIOPOLIS

Suddenly doubling up.

OWWW!

LAMACHOS

What *now?*

DIKAIOPOLIS

Please, Sir, a plume from your helmet?

LAMACHOS

Very well—but not an entire plume. One feather.

He extracts a huge, gaudy feather from a cheekpiece plume and hands it to Dikaiopolis.

DIKAIOPOLIS

Leaning over the shield.

Now hold my head, please.

Lamachos obeys almost mechanically. Dikaiopolis prepares to tickle his throat with the feather.

Thanks, I have to vomit.
It's those crests—I'm allergic to horsehair.

LAMACHOS

Letting go with a start.

What? Vomit?
By god, you DARE to vomit with LAMACHOS' feather?

DIKAIOPOLIS

Yours, O bird most rare?
What species?—Don't tell me,
let me guess. Could you be the Great-Crested Peewee? No?
the Blabber-Breasted Boastard?

LAMACHOS

Reaching for his sword.

You scurvy canaille,
you die!

*The sword is inextricably twined in his belt. Dikaiopolis
watches his struggles.*

DIKAIOPOLIS

Tut, Lamachos, old man. Out of the question.
Your strength is helpless here.

He flips open Lamachos' cloak, exposing the phallus.

Besides, you're not equipped
for frontal attacks—more for distending the rear.

LAMACHOS

You whoreson beggar, do you DARE address a GENERAL*
in this insolent, unseemly fashion?

DIKAIOPOLIS

Beggar?

He throws off the rags.

I'm a beggar,
am I?

LAMACHOS

Well, what *are* you, then?

DIKAIOPOLIS

I shall tell you.
I am that bird least rare, but unknown to you:
The Honest Citizen. Not the Very Important Person.
Contrast us, Lamachos. Since the War began,
I've been in the ranks, the plainest of private soldiers.
But *you,* my fine feathered friend—since the War began,
you've been in the banks, a commissioned officer—let's say
supercommissioned. Commission Plus Ten Per Cent.

LAMACHOS

I was Duly Elected, Sir—

DIKAIOPOLIS

—by three jibberjabber
whippersnapper mocking birds, camouflaged as a quorum.
That's the sort of flimflam that stuck in my craw
and made me strike this Truce. I looked at the Army
and saw gray-haired old men filling the front lines,

53

because the strong young hulks—like you—had dodged
enlisted service by a perfectly legal device:
viz., Due Election.
From the city of Athens there poured
a bewildering stream of beardless civil servants—
ambassadors, messengers, attachés, chargés d'affaires—
functionaries with a single function: to save their skins
by scattering to the points of the compass at State expense.
Oh, what a crowd—the crudded cream of Athens:
the scions of bluebloods, robber barons, plutocrats,
First Families fifteen years off the boat from Skythia—
nouveaux riches, anciens riches, just plain Filthy *riches*—
industrial giants, moral pygmies, experts
in public calumny, and specialists in self-abuse . . .
What a comical bunch! And their ridiculous destinations:
Thrace, to chaff with Sitalkes; Chaonia,* where it's always
Open House, to bugger the obliging Natives;
Sicily, to joy-ride from town to silly town
and show off our Navy in the middle of the War—ridiculous
isn't the word! And the pay—three drachmas per day
per man—an absolute howl!—We nearly died laughing.

LAMACHOS
Those men were Duly Elected, Sir—

DIKAIOPOLIS
Of course,
but how much was Due?—I mean, doesn't it seem
a wee bit odd that youngsters like you can manage,
now and forever, a niche in the yearly budget,
while Men, mature Men—say, these Acharnians here—
never get an obol? Observe:

To a member of the Chorus.
Dusty, my friend,
in all your life—and I can see it's been a long one—
have you ever been an envoy, or held *any* paid position
with the State?

Dusty shakes his head. Dikaiopolis turns back to Lamachos.
Never! And yet he's a prudent, frugal
man—a worker—sound as they come.

To other members of the Chorus.
What do *you* say,
Collier?
—Or *you,* Aschmann?
—Or Kendall here?

—Have you ever seen glorious Ekbatana?
They shake their heads. He turns to others.

—Well, Birnham, you?
—Or maybe Stoker?
—Ever have an all-expense tour
of awe-inspiring Chaonia—The Buggery Coast?
They shake their heads.

Never! So much for Virtue and Thrift—Those appointments
go to aristocratic young decadents, spendthrifts, welshers
like friend Lamachos here. Behold Success!

He points dramatically to Lamachos.

Barely yesterday, friends, Lamachos was up to his clavicle
in unpaid dues and debts. He was the type
whose Best Friends *Told*—they touted perfect strangers
away from him. Socially, friends, the man was a Slum—
possessed of all the popularity of used bathwater . . .

LAMACHOS

In DEMOCRACY'S name! Is such corrupt depravity
to be borne? Is such depraved corruption to be brooked?

DIKAIOPOLIS

Certainly not—unless you continue on the payroll.

Lamachos starts for his sword. Dikaiopolis feints a blow at him.
Lamachos jumps back, cowers briefly, then gathers up his weapons,
clutches his cloak about him, and addresses the audience.

LAMACHOS

Attend my Program and Declaration:
I SHALL PROSECUTE THIS WAR.
I SHALL STRIKE DEEP INTO THE SOFT UNDERBELLY OF
THE PELOPONNESIANS.
I SHALL NOT FLAG OR FAIL. I SHALL FIGHT IN SPARTA.
I SHALL FIGHT ON THE SEAS AND OCEANS, I SHALL FIGHT
ON THE FIELDS
AND IN THE STREETS, I SHALL FIGHT IN THE HILLS: I
SHALL NEVER SURRENDER.

He stalks off, tripping over his sword. Dikaiopolis watches him
leave, then turns to the audience.

DIKAIOPOLIS

Attend my Prospectus and Proclamation:
I SHALL INSTITUTE A MARKET.
I SHALL SELL DELIGHTS FOR THE SOFT UNDERBELLY OF
THE PELOPONNESIANS,
THE MEGARIANS, AND THE BOIOTIANS: I SHALL NOT LACK
FOR SALES.

I INVITE THEM TO LEAVE THEIR HILLS, I INVITE THEM TO
  QUIT
THEIR FIELDS, I INVITE THEM TO TRAVERSE THE SEAS
  AND OCEANS.
I SHALL MEET THEM IN THE STREETS AND THERE ENGAGE
  THEM
IN GOOD OLD ATHENIAN TRADE. I SHALL NEVER
  SURRENDER
MY MONOPOLY. THEY MAY TRADE WITH ME—BUT NOT
  WITH LAMACHOS.

He enters his house.

The Semichoruses reunite and hold a brief whispered consultation.
The First Koryphaios advances to address the audience.

FIRST KORYPHAIOS
RESULTS OF THE DEBATE:
                    FIRST, DIKAIOPOLIS.
                              SECOND, LAMACHOS.

A RINGING POPULAR ENDORSEMENT OF THE PEACE!
                              —And now, the customary
Choral Interlude.

To the Chorus.
                    Places, men! It's time for the ANAPESTS.*
Off with the cloaks—let's get this atrophied ritual on the road!

The members of the Chorus remove their cloaks and form behind him.
He comes to the front of the stage and makes his formal address
to the audience.

Gentlemen, our Playwright is a modest man. Never in his career
has he written his ego into the script, or prostituted his Parabasis
to declare his genius. But now that genius is under attack.
Before the people of Athens (so notorious for their snap decisions),
his enemies charge that he degrades the City and insults the Populace.
And thus our Poet requests this time to defend his Art
before the people of Athens (so illustrious for their reasoned revisions
of their snap decisions).
                    Our Poet gives his accusers the lie.
He protests that he is a Public Benefactor, instilling in the Body
Politic a healthy resistance to rhetoric. No longer, Gentlemen,
are you ceaselessly victimized by foreign oratory, willingly wallowing,
unthinking and blissful, in flattering unction—wearing a wide-eyed,
slack-jawed gawk as your National Mien. But think back three years
from this Enlightened Present: the Ambassadors from the Federated
  States

came yearly (at least) to fleece you, with a never-fail one-two punch
compounded of Pindaric epithets—and you never caught on. STEP
  ONE:
They'd hail you as VIOLET-WREATHED. And up to the tips of your
  rumps
you shot, panting for more. And more you got—STEP TWO:
O GLISTERING ATHENS! they'd howl. Thus graced with a term
  quite apt
for sardines, you were hooked—and handed over the whole damned city.
But this is all past, thanks to our Poet—our Public Benefactor.

Consider a second benefit. Gentlemen, why do you think
that the Allies keep flocking to town to pay the tribute you exact?
Because they love you? Because they hate money?
                                        Not in the least.
Because last year, in *The Babylonians,* a Certain Comic Poet
ripped the lid off the relations between Athens and the rest of the
  Federation,
exposing how we democratically democratize our Allies into Complete
  Equality—
with each other, like slaves. So now these Allies are wild to see
this nonpareil among poets with the Courage to Tell the Truth in
  Athens.
And they come—and you get the money.
                            This Courage, in fact, is famous
throughout the world, as witness a recent report from Persia:
It seems that the Great King was sounding out a delegation from Sparta,
and asked about the relative strength of their side and ours.
First, of course, he wanted to know which State had the larger
Navy; but THEN he turned to the question of the famous poet
who criticized his own city without mercy. Which side had HIM?
"The men who have been guided by that adviser," he said,
"are necessarily far superior; their decisive victory in the War
is only a matter of time." And *there* is the reason for the Spartans'
recent suit for Peace—AND their demand for Aigina.
They don't give a damn for Aigina *per se;* they only desire
that island in order to appropriate one of its Summer Residents*—
your Fearless, Peerless Poet, ARISTOPHANES. I urge you, Friends,
don't give him up! Don't discard the Voice of Justice!
—Hear now the pledge of the Poet as Teacher.
                              His subtle stagecraft
will bear you along to perfect happiness, public and private.
His integrity remains absolute. He will not knuckle, truckle,

hoax, or coax his way into favor. He will not adulterate
the pure matter of his plays with soft soap, bunkum, or grease,
simply to win a prize. His aim is not your applause, or votes,
but your EDIFICATION:

ONWARD AND UPWARD WITH HIS ART!
Hence—and I quote:*

> *Let the crafty* Kleon *forge and frame*
> *each fell, nefarious plot.*
> *My aide is Justice; my adjutant, Right—*
> *I defy such scheming! I'll not*
> *be caught!*—But his charge of perversion and fear
> could lead to arresting ends . . .
> since the versatile Kleon turns tail to our Foes—
> and repeats the maneuver for Friends.

He rejoins his Semichorus, which steps forward to invoke its Muse.

FIRST SEMICHORUS
Muse of charcoal,
Muse combustible,
Muse of Thermogenesis,
Muse Acharnian,
Muse of Arson,
come, inspire your townsmen—us.

Swiftly fly as
when the bellows
frees your godhead from the coal,
when your essence
sweeps to ovens
and invades the mackerel,

heats to ardenc-
y the sárdines
fillèted in glistering oil,
then enkindles
on the griddles
fervid seethings in the sole—

Thus our singing
turn to singeing
sure to scorch and char—and may
your afflatus,
Muse, ignite us:
We have other fish to fry.

FIRST KORYPHAIOS

—Specifically, YOU, you greathearted guppies! We Long-Time
   Residents
and Senior Citizens have a bone to pick with the City of Athens.
We'd like to point out a slight discrepancy between the glorious
sea-battles we fought for you once, and the treatment you give us now.
WHOSE SIDE DO YOU THINK WE WERE ON?
                                 Look at it fairly: what is our
reward for Age, Service, and, *passim*, Saving the State?
TORTURE! You grease the skids under our declining years,
   and slide us
straight into court, to serve as butts for youngsters-at-law—
to supply these tyro shysters with cash and practice, and yourselves
with laughs. Oh, we fill the role admirably. Halt, lame,
deaf, blind, decayed, decrepit—all the eloquence
of worn-out oboe reeds—all outside support, temporal
and divine, lodged in How Firm a Foundation, The Old, Rugged
Crutch. With such as our ample armor, we totter to Court
and stand before the bench to stammer our senile squeaks,
while the wisps of Law curl so thick we fumble, fogbound by Justice.
Enters then our spruce accuser, milk teeth shining
in expectation of Easy Pickings. Swiftly he softens us up
with a hail of insinuations, a mighty barrage of bald accusations,
and attacks at close quarters. He pulverizes poor Tithonos,
and scatters the pieces at random; and the feeble old fossil, tongue-tied
from age as he is, can't collect himself in time to utter
more than a splutter. Which is not enough. He loses, of course.
And is fined. And, sick with shame, staggers off to die. And can't.
Why? Well, hear him tell it to his friends with sobs and wails:
"How can I buy a coffin? My savings all went for that case!"

SECOND SEMICHORUS

         Clock of Water,*
         Courtroom-Meter,
   Hear your drip-drop's dread result:
         Law diluted,
         Honor spotted,
  Right and Justice warped and spoilt.

         See the Veteran:
         Once his sweat ran
     hot and fierce at Marathon;
         now his hopes flow
         cold, through loopholes,
  litigated down the drain.

Once the Persian
inundation
broke before us, checked and dammed;
now the verdict's
swirling vortex
leaves us broken, charged, condemned.

Clock, forswear your
Rain of Error;
let not lawyers, flush and fee'd,
clear their knavery—
claiming every
silver lining has a cloud.

SECOND KORYPHAIOS

Are these soggy proceedings Justice? Consider some dry specificities.
Inspect the demise of THOUKYDIDES:*
In the midst of Athens, there lurks
a shifting Skythian desert, a howling wilderness—in short,
a Public Prosecutor. Its name is EUATHLOS. It's the son of that eminent
immigrant, KEPHISODEMOS (no wee wasteland himself)—and recently
engulfed Thoukydides, smothered and choked him with writs and ropes
of sand.
—I ask you, Gentlemen, was *this* a Just Desert?
I had to wipe away tears of pity at the sight of this aged
hero, statesman, general, wrestler, and purebred Athenian
drawn, flexed, snapped, and unstrung in the hairy paws
of a half-baked, half-breed bowman! When he was still Thoukydides
the Famous, he wouldn't be flexed by anyone—by Demeter,
not even
by Demeter! He'd have gone to the mat with TEN of those worthless
Euathloses,
and pinned the pack; and then out-bawled, out-bellowed THREE
THOUSAND
Skythian archers (cousins of Kephisodemos), unslung his bow . . .
with a single shot, he'd have shafted the lot!

He pauses and shrugs.

It's useless to plead.
To you, Age Must Be Served—until you run out of subpoenas.
Facing which sleepless prospect, we oldsters propose an addition
to Judicial Procedure: Partition the populace into OLD and YOUNG,
and decree that defendants and plaintiffs belong to the same Division.
The Old Man's prosecutor must himself be Old and toothless;

the Young Man's prosecutor must himself be a compulsive babbler,
a compliant bugger, and a—well, save time: just say ALKIBIADES.*
Impose a fine for failure to comply; then back to the Great
Athenian National Sport—Courtroom Catharsis. Be regular
in elimination:
Purge Age with Age, and Youth with Youth.

*The Chorus divides and moves to the sides of the stage. Dikaiopolis
enters from his house and marks off a large area before the door.*

DIKAIOPOLIS
I herewith fix the boundaries of my place of business
and send abroad a blanket invitation to the citizens
of Megaria, Boiotia, and the Peloponnese.

HURRY ON DOWN

TO DIKAIOPOLIS' FREE BAZAAR!   Contract Acceptance
Contingent on Absolute Avoidance of Business with Lamachos.

He produces a huge paddle.

I now present my Board of Trade—the pick of a
large panel—well-seasoned, rigid and unbending
in its application of the solitary Rule of Commerce, *viz.:*
THIS IS NOT A BIRD SANCTUARY! ALL STOOL PIGEONS,
    PEEPERS,
MEDDLING NARKS, AND FINKS ARE HEREBY INFORMED:
OFF LIMITS! STAY OUT! THIS MEANS YOU!

—And now

to fetch that enlarged copy of the Treaty and post it
in a conspicuous spot along the Rialto here.

*He enters the house. After a short pause, a poverty-stricken,
emaciated Megarian* enters from the right, carrying a large and
seemingly empty sack. Two Little Girls follow fearfully at a
distance. They look more wretched than he, if possible.*

MEGARIAN
Empohrium of Athens, highes' hope an' deepes'
desiah of all mah people, Ah take this oppuhtunity
t'extend to y'awl a heartfelt Megarian Howdy-Do.
Bah Hermes, God of Profit an' Loss, Ah've missed yo'
like mah deah ole mammy—bless her greedy soul.

He turns to the Little Girls.

—Dahlin daughtuhs, yo' mizzuble offspring of a sire
whom the clutch of circumstance conspires to mold into a bum,
come heah to yo' daddy, an' prepare to take that first
great step to'd the Ultima Thuley of Worldly Wishes—
Ah refer, of co'se, to FOOD.

—Ef'n yo' kin find any.

The Little Girls break into wails. He raises his voice.

> Ah retain the floor, an' Ah request the respeckful attention
> of yo' bellies! Fill 'em with advice, 'n' yo' *may* git vittles.

The Little Girls subside.

> That's bettuh.—Now, heah are the altuhnatives facin' you two.
> Yo' kin eithuh be sold in the mahket, or else go Home . . .
> to expiah in awful agonies of Uttah Stahvation.
> —Which is yo' pleasure, dahlins?

LITTLE GIRLS
> Sell us! Sell us!

MEGARIAN
> A credit to the fam'ly—just what Ah'd say mahself.
> Still, look at you. Ah shuddah to say it of mah own
> flesh an' blood, but the man who's fool enough
> to invest in yo' ain't bo'n yet. Ah sadly feah
> the slave-trade is OUT. Lessee . . . Hold on, Ah got
> a plan—so underhanded, it proudly declares
> its origin just by *bein'*—a MEGARIAN Plan!
> Heah 'tis. If yo' won't sell as chilluns, yo'll sell as chitlins . . .

The Little Girls recoil in terror. He puts out a reassuring hand.

> more or less. Ah'll dress yo' up in a clevuh disguise
> an' announce to all an' sundry that Ah'm purveyin' *Pigs.**
> —By an odd coincidence, Ah have the costumes with me.—

He procures the disguises from the depths of the sack and hands them to the Girls.

> Heah, now, put on these piggie shoes—those neat
> li'l trottahs, an' make evvy effort to ack like the farrow
> of a well-bred sow—because, bah Hermes, God
> of Diddlin' an' Double-Dealin', ef yo-all don't sell,
> Ah'll tote yo' back to Meg'ra an' REAL Stahvation!
> —Next, slip into these snouts.
>   —Now into the sack.

They obey.

> Make yo' daddy proud, guhls. Oink, an' squeal, an' grunt
> in the tones of pigs predestined fo' a highah puhpose—
> patrician pigs earmahked fo' immolation at the Myst'ries.
> Ah'll send the Herald around to summon Dikaiopolis.

He closes the sack carefully, walks off a few paces, and attends to the heralding himself.

> DIKAIOPOLIS! FRESH PO'K FO' SALE! YO' WANT TO BUY?

DIKAIOPOLIS

Emerging from his house.

What's this? I don't believe it—but the signs are unmistakable:
the shifty eye, the mangy mantle on a wasted
frame, that shabby-genteel drawl—it's incredible
but obvious: a MEGARIAN!

MEGARIAN

We've come to mahket, Suh!

DIKAIOPOLIS

Well, Sir, and how are you getting along in Megara?

MEGARIAN

Porely. We tighten ouah belts to the final notch,
we reel th'ough the streets, an' then we kick the bucket
an' shuffle off ouah mo'tal coil.

DIKAIOPOLIS

Folk-dancing?
Uh—delightful! I imagine it keeps you warm in winter.
—well, now . . . what else is doing in Megara these days?

MEGARIAN

Outside of dyin', things tend to be rathuh slow.
But the Senate's fixin' to liven the State up considerably.
Just as Ah left, they were engaged in a grand filibustah,
debatin' a method of savin' Meg'ra.

DIKAIOPOLIS

Really?

MEGARIAN

Yup. The main aim is cleah: to make the FOOD
go furthah. Evvythin's set ceptin' Implementation.
They're figgerin' ways an' means to exterminate non-Senatuhs—
like me—as swiftly as possible.

DIKAIOPOLIS

. . . And thus provide
a speedy end to your troubles?

MEGARIAN

Precisely, Suh.

DIKAIOPOLIS

Somewhat desperately.

What more from Megara?

He notices the sack and jerks a thumb at it.

What's the price of grain?

MEGARIAN
We reckon it's Divine—it's higher'n Mt. Olympos.

DIKAIOPOLIS
Of course. . . . I presume you must have *salt* in that sack?

MEGARIAN
Well, Ah might—ef yo' Athenians hadn't blockaded
ouah mines fo' the past two yeahs.

DIKAIOPOLIS
                                    You've brought *garlic,* then?

MEGARIAN
Well, Ah might—ef yo' Athenians hadn't raided
ouah fields fo' the past six yeahs. Not that Ah'm complainin',
but yo're more mice than men. Evvy attack,
yo' grub out those cloves. The whole plantation's perforated.

DIKAIOPOLIS
I give up—what DO you have in the sack?

MEGARIAN
                                    Heah, Suh,
are Pigs fo' sackifice at the Myst'ry Rites.

DIKAIOPOLIS
                            Excellent!
Display them.

MEGARIAN
            Ah assure yo', Suh, they're beauties. But since
yo're not the type to buy a pig in a poke—
He pulls the First Little Girl from the sack.
    you jus' poke away, Suh! Feel it out, an' probe.
    Yo'll find it Juicy! Tenduh! Satisfaction Guaranteed!

DIKAIOPOLIS
But I've never seen anything like this—what is it?

MEGARIAN
                                        A piggie,
    bah Zeus!

DIKAIOPOLIS
            A piggie? *That?* What breed of piggie?

MEGARIAN
    It was bo'n in Meg'ra, Suh—
With a sly nudge and a wink.
                    but, ef'n yo' want,
    it kin be bred in Athens.

                              —Suh, do yo' dispute mah word?
Do yo' claim this is *not* a pig?

DIKAIOPOLIS

                              It doesn't look
very much like a pig to me.

MEGARIAN

                    SACRILEGE, SUH!
Ah respeckfully request that yo' put yo' money wheah yo' mouth is!
A wager, Suh, fo' high stakes. Salt! A whole peck!—
An' none of yore ordinary salt, but *Seasoned* Salt!

He points very specifically at the Girl's groin.

Now, do yo' still maintain that this luscious, savory
mo'sel is not what we, followin' the folk-usage
of the Greek people an' the genius of the Greek language,
refer to as a *Piggie?* Well, Suh?

DIKAIOPOLIS

Puzzled; inspecting the indicated spot closely.

                              Not to be crotchety,
but *this* belongs to a human being.

MEGARIAN

                                        Ah should hope so!—
It belongs to ME, Suh! Do yo' take me fo' a hired dealuh?
How would yo' like to hear it squeal?

DIKAIOPOLIS

                              This?
Squeal?—By all means, yes!

MEGARIAN

                              —Quickly, dahlin
piglet, give us a squeal.

*Dumb with fright, the Girl shakes her head. He changes to a
vicious aside.*

                         Yo' REFUSE? Yo' stay
shet up, yo' no-count trash? Bah Hermes, God
of Conductin' the Dead to Hades, Ah'l tote yo' back
to the Ole Plantation!

FIRST LITTLE GIRL

                              Oink!   Oink!   Oink!

The Megarian turns expansively to Dikaiopolis.

Now, *that,* Suh, is a *Piggie!*

DIKAIOPOLIS

                              For the moment, you have me convinced.
It does appear to be a pig.

MEGARIAN

An' in five mo' yeahs,
ef it's constantly crammed, it'll swell to the puhfeck facsimile
of its mothuh, an' fulfil its Destiny, Suh.

As a cunt.

DIKAIOPOLIS

That's all very interesting, but this is *not* a sacrificial
animal.

MEGARIAN

Ah disagree, Suh. Would yo' kindly info'm me *why*
it's not sackificial?

DIKAIOPOLIS

Pigs for the Mysteries must
be perfect specimens—and this one is deformed. It possesses
no trace of a tail.

MEGARIAN

But that's not bein' DEFO'MED!—
It's teeny yet. Howevah, when it's grown to the bloom
of glorious sowhood, it *will* acquiah a tail—
monstrous, an' thick, an' red.

He produces the Second Little Girl from the sack.

Might yo' be willin'
to fatten anothuh? Ef yo' want, heah's a beautiful po'kuh.

DIKAIOPOLIS

Looking from one Little Girl to the other.

What a close resemblance—they appear to have more than country
in common. Could this be a case of congenital relationship?

MEGARIAN

Striking a tragic attitude.

In the words of that immo'tal bahd (who shall be nameless):
delivuhed of the self-same dame an' self-same siah,
Suh! An' once it swells, an' downs itself
with hair, yo'll find no prettiuh piece of po'k,
f'um chine to chin, to spread on the altuh and sackifice
to Aphrodite.

DIKAIOPOLIS

Pardon—a correction. Pigs are sacrificed
to *Demeter*—never to Aphrodite.

MEGARIAN

Beggin' *yo'* pahdon,
but when this pig is impaled, it'll be in the rites
of Aphrodite, an' Aphrodite alone.

Conspiratorially.

But why delay
yo' delights until they're grown? Ah tell yo' truly—
theah is nothin' mo' sweet or tenduh than a pigmeat bahbecue:
thet juicy pigmeat done to a turn on yo' spit.

DIKAIOPOLIS
Are these pigs weaned?

MEGARIAN

Ah hope to tell yo' they are, Suh!
These pigs don't need theah daddy in orduh to eat!

DIKAIOPOLIS
Weaned from their daddy?

MEGARIAN

Precisely—yo' know the proverb:
Theah's no separatin' a sucklin' pig f'um its pap.

DIKAIOPOLIS
And what is their favorite food?

MEGARIAN

They're mighty peckish.
Whatevah yo' give 'em—just hold it out, 'n' they'll gobble it.
Ask them yo'self.

DIKAIOPOLIS
To the Little Girls.

Soo, pig! Soo, pig!

LITTLE GIRLS

Oink!

DIKAIOPOLIS
Tell me—do you like peapods?

LITTLE GIRLS

Oink! Oink!

DIKAIOPOLIS
So? How about cockles?

LITTLE GIRLS

Oink! Oink!

DIKAIOPOLIS

Nuts?

LITTLE GIRLS
Oink! Oink! Oink!

DIKAIOPOLIS

Prickly pears?

LITTLE GIRLS
Oink! Oink! Oink!

DIKAIOPOLIS

Well—what do you say
to a succulent, sappy, juice-filled, well-stuffed, six-inch
FIG?

LITTLE GIRLS
Wildly jumping up and down.

OINK! OINK! OINK! OINK!

*The Megarian abandons all pretense and throws himself down beside
his daughters, startling Dikaiopolis considerably.*

DIKAIOPOLIS
—What's this? Do *you* want a fig, too?

MEGARIAN

OINK! OINK!

DIKAIOPOLIS
Surveying the three.

Fascinating reaction. To elicit the shrillest of squeals
from you, I have merely to pronounce the solitary syllable,
Figs, and. . . .

MEGARIAN AND LITTLE GIRLS
OINK! OINK! OINK! OINK!

DIKAIOPOLIS
Calling into the house.
Bring the piglets some figlets.

—I wonder, will they really eat them?

*A slave emerges from the house with a dish of figs, places it
before the Little Girls, then jumps back and races into the
house as they dive for it and begin gobbling. The Megarian
daringly reaches in and abstracts a fig, then removes himself
to safety. Dikaiopolis stares astounded at the Little Girls.*

Shades of Herakles! Listen to the scrunch of those jaws!
What untamed gluttony—what passionate, lawless guzzling!
Domestic swine?

They're wild! Wart hogs?

—No, PECCARIES!

MEGARIAN

That may be, Suh, but they didn't peck 'em *all* down—
as witness this solitary fig. Appropriated bah me.

He holds up the fig, looks at it lovingly, pops it into his mouth,
and swallows it.

DIKAIOPOLIS

I am forced to admit that I have never seen a more charming,
urbane, and polished pair of slubbering swine.
—I wish to purchase your pigs, Sir. Name your price.

MEGARIAN

Taking a tablet and stylus from his cloak, he begins to figure.
After a long pause, he looks up slyly.

Friend, Ah'll be candid. Ah can't affo'd to haggle.
Ah'm ovah a barrel.—Now, take that fust pig.
Absolutely the lowest Ah kin possibly go on her is

With the air of a man forced against his will to deal in billions.

A Bunch of Gahlic!—Ah'm adamant, Suh! Ah can't
be moved!

Perceiving that Dikaiopolis is not protesting, he points to the
Second Little Girl.

Ah'll throw *her* in fo' one Peck of Salt.
Suh, theah's mah rock-bottom offuh—Take it or Leave it!

DIKAIOPOLIS

Sir, you have found yourself a buyer. Wait here.

He enters the house.

MEGARIAN

Done, Suh!

In a transport of joy, he begins to stuff the Little Girls back into the sack.

O Hermes, God of Bahgains an' Mahk-Ups,
fo' such a princely price as this may Ah dispose
of the Fam'ly Honuh, the Ole Plantation, mah wife,
an' mah deah ole mammy—bless her glutton heart.

As he finishes replacing the Little Girls in the sack, an Informer
enters briskly from the right and accosts him. The Informer has a
loud voice, an official manner, and a small phallus.

INFORMER

You, there! Occupation? Nationality?

MEGARIAN

Ah travel in pigs, Suh.

F'um Meg'ra.

INFORMER

Ah-hah! As I thought.

I HEREBY DENOUNCE
THESE PIGS AS *MEGARIAN CONTRABAND!*

—Incidentally, you, too.

He grabs the sack and makes as if to drag it off, right.

Come along!

MEGARIAN
Heah we go again—INFO'MUHS!
Thet infamous fount an' origin of all ouah mis'ries!
—Is the Wah stahtin' up again befo' it's ovah?

He grabs the sack and pulls in the opposite direction.

INFORMER
This Curious Affinity for Megarian Causes can only
bring you to grief!

HAND OVER THE SACK—THAT'S AN ORDER!

*The tug-of-war continues, to the shrill accompaniment of the Little
Girls' cries. At length, nutrition tells, and the well-fed Informer,
gaining the upper hand over the emaciated Megarian, drags both him
and his sack toward the right.*

MEGARIAN
DIKAIOPOLIS!

DIKAIOPOLIS!

HALP! AH'M BEIN' CONFISCATED!

DIKAIOPOLIS
Rushing from the house with a bag of garlic and bag of salt.
By whom? Who's turning you in?

He sees the Informer and stops.

Where's the Board
of Trade?

*He drops the bags on the stoop, picks up the paddle, and,
swishing it, advances on the Informer.*

I request a ruling on these Informers.
Bar them from the Mart!

*Savagely arrived before the terrified Informer (who has loosed
his hold on the sack), he stops in astonishment, and indicates, with a
wave of the Board of Trade, the small phallus of his intended victim.*

—Have you no pride in your tools?
A finger-man with a digit like that? How can you shine
as Justice's Hurricane Lamp—without a wick?

He brandishes the paddle. The Informer backs away nervously.

INFORMER

STOP! You can't beat a man for exposing the enemies
of Athens! I was only performing a patriot's duty!

DIKAIOPOLIS

If expose you must, I suggest, my Patriot Beauty,
you expose yourself. But not here—unless you want
to lose your scanty equipment. HURRY—OUT!

*He beats the bawling Informer out of the market area and off the
stage, then returns to a still shaken Megarian.*

MEGARIAN

Mah sympathy to Athens, Suh. These Info'muhs—what a civic
affliction!

DIKAIOPOLIS

Retrieving the bags from the stoop.

Cheer up, Megarian. Hand over the piggies;
here's your price. Take your garlic—and your salt—
and all Good Luck go with you back to Megara!

MEGARIAN

Mournfully.

Good Luck just isn't ouah National Fashion, Suh—
it's not the Megarian Way.

DIKAIOPOLIS

Damn me for a busybody!
Please don't be offended, Sir. If Good Luck bothers you,
I'll take it back—I'll even wish it on myself!

*The Megarian smiles broadly. He opens the bags, tries the contents,
then turns to his daughters and makes a manful attempt at a sorrowful
farewell—an attempt which is hampered by his constant salt-eating.*

MEGARIAN

Yo' po' li'l piggies, abandoned to be banged around
f'um pillah to post without a fathah, Ah leave you
this lump of advice: Nevvuh . . . *yum* . . . fo'get . . . *yum* . . .
throughout yo' lives . . . *yumyumyum* . . . that a slice of bread
makes mighty fine eatin' with salt—ef they give yo' any.

*He saunters off right, eating. Dikaiopolis looks after him,
shakes his head, then conducts the Little Girls into his house.
A pause, and the Chorus forms.*

FIRST SEMICHORUS

Pointing with pride at Dikaiopolis' house.

His Marketing Acumen shows the Acme of Finesse.
His Luck, and Pluck, and Policies can only spell SUCCESS!

See how he undertakes
these radical techniques.
Informers caught within his street will have to stand for weeks!
While he can sit at ease upon his assets as they swell,
because his law of Commerce reads: RESTRICT YOUR CLIENTELE!

SECOND SEMICHORUS
*To the audience, intimately.**
Imagine if you can, Dear Shopper, just what this can mean
for YOU: No thugs will pinch your lunch! What's more, you'll go home
clean:
your cloak not soiled with scores
of sticky souvenirs—
KLEONYMOS's cowardice or PREPIS' vile amours.
Nor will you have to fumigate and disinfect the traces
of courtroom-sick HYPERBOLOS and his contagious cases!

FIRST SEMICHORUS
Your tortured nose can take a rest: It won't meet in this mart
that poet who offends in both his armpits and his art,
that overfacile scratcher,
that drooling fossil lecher,
his head no balder than his name is void of any virtue,
that staggering aesthetic zero, mighty moral minus,
and ninety-year-old nullity
(we mean, of course, KRATINOS!*)

SECOND SEMICHORUS
No character-assassins will amuse the noonday rush
and ridicule your foibles with their feelthy pen or brush.
Not that disgusting person
the pornographic PAUSON,
that living, breathing synonym for Ultimate Perversion;
nor shriveled-up LYSISTRATOS, the dyed in vice, the dirty—
whose phthisic fast days every month amount to more than thirty!

ENTIRE CHORUS
We hymn and celebrate
the Secret of his Might:
THE CUSTOMER—if wrong ones are debarred—IS ALWAYS
RIGHT!

*A languid Theban, carrying a tiny bunch of mint, enters from the
right. He is followed by his personal slave, Ismenias, who struggles
under a towering load of comestibles, mostly birds. Bringing up the*

*rear of this procession is a cluster of flute players, piping away
at what might pass for a march. They continue playing even when the
Theban and Ismenias stop within Dikaiopolis' market place. Ismenias
unloads his burden.*

THEBAN*

I say, this Trade *is* fatiguing, what? I rawthah feel
as though I'd maimed my shouldah.

He hands the bunch of mint to the still struggling Ismenias.

                             Ismenias, old thing,
do try to deposit this gently. Mustn't splinter
our mint, you know.

To the flute players.

                  I say, you chappies with the whistles,
you've been awf'ly decent to tweet us all the way from Thebes,
but could we have another tune? Something spicy, don't you know?
Could you whistle up *"The Sphinx's posterior opening . . ."?**

*The flute players try. Their resultant cacophony brings Dikaiopolis
from the house. He lays about him with the paddle.*

DIKAIOPOLIS

STOP! A plague of crows on this plague of locusts!
I'm finished with screeching flutists, with Chairis and his tribe—
so OUT! Remember, insecticide is not considered a crime!

He shoos the flutists off-stage.

THEBAN

Dreadf'ly grateful, old boy, actually. Never
could stand that wheezing. All the way from Thebes.
Poor mint's completely leafless. Beastly bother.
To show my gratitude, anything here is yours.
Consideration, of course. But still, your choice: the Birds
of the Field or the Beasts of the Air! Or something like that.*

DIKAIOPOLIS

What's this? A highborn omnivore—a Boiotian crumpeteer.
—Good day, most gracious glutton. What do you have?

THEBAN

Produce of the Realm, don't you know—Boiotia's Best:

Reciting by rote.

Marjoram, Carpets, Pepper, Mint, Peppermint,
Lampwicks, Spring Chicks, Teal Ducks, Ruddy Ducks, Bloody Ducks,
Jackdaws, Macaws, Hens, Wrens, Loons,
Partridges, Petrels, Pigeons, Finches, Thrushes,
Doves . . .

DIKAIOPOLIS

Rubbing his hands.

I feel exactly like Nobody in the proverb:
It's a fowl wind that blows Nobody good.

THEBAN

I say,
I've barely begun:
Geese, Weasels, Easels,
Foxes, Ferrets, Rabbits, Bobcats, Otters,
Gophers, Moles, Voles, and

Pointing to a basket.

Eels from Lake Kopaïs!

DIKAIOPOLIS

Mock-tragic.

O dealer in delight, retailer of toothsome tidbit,
vouchsafe me thy fairest morsel for mortals: grant
that I greet the Eel, if her in truth thou bearest.

THEBAN

Avaunt, O venerable emissary of the fifty virgin
daughters of Kopaïs!

Peering into the basket.

I say, old girl, could you see
your way clear to a brief appearance for our friend's amusement?

He reaches into the basket and brings out a huge eel, which he
hands to Dikaiopolis, who stretches it to its fullest extent
and continues in the mock-tragic vein.

DIKAIOPOLIS

At length, Dear Love? At last, O focus of my lust?
Dost thou return to rush the humor to mine eyes
and mouth, delight gourmets, and grace the table
of the Chorus when this play is done?

Toward the house.

—Vassals, attend
this lady! A stove! A bellows! Haste!
—Children,
come feast your gaze upon this enfinnèd excellence,
la Princesse d'Anguille, who lays to rest our anguish
after six lean, hungry years! Embrace her, children;
whilst I prepare burnt offering: this dish of charcoal.
—BRING that stove out!

To the eel again.

　　　　　　　　—O Love, henceforth may we
be joined as one, heart to heart, through Death;
and may his crimson beets lie light upon thee.

The slaves bring the stove. He planks the eel upon it.

THEBAN
Don't mean to be pushy, but, dash it all, one is generally
paid, isn't one? The Usual Thing?

DIKAIOPOLIS
　　　　　　　　　　　　　Ah, but not
in this case. She's a gift. From Gentleman to Gentleman. An eel
to seal our dealings—and pay for your license to sell.
What else *are* you selling, by the way?

THEBAN
　　　　　　　　　　　　　The lot, what!

DIKAIOPOLIS
Have you set a figure? Or are you set on barter?

THEBAN
Oh, definitely barter. Your surplus for our shortage, and all that.

DIKAIOPOLIS
Hmmm. A shipment of sardines? Perhaps some pottery?

THEBAN
Sorry, old chap. We're simply sated with sardines,
and there's a vile surfeit of vahzes. Any other overstocks?

DIKAIOPOLIS

Thinking.

Surpluses? Overstocks?—Of course! Export an INFORMER!
Ship him like crockery; standard wrapping.

THEBAN
　　　　　　　　　　　　　Ripping,
by Jove! One could simply make pots of money, what?
We don't have any of *them!* Thebes would be *wild*
to see a monkey like that, just full of deviltry!

Enter, suspiciously, Nikarchos.

DIKAIOPOLIS
Speak of the devil—here's Nikarchos to denounce you.

THEBAN
Awf'ly teeny Informer, what?

DIKAIOPOLIS
　　　　　　　　　　　Concentrated:
100% Pure, Perverse Viciousness.

NIKARCHOS

Espying the Theban's goods.

Whose stuff is this?

THEBAN

It's mine. I brought it from Thebes.
Word of Honor. As sure as I'm standing here.

NIKARCHOS

From where I stand, it looks like ENEMY CONTRABAND!
I denounce it!

THEBAN

Oh, I say! Have you Athenians come
to declaring war on canaries? Simply Not Done!

NIKARCHOS

And I'll denounce YOU, too!

THEBAN

Me? What have *I* done?

NIKARCHOS

It's not Standard Procedure to tell in these cases, but the audience
has to find out somehow: Gentlemen, from enemy soil,
this man has slipped in with an alien lampwick! The charge
is WICK-SLIPPING!

DIKAIOPOLIS

It's sloppy logic—you'd report a man
for a lampwick?

NIKARCHOS

That wick could set the docks on fire!

DIKAIOPOLIS

The docks? A *wick?*

NIKARCHOS

So I believe.

DIKAIOPOLIS

Well, how?

NIKARCHOS

Sound Reasoning. First, if the Theban should stick
his wick on the back of a cricket, and next touch it to a torch
and pitch it into a ditch—presuming the ditch ran into the locks
by the docks—and further, if the wind hadn't thinned—THEN,
if the wind should flick a spark on the deck of a barque,
the docks would go up in a flash!

DIKAIOPOLIS

                    I never heard such trash—
to wreck the docks with a wick on the back of a cricket!

He grabs the Board of Trade and beats Nikarchos.

NIKARCHOS
Spectators! Be prepared to testify!

DIKAIOPOLIS
To the Theban.

                    Impound his mouth!

*Nikarchos is grabbed, laid on the ground face down, and sat upon
by the Theban and Dikaiopolis, who calls to his slaves.*

—Slaves! Some straw and rope for wrapping! If I bale
him up like a bowl, he won't get broken in transit.

*Straw and rope are brought, and Dikaiopolis begins to pack Nikarchos,
a process which takes some little time.*

FIRST KORYPHAIOS
Now crate the freight with care, my friend,
and pack it with finesse.
We mustn't have our customer
import a shattered mess.

DIKAIOPOLIS
No fear; I'll see to it myself.
This pot's no masterpiece.

Kicking Nikarchos savagely and listening to the ensuing muffled cries.

It's cracked, it chatters, it's charred—
a bowl of botcheries.

FIRST KORYPHAIOS
But is it really usable?

DIKAIOPOLIS
All-purpose *and* reversible.
A mortar for malfeasances,
crime-cup, judgment-jug,
audit-lantern, evil-vial . . .
a patent thunder-mug!

SECOND KORYPHAIOS
For daily use around the house,
how could you trust this crock?

Kicking Nikarchos and listening in turn.

What an awful clatter! It starts
at the merest little shock.

DIKAIOPOLIS
Still wrapping.
>No fear. It's shock-resistant. Has
>a break-proof guarantee.
>You can hang it bottom-up without
>a sign of damage—

He stands Nikarchos on his head and continues wrapping.
>See?

SECOND KORYPHAIOS
To the Theban.
>He's done. What glorious packaging!

THEBAN
*Gazing reflectively at Nikarchos, inverted and swathed in yards
of rope and straw.*
>How Jolly! Bringing in the Sheaves!

SECOND KORYPHAIOS
>Harvest it, friend. It's ready now
>for any sort of work—
>The Adaptable Informer, or
>The Universal Jerk!

DIKAIOPOLIS
Putting the finishing touches on Nikarchos, then standing up with a sign.
>I didn't think I'd make it; but the rat is packed.
>Collect your crock and cart it away, my friend!

THEBAN
>I say, Ismenias, old thing, would you bend down and lend
>me your shoulder again? Thanks awf'ly.

*Ismenias obeys, the Theban and Dikaiopolis lift Nikarchos onto
his back, and the Theban and Ismenias move off slowly.*

DIKAIOPOLIS
>A word of advice.
>Please exercise a modicum of care in transport.
>The fact that it's damaged merchandise in any case notwithstanding,
>if this shipment *should* show a profit, your fortune's made
>in Informers. The supply here is absolutely unlimited.

*He starts to enter his house. A Servant runs from Lamachos'
house to the market place, shouting.*

LAMACHOS' SERVANT
DIKAIOPOLIS!

DIKAIOPOLIS
>What's all this racket?

LAMACHOS' SERVANT

                      I bear the exactions
of Lamachos, who now desires to visit the drinking-feast.
Whereto, he demands from you this drachma's worth
of thrushes, and deigns to triple the price for one
Kopaïc eel.

DIKAIOPOLIS

           Hmmm. Lamachos? Don't seem to recall
the name. What's he like?

LAMACHOS' SERVANT

               His eyes flash fire! He knows
no fear! He gyres the grim-visaged Gorgon, and swirls
three huge, umbrageous plumes in triple terror
about his casque!

DIKAIOPOLIS

            Oh, him?—Fat chance. I wouldn't
take his *shield* in trade. Let him swirl his plumes for sardines!
One word out of him, and I'll make a complaint to the Board!

*He grabs up the paddle. The Servant runs back to Lamachos' house.
Dikaiopolis surveys his comestibles proudly, then begins to stuff
birds under his arms.*

    This merchandise is *mine*. I'll take it in to my home
wafted on the high panache of blackbird and thrush.

FIRST SEMICHORUS

As Dikaiopolis carries part of his merchandise into his house.

    Citizens all, this man is an ace,
              the sagest of entrepreneurs!
    Behold his monopoly, sprung from his Truce,
              on items not stocked in our stores:
    pre-War delectables, tasty and choice—
              he's cornered our dearest desires!
          No toil, no spin—
          but the yummies roll in!

FIRST KORYPHAIOS

TO WHOM IT MAY CONCERN:
               BE IT KNOWN THAT I HEREBY DECLARE
H. O. POLEMOS, BETTER KNOWN AS *WAR,* PERSONA NON
    GRATA,
AND ENJOIN HIM FROM THE FOLLOWING ACTIVITIES ON
    OR ABOUT MY PREMISES:

A. ENTERING.
   B. WINING.
      C. DINING.
D. RECLINING.
   E. SWEET-ADOLINING.
         —Friends,
I've had a bellyful. I tried to be a True-Blue Host to WAR—
and found myself a host of troubles. He is simply a brutal drunkard.
You be the judge. It began with a joyous family feast,
food and frolic in abundance, not a worry in the world.
Life was Simply Perfect—and then WAR crashed the party
and smashed the table. Did I—Hospitality Itself—object?
Not me. "That's it; pull up," said I. "Always room
for one more, War." War mashed the rest of my guests to pulps,
and squashed all the food to atoms. "A drink, old man?" said I.
He was burning my vineprops. The place was a shambles. I smiled. A
 guest
is a guest.
   But THEN War trampled my vines and spilled every drop
of my wine in the dust! Well, that did it. I got this Injunction.
If there's one thing I refuse to entertain in my house, it's BAD
MANNERS!

*Dikaiopolis emerges, collects the rest of his merchandise, and
re-enters his house.*

SECOND SEMICHORUS
Our man is aloft, he's on the wing
    for his dinner; he's got big ideas.
His life has breadth, and expanse! There's a sign—
    those feathers he dropped on the stairs.
And it's PEACE!* Companion of Kypris divine
    and heaven's own Graces! O Peace!
   How lovely and refined!—
   (By god, I must have been blind!)

SECOND KORYPHAIOS
PERSONAL TO MISS EIRENE ADORÉE, BETTER KNOWN AS
 MISS *PEACE:*
DARLING:
   HAVE NOT FORGOTTEN. WILL YOU FORGIVE?
   MY FAULT.

PLEASE TAKE ME BACK. BIG WEDDING. EROS TO PRESIDE
   IN FULL VESTMENTS:
FLOWER CROWN.
               FOREVER YOURS.

He looks over the heads of the audience and speaks as though to
his beloved.

                            Peace, Darling, I *know.*
You've tried to hide it, but I know you think I'm just a dried-up,
petered-out, little old man, who can't give you the one thing
that every girl has a right to expect. Don't cry—it's all right.
Because you're wrong about me—and I'll prove it three times over
when we reach our honeymoon spot. There I'll plant your garden
   properly.
First, I'll embed a long, unbroken series of sprays
from the passion flower, and raise them for seed. Second, quite close,
I'll lay out a parallel plat of succulent suckers from the fig.
Third, in the center of the bed I'll raise an astounding stand
of lusty vine. And around this fertile plot, Sweetheart,
a circle of olive trees—unlimited oil to anoint us
for Feasts when we take a rest from our toil in the garden—say,
one day a month. Then, Pet, you'll change your opinion of me,
and proclaim to the world:
                 "HIS HAIR IS SILVER,
                   BUT HIS—er—THUMB IS GREEN!"

The Herald enters.

HERALD
OYEZ! OFFICIAL ANNOUNCEMENT:
                      THE ANNUAL GRAND
ANCESTRAL DRINKING PARTY* IS HERE AGAIN!
You're all familiar with the rules. At the sound of the trumpet,
swill down your gallons! A Prize to the first man done:
a skin of Old Dry Sack—
                   (of-guts Ktesiphon)!
He exits. A short pause. Then Dikaiopolis, loaded with fowl and
kitchen implements, bursts from his door. He is followed shortly
by the members of his household, similarly laden.

DIKAIOPOLIS
Rousing everyone to furious action.
Women! Slaves! Did you hear what he said?
                         —Well,
what are you waiting for? Didn't you hear the Herald?

ACTION!
>These rabbit-chops—Sear them!
>>Now roast them!
Now cook the other side—
>Now take them off!
Next, weave the wreaths.
>Now skewer the larks! RUSH!

FIRST SEMICHORUS
>I dote upon your Wisdom,
>your Reason I adore—
>but I envy you your Rations
>considerably more.

DIKAIOPOLIS
Save your praise. You haven't see *anything* yet!

FIRST KORYPHAIOS
I bow to your logic—worse luck.

DIKAIOPOLIS
To a Slave.
>Poke up the fire!

FIRST SEMICHORUS
>Such range! Such scope in service!
>Such restaurantial vim!
>He's chef, he's cook, he's waiter.
>And who's the diner?
>>HIM!

*A cretinish farmer, wearing a white cloak liberally smeared with
cow dung, enters from the left. Something seems wrong with
his vision; his progress is erratic and he keeps bumping into things.
He is crying throughout the scene.*

FARMER
Oh, unhappy day! Oh, Woe!

DIKAIOPOLIS
>And who in the world
might you be, I beg to ask?

FARMER
>I'm an onlucky man.
I am.

DIKAIOPOLIS
>You'll oblige me, Sir, and keep it to yourself.

FARMER

Shucks, Friend, be neighborly. Don't keep that Treaty to *yourself*
Measure me out a little? Five years'll do.

DIKAIOPOLIS

Just what is your trouble?

FARMER

                    I'm a ruint man. I am.
I lost my pair of bulls. I did.

DIKAIOPOLIS

                    What from?

FARMER

From Phyle. I live there. Boiotian rustlers rustled 'em.

DIKAIOPOLIS

Deplorable—a bucolic tragedy, in one act!

Looking dubiously at the Farmer's dung-smeared white cloak.

                                        But shouldn't
you be in mourning? At a time like this, how
can you dress in white? (Correction: Off-white.)

FARMER

                                    I kin afford it.
I ain't no peasant. I ain't. Them bulls perduced—
they kept me rollin' in shit!

DIKAIOPOLIS

Sniffing and backing away.

                    So it appears.
But what do you wish from me?

FARMER

                              It's my eyes. They're gone.
I missed them bulls so much I cried 'em out.
I did. So please, if Farmer Squint from Phyle
means anythin' to you, come on, gimme just a dab
of that there Peace-salve for my poor eyes. Please!

DIKAIOPOLIS

What do you think this is, you yokel? The clinic?

FARMER

Neighbor, I plead you. If my eyes git fixed, mebbe
I kin find my bulls!

DIKAIOPOLIS

                    Impossible. Remove your bawls
and laments to Dr. Pittalos—Painless Pittalos,
the Public Physician.

FARMER

                Cain't you hearken to the plead
of a friend in need, and dribble one teentsy drop
of that Peace inside of this here hollow reed?
Peace on me!

DIKAIOPOLIS

           Not a scruple. Not a dram. Not a **minim**.

The Farmer redoubles his wails.

       Hence these tears. Hence, in addition, you.

He ushers the Farmer out.

FARMER

Onhappy day! Them poor, mizzuble bulls!

SECOND SEMICHORUS

             He can't be thawed or melted
            to share his Fluid Bliss—
            no Solvency was ever
            insoluble like this!

DIKAIOPOLIS

To the slaves.

    SET THE SQUID ON THE FIRE! GLAZE THE SAUSAGES!

SECOND KORYPHAIOS

Did you ever hear such volume?

DIKAIOPOLIS

                     ROAST THE EELS!

SECOND SEMICHORUS

To Dikaiopolis.

             You can choke us up with hunger
            and stifle us with smells,
            but keep your menu quiet:
            we'll die of decibels!

DIKAIOPOLIS

KEEP THEM ON THE FIRE UNTIL THEY'RE NICE AND
    BROWN!

*Two members of a wedding party enter from the left: the Best Man
and the Maid of Honor. The Best Man is young and pompous.
He carries a dish of cutlets and a tubular alabaster flask.
The Maid of Honor, pretty and shy, follows him at a distance.
She stops and waits shortly after she has made her entrance.*

BEST MAN

Dikaiopolis! Dikaiopolis!

DIKAIOPOLIS

        And whom do we have here *now?*

BEST MAN

For you, my good man, Compliments of the Groom. This dish
of tasty cutlets from the wedding feast . . .

DIKAIOPOLIS

Taking the dish.

                          Well, now,
I call that thoughtful. Splendid fellow, the Groom—
whoever he is.

BEST MAN

           . . . with a request. That you, in gratitude
for this dish of tasty cutlets, enable him to avoid
his Army service and bide at home in bed—
the better to pleasure his new-found bride—by pouring
into this flask one dram of liquid Peace.

DIKAIOPOLIS

Thrusting the dish back at him.

        Enough! Never! Return these gobbets to the Groom!
Not for One Thousand Drachmas—cash in hand—
would I grace his wretched flask with Peace!

He notices the Maid of Honor.

                          But hold—
who is this lovely thing?

BEST MAN

                 The Maid of Honor,
commissioned by the Bride with a private request for you.

DIKAIOPOLIS

Well, dear, what was it? A private request?

The Maid of Honor whispers in his ear. He laughs.

        Private, indeed. An odd request, but modest.
A stopgap measure that goes to the root of the matter.
Better for a Bride to keep part of a husband at home
than *no* husband at all. Why kick against the pricks?
Bring out the Peace! I'll do it. For her. *Just her.*
She's only a woman. And you don't make war on women.

A slave brings the bottle of Peace. He turns to the Maid of Honor.

        Would you kindly assist me? Hold this flask. Be careful.

He pours a drop of Peace into the flask.

        You know the directions, of course?

The Maid of Honor shakes her head.

Repeat this to the Bride:

For External Use Only.

At the first sign of a draft,
confine the husband to bed. Apply in the evening,
locally. Rub in well with a vigorous stroke,
until swelling subsides. This Prescription is *Not* Refillable.

The Maid of Honor and the Best Main exit left. Dikaiopolis turns
to the slave.

Return the flagon of Peace to the house. And bring me
a ladle. The time grows short, and I have yet to fill
the containers with wine, and ready my weapons for the Festival.

Preceded by the slave with the bottle of Peace, he returns to
his front door.

FIRST KORYPHAIOS
Mock-tragic.

But lo! A wight with brangled brow hastes hotfoot
hither, mayhap the harbinger of fortune foul.

The Herald enters on the run, races to Lamachos' house, and
bangs at the door.

HERALD
Ah, toils,

      ho, battles,

            ha, lambastings and Lamachoses!

LAMACHOS
Opening the door.

Who beats before my bronze-embossèd halls?

HERALD
Reading from a scroll.

FROM: GENERAL STAFF.

      TO: MAJOR LAMACHOS, COMMANDING.
RE: OPERATION SNOWDRIFT.

      LEAVE CANCELLED. DETACH
AVAILABLE CRESTS AND COMPANIES. PROCEED QUICKEST
WAY NORTH TO COLD REPEAT COLD BOIOTIAN FRONTIER.
INTELLIGENCE REPORTS BUILD-UP OF BANDITS. STOP
INCURSION SCHEDULED HEIGHT OF FESTIVITIES HERE.
THIS IS AN ORDER. REPEAT. THIS IS AN ORDER.

He races off.

LAMACHOS
General Staff! General Stuff and Stupidity!
Perish the purblind idiots who hinder me from holiday!

DIKAIOPOLIS

And pity your poor legions—led by a Major Catastrophe.

LAMACHOS

Again to endure the affliction of your gibes and gibbers?

DIKAIOPOLIS

You'd prefer to fight a Fabulous Monster? The Manticore?
The Cockatrice?

Snatching up two birds and waving them at Lamachos.

Perhaps the Flapwinged Flibbertigibbet?*

LAMACHOS

The times torment me! Woe, the tidings of the Herald!

A Messenger enters from the right and advances toward Dikaiopolis.

DIKAIOPOLIS

Well, times and tidings wait for no man. Here's mine.

MESSENGER

Dikaiopolis?

DIKAIOPOLIS

What is it?

MESSENGER

Apologetically.

We don't mean to rush you, Sir,
but the Priest of Dionysos sends his compliments, and could you
step 'round to the drinking-feast and grace us with your company?
At your convenience, of course . . . but you're Guest of Honor,
and the whole celebration has been waiting on you for hours!
Those plushy couches, the cushions, the festal board,
the scents and essences, the garlands and bowers of flowers,
and all those perishables! Cakes, Pastries, Pies,
Sweets, Tidbits, Tarts—and all those GIRLS!
Those supple, sumptuous, raving beauties, burning
for your beck, crying for your call, ravenous and wild
to warble you a song, or whirl you in the dance, or—well,
if you don't come quickly, Sir, they might get COLD!

He exits right.

LAMACHOS

Alackaday! The smart of fortune!

DIKAIOPOLIS

You outsmarted yourself—
blazoning that bellicose Gorgon all over your shield.

To the house.

Time to lock up! Someone come pack my dinner!

*Throughout the ensuing exchange, Lamachos and Dikaiopolis, with
their servants, make their preparations for departure before
their respective houses.*

LAMACHOS
To his servant.
> Break out my fieldpack! Issue Emergency Rations . . .

DIKAIOPOLIS
To his servant.
> An emergency's broken out. Bring our largest lunchbasket.

LAMACHOS
> Moldy biscuits, a stack of mildewed hardtack . . .

DIKAIOPOLIS
> The fresh-baked bread, the buns, the *petits fours!*

LAMACHOS
> . . . some lumps of salt, a bag of wormy beans . . .

DIKAIOPOLIS
> That tasty filet of sole! Never could stand beans.

LAMACHOS
> . . . the dried and dessicated heads and tails of scrod.

DIKAIOPOLIS
> The sweetbreads *en brochette*—I'll roast them there.

LAMACHOS
> The swirling plumes to deck my hero's helm!

DIKAIOPOLIS
> Now for *my* birds. Let's pack those yummy thrushes.

LAMACHOS
> Ah, the blazing glint of this ostrich plume!

DIKAIOPOLIS
> The delicate, brownish tint of a roasted thrush!

LAMACHOS
> —Avaunt, Sirrah! Cease your fleering at my panoply!

DIKAIOPOLIS
> —Well, tit for tat. You stop leering at my pigeons.

LAMACHOS
To his servant.
> Hither with the case that cradles my triple panache!

DIKAIOPOLIS
To his servant.
> The pan and ladle for that savory rabbit casserole.

LAMACHOS

A murrain on the moths who sneaked in to feast on my crests!

DIKAIOPOLIS

If I hurry, just time for a tasty snack before dinner.

He picks up a partridge leg and begins to eat.

LAMACHOS

You gabbling glutton, forbear to mock me with your menus!

DIKAIOPOLIS

I wasn't talking to *you*. The boy here and I
have a wager going. You can hold the stakes and decide
the issue, if you wish.

Waving the partridge leg at Lamachos.

Here's the Bone of Contention:
which is more delicious—Partridge or Duck?

LAMACHOS

OUTRAGE!

DIKAIOPOLIS

I agree: Partridge. —Pay me, boy.

LAMACHOS

STINKING PEASANT!

DIKAIOPOLIS

So? No accounting for tastes.

LAMACHOS
To his servant.

Lift down my deadly, lethal lance from the rack!

DIKAIOPOLIS
To his servant.

We'd better take that lovely sausage off the stove.

LAMACHOS

Grasp tight the haft, whilst I uncase the spear!

DIKAIOPOLIS

Hold on to the spit, while I strip off the sausage.

LAMACHOS

Assemble the sturdy tripods to support my shield!

DIKAIOPOLIS
Rubbing his stomach.

That tempting stew of tripe—*mine* needs supporting, too.

LAMACHOS

Now fetch the Peerless Prime of my *Apparatus Belli* . . .

DIKAIOPOLIS
Still rubbing his stomach.

You heard the man, boy. Hurry. I'll take the same.

LAMACHOS
The Ghastly Gorgon-Bedizened Orb of my Shield!

DIKAIOPOLIS
That sugary shortcake for dessert. Don't forget the cheese.

LAMACHOS
—I term that a Rank Offense—Flat Insolence!

DIKAIOPOLIS
—As you choose. *I* call it Fresh Three-Layer Spice Cake.

LAMACHOS
To his servant.

Furnish my buckler. In its shimmering, mantic surface
I behold a gaffer, soon to shiver in the dock
on the cowardly charge of Shirking his Country's Service!

DIKAIOPOLIS
To his servant.

Ice the spice cake. In its candid, candied surface
I behold the very same gaffer guffawing at cheese-head
Lamachos, son of Gorgonzola.
To Lamachos.

                         —Tune up your threnodies!

LAMACHOS
Bring now my brazen breastplate against the battles!

DIKAIOPOLIS
And now for the drinking-festival—bring the bottles.

LAMACHOS
Putting on the breastplate.

Thus firmly carapaced shall I defy the foeman!

DIKAIOPOLIS
A wee bit of fortification against my competitors.
He drinks from the bottle.

LAMACHOS
Bind up my blankets tight against the shield!

DIKAIOPOLIS
We'll have to tie the rest of the banquet to the basket.

LAMACHOS
I hoist the burdensome fieldpack and bear it forth!

DIKAIOPOLIS

It's hard to get help these days. I'll carry my cloak.

LAMACHOS

Struggling under the pack.

Raise high the laden shield, boy! FORWARD, MARCH!
—"Snowdrift," quotha! Welladay—the Winter of my Discontent!

He moves off slowly to the left, followed by his servant.

DIKAIOPOLIS

Raise high the viands—Supper is Icumen In!

He moves off briskly to the right, followed by his servant.

FIRST KORYPHAIOS

To the departing pair.

Now each to his own, campaigners!
May each good fortune pursue!

To Lamachos, with a gesture at Dikaiopolis.

His creature comforts compel us
to wonder what motivates *you:*
Why freeze in the snow as a sentry
and stiffen erect at attention?
He'll stiffen in bed, while a beauty
attends to his seething erection.

*No reply. The processions exit. He turns and addresses the
audience, recitatif.*

A compact prayer *in re* that greediest of civil servants,
that blubber-lipped bard of blather, ANTIMACHOS, son of Spittoon:
BLAST HIM, ZEUS!

He conducted our Chorus in last year's performance,
and barred us from the post-play supper. We didn't get a bite—not one!

FIRST SEMICHORUS

Singing.

We've planned a little dinner for Antimachos.
We'll sit him down and watch him salivate,
impatient for our subtle dish,
a finely roasted cuttlefish
au gras, au jus—and oh, so very late!

We've planned a little dinner for Antimachos;
at last we'll bring it, sizzling, sweet, and brown.
The sight of squid will ravage him;
he'll reach—but, by our stratagem,
a dog will get there first and gulp it down—
Yes, a dog will get there first and gulp it down!

SECOND KORYPHAIOS

So much for his gluttony, Gentlemen; now to do his lechery justice.
Some night, when this boudoir cavalier dismounts from the mattress
    for home,
on the way we envision him, shaken with ague, meeting ORESTES
the madman,* drunk, who will smash in his skull with a satisfying *boom*.

SECOND SEMICHORUS

    We've planned some entertainment for Antimachos.
        He'll venture to avenge his broken head;
            the moment that he topples prone,
            he'll fumble for a cobblestone—
        but grab a newly minted turd instead.

    We've planned some entertainment for Antimachos.
        He'll struggle up and give Orestes chase.
            He'll draw his deadly pellet back
            and launch his aerial attack—
        and miss, and hit KRATINOS in the face—
    Yes, he'll miss, and hit Kratinos *in the face!*

*Lamachos' Servant runs in wildly from the left and bangs at
the door of his master's house.*

LAMACHOS' SERVANT
*In the style of a Euripidean messenger-speech, with footnotes.**
    Ho! ye vassals, and ye serfs Ahoy! who habit
    the halls of Lamachos! Water, water! Enchafe
    the healing flood! Warm up about a cupful.
    Prepare ye plaster and poultice, ply splint and sponge,
    fix fomentation and embrocation! And some tape for his ankle.
    Succor our shattered Hero, our shivered Lord,
    most fell and foully pierced by a stick. He tried
    to hop a trench. Aye, and worse! Oh, curse
    the abrupt peripety, the wrenching reversal! He sprained
    his ankle. His crown is cleft. Remorselessly cleaved.
    Cloven by a craven rock. He tripped and fell on it,
    so hard that he waked the ghastly, grim-visaged Gorgon
    from her shield and snapped that great big Boastard feather
    off short on the stones. He raised his awful song:
    "Divine Effulgence, Glorious Orb of Radiance,
    O Lambent Eye of Day, receive thou now,
    at this my finest hour, my final gaze.

I leave this light. I am no more. . . ." And SPLASH!
headlong into a ditch kerflop,
> face down. And yea,
he rose once more, to harry and rout the rabble
brigands into flight. Oh, what a charge was this!
Straight into a lance.

> But lo, he comes! Behold
the peerless paladin! Ope wide the portals, ho!

*Lamachos, badly battered, is brought in from the left on the arm
of two slaves.*

LAMACHOS
> Cry Woe! the Injustice of War!
Racked with torture, with torment rent, I writhe
at agony's onslaught, a riddled wreck of body!
Oh, I am slain, sped stiff to ruin by the edge
of enemy staff!
> But pen me from the peak of pain.
Let me, undone, be not descried by Dikaiopolis,
whereat my woe might make me meat for mockery!

*Dikaiopolis, very drunk, reels in from the right, with a whore
on each arm. He carries an empty wineskin.*

DIKAIOPOLIS
> Sing ho! for the breasts of a whore!
So packed with pleasure! So firm and tense! I seethe
as passion's upsurge readies me for work so bawdy!
Oh, am I primed, made stiff for love by the nudge
of a friendly bosom!
> So kiss me, Golden Girls!
Cover with love, both inside and out, the mouth
that drank the wine to win the drinking-feast!

LAMACHOS
With a horrified glance at Dikaiopolis.
I shudder at Suffering's icy summit; my tale is told.
Cry woe, woe, for wounds which pain and pain again!

DIKAIOPOLIS
The Knight-Aberrant Lamachos! Good day, O Hero, j.g.!

LAMACHOS
MISERY!

DIKAIOPOLIS
To the First Whore, with a shiver of pleasure.
> Why did you kiss me?

LAMACHOS

ADVERSITY!

DIKAIOPOLIS
To the Second Whore, with another shiver of pleasure.

Why did you bite me?

LAMACHOS
Alas the charge! The cost! My cup runneth over with gall.

DIKAIOPOLIS
I don't know what you've been drinking, but Festival wine is free.

LAMACHOS
Apollo Paian! Healer! Send thy servant succor!

DIKAIOPOLIS
You'll have to wait for the Feast of Panacea—the All-Day Succor.*

LAMACHOS
To the Slaves.
A hand to soften my affliction!

DIKAIOPOLIS
To the Whores.

A hand to harden my erection!

LAMACHOS
I swoon, smitten by a rock!

DIKAIOPOLIS

I'm swollen as mighty as a boulder.

LAMACHOS
Wretched shall I lie in the dark!

DIKAIOPOLIS

I'm rigid. I'll lay in the dark.

LAMACHOS
To his comrades.
Tenderly bear me with hands that heal to Pittalos' clinic.

DIKAIOPOLIS
Take *me* to the judges. Who's in charge here? Award me the prize!

LAMACHOS
As he is carried off.
A baleful bolt impaled my bones and drained my soul!

DIKAIOPOLIS
Brandishing the empty wineskin at the Chorus.
The evidence of victory—it's empty! *All Hail, the conquering Hero!*

FIRST KORYPHAIOS

We bow to an elder's wisdom. *All Hail, the conquering Hero!*

DIKAIOPOLIS

What's more, I poured it neat and swallowed it down at a gulp!

FIRST KORYPHAIOS

The hallmark of true nobility! Proceed in triumph with your prize!

*A huge, full wineskin, the prize for the drinking contest, is
brought to Dikaiopolis. He clutches it, and, still supported
by the whores, starts off-stage.*

DIKAIOPOLIS

Follow my lead, and sing *All Hail, the Conquering Hero!*

CHORUS

We gladly follow in your train
to glorify your bold design
and raise our panegyric strain
in praise of wisdom mixed with wine:
ALL HAIL, THE CONQUERING HERO!

All exit, singing and dancing.

Notes

page 9. *five talents:* This takes at face value an old solution of a notorious crux and assigns Kleon's punishment, not to some actual event, but to Aristophanes' lost play, *The Babylonians,* produced in 426. Other solutions founder on the amount, really staggering for an individual to pay.

10. *The Executive Board:* Literally, the "prytanies," the members of a revolving executive committee of the Council (*Boule*) of 500. There were ten prytanies, the representatives of one of the ten tribes which made up the 500 members of the Council, and who convened and presided over the Assembly (*Ekklesia*) in turn.

10. *Olympos:* In the Greek, this peripatetic divine's name is "Amphitheos" —"having a god on both sides of the family." There is also a look, reflected in this character's actions, at the verb *amphitheein*—"to run around." The English "Divine" or "Father Divine" or "Brother Divine" is scarcely suitable.

11. *He begat me:* This genealogy is probably a parody and spoof of the elaborate genealogies with which so many Euripidean prologues began. With typical incongruity, Aristophanes juxtaposes the names of bona fide gods (Demeter, Triptolemos, etc.) with everyday Athenian names (Phainarete, etc.).

13. *PERSIA:* Both Athens and Sparta were in constant suit throughout the early years of the War for aid from this traditional enemy. Persia played her cards very closely, then threw in her lot with the Peloponnesians in 412, after the Athenian disaster at Syracuse.

14. *Crapathians:* This is preserved as a monument, if one were needed, to the impossibility of reproducing one of Aristophanes' favorite comic devices, the pun on proper names. The "Golden Hills," whatever they were, must have been in Asia. This attempt does not mean to imply that the Persian Empire, huge though it was, ever permeated to Transylvania.

16. *The All-Athenian Boy:* Literally, "the son of Sibyrtios," who was a noted trainer of athletes. The usual sarcastic jibe at Kleisthenes' effeminacy.

17. *SITALKES:* King of the Odrysians in Thrace, with whom Athens maintained an alliance in the early years of the War. An uneasy alliance,

evidently, since Sitalkes seemed much more interested in attacking Makedonia than aiding in the struggle in Greece proper. Aristophanes' feeling that this alliance, like the representations to the Persians, was an elaborate boondoggle, is pointed up by his making Kleon's notoriously corrupt toady Theoros the Athenian envoy.

page 23. *PHAῙLLOS:* Of Croton, probably, thrice victor in the Pythian games and possibly at the Olympian. Commander of a ship at Salamis. Aristophanes' stock example for swiftness, but swiftness of long ago.

24. *Country Dionysia:* This rustic feast, held in December-January, was seriously curtailed during the war by the necessary retreat of most of the rural population within the City walls during the winter. The other Dionysian celebrations—the Lenaia (end of January) and the Great, or City Dionysia (end of March)—continued.

29. *Breadboard:* The nearest English equivalent to *epixênon*—a chopping block *for domestic use.* This is the first of a string of devices, such as Euripides' rags, which provide the background for and at the same time undercut the tragic *mise en scène,* and thus make workable the parodies of the *Telephos* which now come thick and fast. So the same with the basket of coals parodies Telephos' threat to the infant Orestes in Euripides' play; the address on the Peloponnesian War, Telephos' defense of his (and the Trojans') actions at the beginnings of the Trojan War; the meeting with Lamachos, Telephos' confrontation by Achilles.

31. *Charcoal-lovers:* Acharnai was the largest of the rural demes of Attica, located approximately seven miles north of Athens near the foot of Mt. Parnes and consisting mostly of small farmers and charcoal burners. In 431, at the beginning of the Peloponnesian War, the deme of Acharnai had been ravaged by the Spartans and their allies under the command of Archidemos, and after the establishment of a Spartan post near Parnes, the Acharnians were forced to take refuge in the city of Athens. Ruined by the war and violently anti-Spartan, they became the most bellicose element in Athens, constantly clamoring to take the field against the Spartans. Indeed, Archidemos' strategy appears to have been based on the hope that the Acharnians might force the Athenians to offer a pitched battle with the Spartans—which would almost certainly have resulted in Athenian defeat. Thanks to Perikles' leadership, however, a policy of defensive attrition was adopted and a disastrous land-battle avoided. For the purposes of his play, Aristophanes deliberately emphasizes the extreme belligerence of the Acharnians in order to give point and resonance to the arguments of Dikaiopolis. Typically, it is only through Dikaiopolis' threat to massacre a scuttle of charcoal —the livelihood of most Acharnians—that the Acharnians are persuaded to hear him at all.

33. *Kleon:* Here, as often in the first half of the play, Dikaiopolis seems to speak in the person of Aristophanes. The legal proceedings referred to

here and elsewhere would seem to be an action for something like *lèse-majesté* brought against Aristophanes in 426 following his attack on Kleon in *The Babylonians*. This has led to the conjecture that Aristophanes played the leading role. I think this unnecessary and unlikely; Aristophanes is fond of injecting himself into other characters in other plays of his (such as Bdelykleon in *The Wasps*), and withdrawing at will, so the reader is left with that sort of half-allegory which is this poet's stock in trade. But, supposing Aristophanes *did* play Dikaiopolis, we are left with one great problem. For this to work, the audience would have to know it, in which case the anapests in the parabasis, the usual place for an author's address, would be intolerably deflated.

page 35. *KEPHISOPHON:* The naming of this servant as the musician who was an intimate of Euripides is rejected as a whim of the scholiast by most modern editors except Rogers. The servant is thus labeled "SERVANT." When the source of the objection is sought, it seems to be the undoubted fact that Kephisophon was not, in actuality, a slave of Euripides'. But this sort of sight-humor is surely part of the fun. Further, it does not appear to be what a scholiast would introduce, but reproduce.

42. *Alas, my Soul:* That favorite Euripidean device, the address to one's soul, is parodied here and at the end of the scene. For a famous example see the *Medea* 1056 ff.

42. *in groceries:* Introducing, to be picked up at the scene's end, Aristophanes' favorite gibe at Euripides: that his mother had been a vegetable-seller. The truth of this is not known.

45. *Lenaia:* This feast was not closed to non-Athenians by statute, but by weather, which kept ships from the sea in the winter, and thus kept friendly aliens from Athens, inaccessible during the War by land.

47. *from the skies:* A version of the famous Megarian Decree of 432, so strangely glossed over by the historian Thucydides in his account of the causes of the War. This translation adopts Schneidewin's *ouranōi* for *ēpeirōi* at line 534.

49. *on stage:* This subsequent scene has been inflated somewhat in the translation; Aristophanes could take Lamachos' jingoism as thoroughly familiar to his audience. Insufficient realization of this fact has led some critics to censure the scene, or even posit it as an imperfect second edition—the first edition, of course, would have contained considerable spouting by Lamachos.

51. *Purple Patches:* Emending *lochōn* in 575 to *logōn*.

53. *GENERAL:* As can be seen from subsequent developments, Lamachos is here inflating his rank, a joke which the audience must have appreciated. I have tried to point this up by the references to his probable rank at this time (*lochagos*—imperfectly rendered, "Major"). But the most difficult thing about Lamachos is his name. The root *mach-* means

fight, or battle, and Aristophanes plays on this relentlessly. If Lamachos had not been a real person, one might render his name as "Slaughter." In any case, he *was* elected a general the summer after the production of this play.

page 54. *Chaonia:* A barbarian settlement in Thrace; like Sicily here, a good destination for a boondoggle. There is a play on *chaskein* "to gape wide" as in Shambyses' characterization of the Athenians as *"chauno-prokt"* "gap-assed."

56. *ANAPESTS:* The main portion of the Parabasis—this choral address to the audience, embodying the author's remarks—was cast in anapestic tetrameter.

57. *Summer Residents:* This is a calculated lie of the translator to cover up a hopeless situation. We do not know Aristophanes' relation to Aigina. Most statements such as that it was his birthplace, or that he was a colonist, or that his father had lived there, are rationalizations, either ancient or modern, of this passage. About all we can be sure of (and some doubt *it*) is that the poet in question is Aristophanes, and not his producer Kallistratos. But he was certainly *not* a Summer Resident.

58. *and I quote:* Doubly: the passage as a whole from the mouth of Aristophanes, the italicized portion lifted from Euripides.

59. *Clock of Water:* The *klepsydra* which timed the speeches in the Athenian law courts.

60. *THOUKYDIDES:* Not the historian, but the celebrated general, son of Melesias. The process here referred to must have occurred sometime after his return from ostracism in 434.

61. *ALKIBIADES:* Athens' most famous black sheep, in his mid-twenties, was already being satirized by Aristophanes for dissolute brilliance.

61. *huge paddle:* In the Greek, Dikaiopolis swings three straps, which constitute his *agoranomoi* or "market-inspectors."

61. *Megarian:* The Megarian's speech in the Greek is quite thick Doric, made thicker by some editors who prefer to regard Aristophanes as a dialectologist rather than a comedian. I have made him a combination of Jeeter Lester and Senator Claghorn to try to realize, at least for those who share my feelings in this matter, what a Megarian accent conveyed to Athenians at this time: impoverishment and windy slyness.

63. *Pigs:* The subsequent scene depends for most of its effect on a basic pun: The word *choiros* means "pig" and is slang for the female genitalia. As there is no way to reproduce the pun in English *and* keep the sense of the scene, I have left it as a *sous-entendu* for the reader and tried to heighten the surroundings.

74. *To the audience, intimately:* This stage direction, plus "Dear Shopper," is counter to the usual interpretation, which is that the Chorus is talking about Dikaiopolis in the first stanza and *to* him in the second, third, and fourth. It seems to me that this stems from a misunderstanding of *hypopsōnōn* (here rendered inaccurately, but in the right direction, by

"pinch your lunch"), together with a failure to realize that the Chorus is acting as an intimate shill.

page 74. *Kratinos:* The aged comic poet, one of Aristophanes' chief rivals. Certain commentators, notably Rogers, tie themselves into knots to prove that this is another, younger Kratinos—who is probably the invention of a bothered scholiast.

76. *THEBAN:* Again, the Greek is in dialect. I have made the Theban into a Wodehousian sillyass to approach, according to my prejudices, the feelings Athenians had about Boiotians: effete, impossibly stupid aristocrats.

76. *whistle up "The Sphinx's posterior opening?":* The Greek has *prōkton kynos* "dog's rear." Following Starkie, I think this is a song—a dirty song, probably—and have substituted a modern, or relatively modern, equivalent.

76. *Or something like that:* The Greek has "birds or 4-winged things"— generally taken as a reference to locusts. I think that the Theban, being stupid, simply wants to say "quadrupeds" and gets mixed up. Hence the confusion.

84. *PEACE:* There is a convention, probably derived from the *Lysistrata,* that a picture, or a statue, or a naked woman representing Peace appears here. The Greek does not seem to require it. But this is no firm argument against it, except that it should probably be preceded by a parallel visual presentation of War. People seem less concerned about this.

85. *DRINKING PARTY:* The *Choēs*—"Pitcher-Feast" or, better, "Gallon-Feast"—the second day of the *Anthēstēria* or Festival of Flowers, which took place in February-March.

92. *Flapwinged Flibbertigibbet:* Literally, the "four-winged Geryon." Again, commentators see locusts.

97. *Orestes the madman:* Not an existent Athenian, but the tragic hero, pursued by the Furies, whose name had become the stock reference for "footpad."

97. *with footnotes:* The odd syntax and patchwork construction of this speech have led to the ejection of much of it by many critics—so many that I feel justified in resorting to typographical overstatement of what I believe to be the true interpretation: The Servant alternates between two tones of voice. The approved tragic declamation is steadily undermined by flat, ironic statements of the scarcely tragic facts.

99. *All-Day Succor:* In the Greek, Dikaiopolis protests that today is not the feast of the healer Paian. As the translation tries to demonstrate, there was none.

Glossary

ACHARNAI: Largest of the rural demes of Attika, located about seven miles north of the city of Athens. Its inhabitants were noted, primarily, for charcoal-burning, military valor, and their bitter hatred of Sparta.

AGORA: The main market place of Athens, used for holding trials, public debates, and the transaction of business.

AIGINA: An island in the Saronic Gulf, approximately twenty miles from Athens' port of Peiraieus (q.v.).

AISCHYLOS, AESCHYLUS: The great Athenian tragedian (525-456 B.C.).

ALKIBIADES: An Athenian politician (ca. 450-404) of great ability and brilliance. Of aristocratic Alkmaeonid descent, he was related to Perikles and was, for some time, a devoted disciple of Sokrates. Distinguished by wealth, birth, and spectacular personal beauty, he spent his youth in lavish display and debauchery (Pheidippides in *Clouds* has been thought to be a caricature of Alkibiades). After the death of Kleon in 422, Alkibiades became chief of the belligerent anti-Spartan party in Athens in opposition to the more conservative Nikias and was one of the primary advocates of the disastrous Sicilian expedition in 415.

ANTIMACHOS: A homosexual on a prodigious scale.

APHRODITE: Goddess of beauty and sexual love.

APOLLO: God of prophecy, music, healing, and light; and his two chief shrines were at Delphoi (q.v.) and the island of Delos (q.v.).

ASPASIA: Mistress of Perikles and the most famous courtesan of the age.

BACCHOS: *See* DIONYSOS.

BELLEROPHON: The famous legendary hero of the winged horse, Pegasos, and protagonist of a lost Euripidean tragedy. Toward the end of his career, Bellerophon met with misfortune, and wandered alone, a crippled beggar, shunning mankind.

BOIOTIA: A plentifully supplied state, directly northeast of Attika. Its capital was Thebes (q.v.) and during the Peloponnesian War, it was allied with Sparta.

CHAIRIS: An inept flutist.

DELOS: A small Aegean island sacred to Apollo.

DELPHOI, DELPHI: A town in Phokis, celebrated for its great temple and oracle of Apollo.

DEMETER: The Earth-Mother; goddess of grain, agriculture, and the harvest, worshipped in her shrine at Eleusis in Attika.

DEXITHEOS: A lyre player of considerable talent and onetime victor at the Pythian games.

DIONYSOS: God of vineyards, wine, and dramatic poetry; also called Bacchos, Evios, Bromios, etc.

EKBATANA: A city in Media, once the capital of the Median kingdom, and later the summer residence of the Persian kings. For the average Greek, Ekbatana was a kind of El Dorado, a distant city of fabulous wealth.

EUATHLOS: An orator and informer of no principles; it was he who brought charges against Perikles' rival, Thoukydides (q.v.), after his return from ostracism.

EURIPIDES: Athenian tragedian (480-406 B.C.) whose character and plays were constantly ridiculed by Aristophanes. Euripides' mother may have been (though this is uncertain) a marketwoman who sold chervil, and Aristophanes never tires of twitting the tragedian about his mother's vegetables.

GORGON: Mythological female monster of terrible aspect, frequently used as an emblem of terror on armor, shields, etc.

HERAKLES: Hero and demigod, son of Zeus and Alkmene: renowned for his great labors, his prodigious strength, and his gluttonous appetite.

HERMES: God of messengers and thieves; in Athens in every doorway stood a statue of Hermes (i.e., a *herm,* usually a pillar surmounted by a bust of the god), protector of the door and guardian against thieves—presumably because it takes a thief to keep another thief away.

HYPERBOLOS: An Athenian demagogue, successor to Kleon on the latter's death in 422. Of servile origins, he seems to have been a peddler of lamps and then to have studied with the sophists in order to advance himself politically. (At least these are the charges made against him by Aristophanes.) He was later ostracized and finally murdered by the oligarchical leaders in Samos.

INO: Euripidean heroine-in-tatters and wife of Athamas. She threw herself at her mad husband's feet, begging for mercy, but he refused to listen and threw her into the sea where she was transformed into the sea goddess Leukothea.

KELEOS: Dynastic name of the kings of Eleusis in Attika. The first Keleos was the father of Triptolemos (q.v.) and Demeter's host at

Eleusis. The Keleos who in *Acharnians* is married to Phainarete (q.v.) would appear, in Olympos' genealogy, to be the grandson of the first Keleos.

KEPHISODEMOS: Father of Euathlos (q.v.).

KEPHISOPHON: Secretary to Euripides (q.v.).

KLEISTHENES: A notorious homosexual, and one of Aristophanes' favorite targets.

KLEON: A wealthy tanner; the most notorious and powerful of all Athenian demagogues. After the death of Perikles in 429 B.C., Kleon became, until his own death in 422, the leader of the radical democracy and the anti-Spartan extremists in Athens. An impressive speaker and a thoroughly unscrupulous and venal politician, he was bitterly loathed and attacked by Aristophanes. In 424 B.C., thanks to his coup in capturing the Spartan hoplites at Sphakteria, he reached the height of his power; so unchallengeable was his position that he was able to persuade the Athenians not to accept the handsome terms offered by Sparta in an attempt to recover her imprisoned hoplites. Filled with confidence in his military ability and tempted by the hope of further glory, Kleon took command of an Athenian army in Thrace, where, in 422, he was defeated and killed by the Spartan forces under Brasidas.

In Aristophanes' *Knights,* Kleon is only slightly masked under the name of Paphlagon.

KLEONYMOS: A corpulent glutton and part-time informer; Aristophanes' commonest butt for cowardice (i.e., throwing one's shield away).

KOPAÏS: A large lake in Boiotia. Eels caught there were among the most cherished delicacies of Athenians.

KRATINOS: The aged Athenian comic poet, competitor with Aristophanes in the earlier years of the younger man's career.

KTESIPHON: A fat Athenian.

KYPRIS: Aphrodite, goddess of sexual love.

LAKRATEIDES: An old soldier, probably a veteran of Marathon.

LAMACHOS: An Athenian general belonging to the aggressive pro-war faction and satirized in *The Acharnians* as a blustering warmonger.

LENAIA: An Athenian Dionysiac festival, celebrated in January-February.

LYKINOS: A name, otherwise unknown.

LYSISTRATOS: An acid-tongued demagogue, evidently a starveling and a parasite.

MARATHON: The famous battle (490 B.C.) in which the Athenian forces under Miltiades crushingly defeated the first Persian invasion of Hellas.

MEGARA: The Greek state to the west of Attika. Subject first to the boycott imposed by Perikles' Megarian Decree (432 B.C.) and later to frequent Athenian incursions, plus the inroads of the Peloponnesian forces on their way to ravage Attika in the winters, it was reduced quite early in the war to extreme hunger and poverty.

MYSIA: Warlike kingdom in Asia Minor, allied to the Trojans during the Trojan War, and ruled by Telephos (q.v.).

NIKARCHOS: An Athenian informer.

OLYMPOS: Mountain (approx. 9700 ft. alt.) in Thessaly, covered at the summit with perpetual snow and reputed by the Greeks to be the abode of the gods.

PAIAN: Manifestation of Apollo as god of healing.

PARABASIS: That part of a Greek comedy in which the poet, through his chorus, directly addresses the audience, usually on political and topical matters.

PARNES: A mountain in the northeast of Attika, forming part of the boundary between Attika and Boiotia. Near its foot was situated the deme of Acharnai (q.v.).

PAUSON: An impoverished caricaturist.

PEIRAIEUS, PIRAEUS: The chief harbor of Athens; its initial fortification had been one of the projects of Themistokles.

PERIKLES: Greatest of Athenian statesmen of the fifth century, and from 461 B.C. until his death in 429, the almost unchallenged leader of the radical Athenian democracy. Of one of Athens' most aristocratic families (the Alkmaeonids), he was nonetheless the politician most responsible for the creation of the extreme democracy of the late fifth century. To Aristophanes' critical and conservative eyes, it was Perikles who was responsible for the corruption of Athens, and Aristophanes never tires of contrasting the Athens of the Persian War period with the Athens of Perikles—corrupt, effete, cruelly imperialistic, avaricious, at the mercy of sophists, clever orators, and imposters, cursed with a system (e.g., the law courts) which practically guaranteed further excesses and injustices. Worst of all in Aristophanes' eyes were Perikles' belligerent war policies (e.g., the famous Megarian Decree of 432) and the fact that, after 429, Athens was left to the mercies of men like Kleon and Hyperbolos who lacked Perikles' restraint and political genius. Like almost all the comic dramatists Aristophanes was a conservative (*not* an oligarch), and although he distinguishes clearly between Perikles and his corrupt successors, he nonetheless holds Perikles responsible for creating the political system in which men like Kleon could thrive.

PHAINARETE: A common feminine name, designed to sit incongruously with the divine names in Olympos' genealogy.

PHALES: The personified phallus.

PHAŸLLOS: A famous runner.

PHILOKTETES: Archer-hero of the Trojan War and subject of a lost Euripidean tragedy and Sophokles' extant *Philoktetes*. En route to Troy, he was abandoned on the island of Lemnos because of the stench of an incurable snake bite. Here he remained in utter indigence and desolation until the tenth year of the war, when Odysseus and Diomedes came to take him to Troy.

PHOINIX: Beggared hero in a Euripidean tragedy.

PHYLE: A rural Athenian deme, on the border of Boiotia.

PINDAR: The great lyric poet of Thebes (ca. 518-438 B.C.).

PITTALOS: A doctor, whose clientele seems to have been the very poor, treated at public expense.

PNYX: Meeting place of Athenian assemblies. Like a theater, it was semicircular and cut out of a hillside west of the Akropolis.

POSEIDON: Brother of Zeus and god of the sea. As god of the sea, he girdles the earth and has it in his power, as Poseidon the Earth-shaker, to cause earthquakes. In still another manifestation, he is Poseidon Hippios, patron god of horses and horsemen.

PREPIS: A homosexual; otherwise unknown.

SICILY: Large island, much colonized by the Greeks, situated to the south and west of Italy.

SITALKES: At the beginning of the Peloponnesian War, king of the Odrysai in Thrace and a nominal ally of Athens. Since his part in the alliance consisted mainly of incursions into Makedonia, there was some suspicion of his good faith at Athens.

SKYTHIANS: Barbarians who lived in the region northeast of Thrace. Skythian archers were imported to Athens for use as police, and thus provided the average Athenian with his most immediate experience of the non-Greek.

STRATON: An effeminate homosexual.

TAINAROS: A promontory in southern Lakonia on which a famous temple of Poseidon stood.

TELEPHOS: Legendary king of Mysia (q.v.) and the subject of tragedies by Aischylos, Sophokles, and Euripides. Wounded by Achilles while defending his country, Telephos was informed by an oracle that only the weapons which had given him his wound could cure him. Thereupon, disguised as a beggar, he made his way to Argos where, with the connivance of Klytaimnestra, he covertly took the young Orestes hostage. When the gathered Greeks were condemning Telephos for his hostility to their cause, the disguised hero made a speech in his own defense, but with such warmth and eloquence that the Greeks recognized him. When Achilles demanded his death, Telephos threatened to kill the infant Orestes. Finally, Achilles relented and agreed to give Telephos the weapon which had wounded him and which would cure him.

THEBES: The principal city of Boiotia; during the Peloponnesian War an ally of Sparta.

THEOGNIS: A tragic poet whose plays exhibited such extraordinary frigidity of invention that he was nicknamed "Snow."

THEOROS: Flatterer, perjurer, sycophant of Kleon.

THOUKYDIDES: Son of Melesias; not to be confused with the historian Thoukydides, son of Oloros. Leader of the conservative and anti-imperialist party in opposition to Perikles. In 443 he was ostracized; when in 433 he returned to Athens, he was involved in a ruinous lawsuit on the charges of Euathlos (q.v.).

THRACE: Name given in antiquity to the eastern half of the Balkans and site of many crucial battles during the Peloponnesian War.

THYESTES: Euripidean beggared hero.

TITHONOS: Son of Laomedon: he was granted immortality but not youth by the gods and hence wasted away into a shriveled old age. Proverbially, any decrepit old man was a Tithonos.

TRIPTOLEMOS: Hero of Eleusis, worshipped after his death as a vegetation god. With his father Keleos (q.v.), he welcomed Demeter to Eleusis and founded the Thesmophoria, the sacred festival of Demeter.

XANTHIAS: A common servile name.

ZEUS: Chief god of the Olympian pantheon: son of Kronos, brother of Poseidon and father of Athena. As the supreme ruler of the world, he is armed with thunder and lightning and creates storms and tempests.

The Congresswomen
(Ecclesiazusae)

Translated by Douglass Parker
with sketches by Leo and Diane Dillon

CONTENTS

S. J. PERELMAN
VIRO ERVDITISSIMO
CVIVS ΛΟΓΟΔΑΙΔΑΛΙΑ ΑΡΙΣΤΟΦΑΝΕΙΑ
VIAM MONSTRAVERAT
HVNC LIBELLVM
DOCTIS PRO DICTIS
INTERPRES
D. D. D.

Introduction

The Play

The fourth century B.C. was certainly no more than five years old when a politician named Agyrrhios instituted payment for attendance at Athens' assembly of the people, the *ecclesia*. It was not much older when he increased the payment to three obols per man per day. At this distance, his motives remain obscure; he may simply have been seeking a solution to the constant problem of pure democracy—how to ensure a quorum. But at least one pathologist of things democratic took a darker view. To the playwright Aristophanes, this was one more betrayal of the Athenian ideal, one more step toward statism. A legislative salary was bad enough, but when it approached, however feebly, a living wage, corruption was sure to follow. Given the normal Athenian citizen's urge for security, first his livelihood, and then inevitably his vote, and hence his life, would rest in the hands of demagogues like Agyrrhios, in hands sure to squeeze. Complete control was just around the corner, since the assembly was open to every citizen; it was worse than Kleon and the courts thirty years before.

Kleon's payment of jurors had furnished the occasion for *The Wasps;* why not do the same for Agyrrhios and the *ecclesia?* Why not demonstrate the implications of this latest constitutional disaster by telescoping its process in a comedy, in which the dithering of a three-obol assembly would transform the *polis* into something unthinkable overnight? Why not loot some current Utopian thinking and produce, full-blown, a totalitarian communistic welfare state? And why not, for that extra, tested turn of the screw to underscore Athens' current idiocy and provide manifold chances for comic business—why not have the takeover of the state masterminded by *women?*

As a correct reconstruction of a playwright's thought processes, the effusion above is probably as accurate as most other examples of its

1

genre—which is to say, not at all. But, as a presentation of dramatic motive, it seems tolerably close to the facts of the *Ecclesiazusae,* or *The Congresswomen,* which probably attained production in Athens toward the beginning of spring, 392 B.C. Bearded and cloaked, the ladies of Aristophanes' transvestite Chorus pack the assembly, or Congress, and accomplish a coup d'etat patterned closely and avowedly on Agyrrhios' career. Their leader, Praxagora, using ultraconservative arguments to appeal to the voters' desire for stability, rams through a measure which places her and her followers in charge of the entire conduct of the state. Then, uncasing, she reveals herself not only as a woman but as a wild-eyed radical. The program she unfolds to her stunned husband Blepyros is not the implied return to the old virtues, but a completely collective Brave New World marked by community property, community feeding, and community sex. There follows a series of scenes in which bewildered males grapple with these unsettling new realities: Two men (one dutiful, one mean) argue the propriety of turning one's property over to the state, only to have the argument rendered pointless by the announcement of a free dinner. A tense young man, wild to bed his girl, is nearly dismembered by three disgusting crones who lay legal claim to his prior services. Finally, old Blepyros, who has dallied with a brace of dancing girls through the dinner hour, leads the famished Chorus off to the feast, signaling the play's end.

As often in Aristophanes, the "message" supplies impulse and framework without usurping the play itself. In it, the three-obol fee and the communistic Utopia are tied together by congressional decree, but not as principal objects of satire; rather, they constitute a continuum in which we may behold the Athenian cit in his apparently boundless capability for being conned. As for the women, anyone who holds that this is a tract for female emancipation should ponder again Praxagora's equivocation, or the Three Uglies. *The Congresswomen* neither exalts nor demolishes Congress, communism, or women, but mines them for their comic potential. Which makes for awkward pamphleteering, but excellent good comedy. Cast exemplarily, one might say, in normal, bipartite Aristophanic structure: Part One (through Praxagora's program)—achievement of the *tolmêma,* the "Happy Plan"; Part Two—illustration of the Plan's consequences, almost by the numbers, culminating in a happy ending. In summary, a well-knit Old Comedy.

But only in summary. In spite of this almost diagrammatic structure, any full experience of the play leaves one with a sense of discontinuity. Aristophanes seems finally, in middle age, to have justified the criticism often leveled wrongly at *The Acharnians,* his earliest extant play. *The Congresswomen* is broken-backed; the episodes of Part Two, though they illustrate the program of Part One, do not really grow out of it in any meaningful progression, whether of emotion, imagery, or character.

Within scenes, there is a build; within the play as a whole, hardly.

This disconcerting effect derives partly from the evanescent characters. Praxagora, formulator of the Plan, attains her goal and propounds her program . . . and then, with two-fifths of the play remaining, departs the stage, never to return. The reappearance of Blepyros at the end is scarce compensation for this, nor can the efforts of various editors and translators (including this one) to link the two parts with other male characters help very much, since the longest and most striking scene—the trials of the tense young man—contains no character who might have occurred earlier.

Also contributing to the disjuncture is the silence of the Chorus, whose members return victorious from Congress, listen patiently to Praxagora's program . . . and then fall still, uttering not a syllable until they depart at the play's very end. Of course, they *may* have said something in Part Two: The manuscripts twice give the word *XOPOY* there —i.e., "this spot belongs to the Chorus"—which might be the last vestige of lyrics now lost; but it probably indicates no more than wordless dancing. Regardless, our text lacks the choral counterpoint to the action which, in earlier plays, defines and focuses the episodes.

But these shortcomings are symptoms, not freestanding causes; *The Congresswomen's* difficulty lies deeper. A recent critic of Aristophanes has put his finger on the trouble quite by accident, with the observation that this play "has no *agôn* at all." Technically, this is wrong, since the contest or debate known as the *agôn* occurs, admittedly in truncated form, as Praxagora's presentation of her program to the futile objections of Blepyros. But, in a larger sense, the criticism is just: The play lacks, not an *agôn,* but the overarching conflict which the *agôn* normally crystallizes; it possesses no opposition between Chorus and character, and no continuous opposition between character and character. Dramatically, the great potential battle goes by default: We do not actually experience the takeover of Congress, but see the women alone in one-sided rehearsal, while the facts of their victory are conveyed to us more distantly yet, in Chremes' report. The same women make a great to-do about the possibility of their being surprised by some man, but at no time are they ever in any real danger, nor do they even confront a representative male: Blepyros is an easily confused old husband, and nothing more; the tense young man has a universal complaint, but it does not extend beyond his episode. It is this lack of conflict, this lack of fundamental opposition and confrontation, which makes Praxagora leave and the Chorus lie doggo; they have nothing to do. And the play falls apart.

And yet, when all this is said, *The Congresswomen* remains a curiously attractive piece, not great, but fine in its way, and its deficiencies in unity should not blind us to its splayed excellences, which exist in plenty: The sheer technique, at the episodic level, which can arrange routine comic bits into an artistic whole. The wit which can make a long, tough exposition both dramatically and rhetorically meaningful. The verve which can create the longest word in Greek and then use it as a lyric background. The flawless pacing, which can manipulate the cheyne-stokes rhythm of the tense young man's discomfiture so that it restarts with increased wildness just when it seems to have stopped for good. The tact which can somehow maintain the most substantial defecation scene in comedy, or balance a lyric midway between anatomy and bliss.

And, of course, the obscenity itself. Not keeping statistics on such matters, I am unprepared to pronounce *The Congresswomen* Aristophanes' most obscene play; but the dirt, at least in spots, does appear more concentrated than usual. In my view, a concentrated excellence. Not only is it funny, not only is it psychologically right—grasping old Blepyros' anal-retentiveness should bring post-Freudian man up with a start—but, by sheer repeated and varied impact, it transcends disgust and moves on into art. The encounter of the tense young man and the Uglies was frequently censured, in another age not too long ago, as much too long; but shorten it, cut it, and only the shock will remain. Poetry can be made of the strangest materials, and Aristophanes has made it here. A curious excellence, perhaps, and not the most illustrious ornament . . . but a most fitting ornament for this most curious play.

Tastes differ, of course, and I realize that there are those, even in this day and age, who are unwilling to entertain the possibility that the use of obscenity might amount to a positive distinction. I can only wish them well, and hope that they go elsewhere; this play is not for them. There is another type of astigmatism that may be easier to correct— that born of historical perspective. The modern reader of *The Congress-women* is perhaps uncomfortably aware that the Athenian empire, well-spring and taproot of Western civilization, had crashed into irrevocable ruin a dozen years before. Some critics, obsessed by this knowledge, have let it cloud their vision of playwright and play. To these, it smacks of bad taste and bad form to make fun amid the wreckage; they, therefore, must impugn Aristophanes' skill and sincerity as an artist. One such critic accuses the play of lacking vitality; another marks it the work of an overtired man; a third describes the author as brokenhearted at the cataclysm which had visited his city.

Now, faults *The Congresswomen* has, and they are not to be denied, but nowhere does it give evidence of heartbreak, fatigue, or listlessness. And, as to the charge of laughing in the ruins—well, the participants in a cataclysm are often the last to know. Aristophanes, like most other inhabitants of an Athens still busily combining against Sparta, had not heard the crash.

Translation

The principles governing this translation into American English remain those enunciated in the Introductions to my versions of *The Acharnians, The Wasps,* and *Lysistrata,* to which the reader is referred. There has been one slight change in orientation, however, which should be set down here: In making my earlier translations, I hoped for production without really expecting it; on looking back, I seem often to have aimed for a theater in the reader's head rather than one before his eyes. Stage directions overflowed, explanatory expansions of the text often slowed down pace, rhetoric swelled in compensation for the lack of physical production. These days, however, such production is becoming more and more usual. I don't regret my former practice; any good director knows when to cut. But in translating *The Congresswomen* I have had more of an eye to an actual stage and the problems of immediate apprehension by an audience, and may thus have assimilated the obscure to the familiar, or suppressed proper names, rather more often than formerly. I have tried to rectify such actions in the Notes, but the dedicated antiquary will do well to check the Greek.

Text

Most plays of Aristophanes cry aloud for new editions; the *Ecclesiazusae* shrieks, since its Greek text has normally been edited only to fill out the set. (In all the extant plays of Aristophanes it is occasionally difficult to tell who speaks a given line; in this play it is all too frequently impossible to say with any certainty who is in the cast.) I have done what I could with the best available text, that of Coulon (1930), bolstering it with the editions of Rogers (1916) and Van Leeuwen (1905). Major departures from Coulon's text are indicated in the Notes.

Acknowledgments

This translation was made while I was a fellow of the University of California's Institute for the Creative Arts, and I take this opportunity to express my gratitude and thanks. Also, to William Arrowsmith, my thanks for trust and tutelage. To my wife Haverly, my thanks for trust, encouragement, and endurance throughout the vagaries of an English spring.

DOUGLASS PARKER

Characters of the Play

PRAXAGORA, *an Athenian woman of somewhat radical views*

FIRST WOMAN

SECOND WOMAN

THIRD WOMAN

FIRST KORYPHAIA

SECOND KORYPHAIA

CHORUS OF ATHENIAN WOMEN

PHEIDOLOS, *a mean man*

BLEPYROS, *a suspicious man and part-time barrator, husband to Praxagora*

CHREMES, *a dutiful man*

A CRIERESS

A HAG

A SWEET YOUNG THING

EPIGENES, *a tense young man*

A CRONE

A HARRIDAN

ASSORTED WOMEN AND SLAVES

SCENE: *A street in Athens, on which front three
houses.* These are, at the moment, allotted thus:
House I, center, Praxagora and her husband Blepyros;
House II, stage left, the Second Woman and her
husband Pheidolos; House III, stage right, Chremes.
The time is early morning; it is still dark. Praxagora
emerges stealthily from House I. She wears a long
cloak and red slippers, and carries, in one hand, some
wreaths, a staff, and a long false beard. The other hand
contains a large clay lamp, lit. After a cautious look
around, she puts down wreaths, staff, and beard, strides
purposefully forward, and mock-tragically begins what
seems to be an invocation of the sun* filched from
a Euripidean prologue.*

PRAXAGORA
O beam resplendent,
                    blaze of glazèd gaze,
O horribly gorgeous orb, who wheeled and sprang,
the fairest ware of those who live for the kiln,
Raising the lamp in both hands.
        O Bedside Lamp . . .
                    (I really feel I should
divulge your parentage and fate; you've come so far
from low beginnings.)
                    *Earth thou wert, but spun
to life and tried in the furnace, you quitted the potter's
field for higher pastures, and now your nasal
orifices spurt forth the Sun's effulgent
offices.*
        *Therefore, Lamp, impel abroad
the supersecret signals we have fixed.*
She waves the lamp vigorously.
        You're the only nonwoman who knows our code;
you've earned our trust.
                    *When we, within our rooms,
strain and struggle to rehearse new shapes of love,
in closest intercourse you guard our flanks.
And when we splay our bodies in supine display,
you oversee the action from the rear, an eye inside
the house whom no one shuts or closes out.
Your shaft alone is privy to our inmost nooks,
and privately in those parts its burning glance
defoliates unwanted hair. Or, when from the well-stocked*

9

cellar we sneak away the yield and stream
of Bakchos, you are there, O friend and guide,
O faithful accomplice, never known to spill
a word to the neighbors.

                   Wherefore, friend, you now
shall be apprised, at nearest hand, of all
decisions taken and actions passed last summer*
by my assembled associates.

                   —Except, there's no one
here. They should have come. It's getting on
toward dawn. The Congress* takes up any minute now,
and we've got to get seats . . .

Realizing, with a start, that she has dropped the
paratragic rhetoric.

                     oh, pardon me; forgot . . .
We must dispone our limbs in crafty slyness
on what the noted spoonerizer Phyromachos
once deigned to name those beery wenches.*

                   —But what
could the trouble be? They couldn't follow directions
and sew their beards on? It was too much of a task
for them to snaffle their husbands' cloaks and not
get caught?

She looks off right.

               Oh, there's a lamp. It's coming this way.
I'd better beat a retreat. With the luck I'm having,
this visitor might turn out to be a Man.

She takes up a position beside House I. Shortly, a
gaggle of women, who will later group and form as
the First Semichorus, straggles on from the right.
They bear (and in some cases wear) men's cloaks,
shoes, canes, and beards. Leading them is the First
Woman, who is earnestly trying to counterfeit
maleness.

FIRST WOMAN
Time to be on the march, men. While we were assembling,
the second reveille blew. Two cocks and a doodle.

PRAXAGORA
Stepping forward.

Do tell. And I was reveling here in an all-night
wait for you.

              But just a moment. Let me
summon my neighbor. Just a scratch at her door;
she'll be in a scrape if her husband hears.

10

She taps lightly at the door of House II, which
is immediately opened by the Second Woman.

SECOND WOMAN
Enough.
I heard your nails. Just putting on my shoes.
Not that I had a single wink of sleep.
Never marry a sailor, darling. Always
fumbling around in the stern sheets, catching me
right between wind and water . . . I had to double
the cape all night before I could snitch this cloak.

PRAXAGORA
Looking off left, where a second muddled and motley
group of women, who will form, eventually, the
Second Semichorus, is beginning to enter. They are
led, or better preceded, by the Third Woman.
Well, now. Here comes Kleináretê—better late
than never—that one must be Sóstratê, and there's
Philaínetê.

THIRD WOMAN
To the stragglers.
Better get a move on! Glykê laid us
under an oath: The last one there picks up
the tab for three gallons of wine and a peck of cockles.

SECOND WOMAN
Look, here's Melístichê, slogging along in Smikýthion's
clogs.

PRAXAGORA
Why such a mad dash? With a man like hers,
she had all night to get here.

FIRST WOMAN
Geusístratê's got
a torch. That means lights out in her husband's bar.

PRAXAGORA
Here's Philodorétos' wife, and Mrs. Chairétades. . .
and here come loads of others, perfect crowds
of the very best women—Athens' complete elite!

THIRD WOMAN
Arriving before Praxagora.
Had the godawfullest trouble getting away,
darling. My husband was at it all night.

11

PRAXAGORA

                                 At it

all night?

THIRD WOMAN
           Yes, the pig. He stuffed himself
on sardines at supper and couldn't sleep for burping.

PRAXAGORA
Very well. Be seated.
                      Now that I've got you together,
I'd like to run a check on your performance.
Have you complied completely with all the directives
we drafted and passed at Athene's feast last summer?

FIRST WOMAN
I certainly have. First, as per understanding,
I let my underarms bush up into jungles.
Next, every time my husband went downtown,
I smeared my body with oil and spent the day
standing in the sun and getting an allover tan.

SECOND WOMAN
Me, too. I started by slinging my razor right out
of the house, and now I'm such a mass of fuzz
I don't even look like a woman any more.
Well, not to a casual glance.

PRAXAGORA
                    Another point
in the compact. We each agreed to bring a beard
to this meeting. Do you have yours?

THIRD WOMAN
Producing her false beard.

                           Mine's divine!

SECOND WOMAN
Producing a huge beard.
          And mine's in line with fashion. Epikrates decrees
that this year's beardline's below the knees.

PRAXAGORA
To the crowd of women.

                            Do you

have yours?

FIRST WOMAN
           Boy, do they. Look at those hairy nods.

PRAXAGORA
Well, everything else appears to be in order.
Let's see, now. Slippers, check. And ditto the canes.
And ditto your husbands' cloaks.

>Just as agreed.

FIRST WOMAN
Producing a tremendous club.
I stole this cane from my husband while he was sleeping.
As usual.

PRAXAGORA
>Just what does your husband *do*?

FIRST WOMAN
>>Delivers

logs. You know him—Lamios.*

SECOND WOMAN
>>Oh, yes—the man
who lets those tremendous farts!

FIRST WOMAN
>>It's such a waste
of talent: He carries a big stick, farts like an army . . .
If only he could stay awake, he'd make
a fortune in politics.

PRAXAGORA
>And now, before the stars
decide to leave the sky, we'd better decide
on our next move. We've made all these preparations
to go to Congress, and Congress takes up at dawn.

FIRST WOMAN
God, yes. You'll have to get us over there early;
we want those seats down front by the speaker's stand,
facing the Executive Board.

THIRD WOMAN
*Holding up a large phallos.**
>See what I brought.

PRAXAGORA
What's that?

THIRD WOMAN
>A carding comb. I thought I could work
the snaggles out of my wool until the men
started Congress in earnest.

PRAXAGORA

What's the point,
you nitwit?

THIRD WOMAN

I'm sure there's bound to be some connection . . .
and anyway, I can listen just as well
while I flog away at my fleece.

I *have* to do it.
My kids are positively *nude*.

PRAXAGORA

That's all we need.
Card your wool, indeed. *No man must see
the slightest bit of your body.*

We've got to hurry;
the littlest slip and we're undone. I can see it all:
The people assemble, Congress commences . . . and then
we arrive in a flap, some woman climbs over a bench,
flips up her cloak, and exposes, to all and sundry,
some misplaced whiskers.

But if we get there first
and take our places, we can adjust our clothing
and no one'll be the wiser. And once we're there,
with proper beards tied on and arranged in place,
what casual observer will say that we're not men?

FIRST WOMAN*
You're right. Agyrrhios started out as a woman,
but then he stole a fluteplayer's beard, and pulled
the wool over everyone's eyes, and look at him now:
He runs the city.

PRAXAGORA

And Agyrrhios, girls, is our model.
By the gods of daylight robbery, let's try to pull
a *coup* as big as his. Let's devise a device
to take command, take charge, take over. *We'll* run
the city, run it right and proper and well.
No more sitting and drifting in a ship of state
with empty oarlocks and barren masts!

THIRD WOMAN

Now, look:
We're *women*! What place is there on the floor of Congress
for feminine intercourse? How can we fit in?

PRAXAGORA
You'd be surprised. It's agreed that the most persuasive
speakers are smoothskinned, softvoiced boys who've been screwed
to a pitch of eloquence—and *that* is a qualification
that we possess in plenty.

THIRD WOMAN
                    That may be okay
for rump sessions, but what's our official position? The thing
we lack is practice.

PRAXAGORA
                    And that, in case you've forgotten,
is precisely why we're here—to rehearse our speeches.
Now hurry and get that beard tied on.
                                    The same
for those of you who've been practicing how to talk.

SECOND WOMAN
You mean there's someone here who doesn't know how?

PRAXAGORA
You tie your beard on. Quickly. Be a man.
I'll set these wreaths down here and put mine on
with the rest of you. I just might want to speak.

*All the women adjust their beards. The Second
Woman, still beard-proud, points at the women
before her.*

SECOND WOMAN
Praxagora, honey, look over here. The funniest
thing I ever saw.

PRAXAGORA
                    The funniest? How?

SECOND WOMAN
                                    That fringe
around their chins. They look like roasted squids.

PRAXAGORA

As a herald.

*Attention, please! The ritual purification will now
commence. The Chaplain will pass among you, bearing
the sacrificial polecat.*

FIRST WOMAN
                    I thought they sacrificed pigs.

PRAXAGORA
We couldn't get a pig.

FIRST WOMAN

But why a polecat?

SECOND WOMAN

It gives an odor of holiness.

PRAXAGORA

Move down front!

As if to an inattentive member of Congress.
(Ariphrades, hold your tongue. Come up and sit down.)
—Who wishes to address the assembled Congress?

SECOND WOMAN

I do.

PRAXAGORA

Wear this wreath on your brow.* May fortune attend you.

SECOND WOMAN

Adjusting the wreath.

This look all right?

PRAXAGORA

You may proceed to speak.

SECOND WOMAN

Before I've had a drink?

PRAXAGORA

What drink do you mean?

SECOND WOMAN

Well, isn't this party politics?

PRAXAGORA

Yes . . .

SECOND WOMAN

So where's

the party?

PRAXAGORA

Snatching back the wreath.

Get out of here. A fat lot of help
you'd be up there.

SECOND WOMAN

You mean they *don't* drink in Congress?

PRAXAGORA

Of all the fatuous questions . . .

SECOND WOMAN

They do *too* drink—
what's more, they drink it straight. They pass decrees
that sound just like D.T.s.

FIRST WOMAN

She's right. They pour
libations, too. I know they do: They're always
praying, and prayers without wine are perfectly pointless.

THIRD WOMAN

And the language. They slander each other like men on benders,
and then the police come along and sling out the drunks.

PRAXAGORA

Move along and sit down. You're worse than useless.

SECOND WOMAN

I wish to god I'd never grown a beard.
This thing absorbs saliva. I'm positively parched.

PRAXAGORA

Is anyone else desirous of speaking?

FIRST WOMAN

I am.

PRAXAGORA

Then get this wreath on. Don't hold up the agenda.
Give us a firmly grounded masculine speech . . .
and don't fall over. Use your cane for support.

FIRST WOMAN

Unaccustomed as I am, I would have preferred
to yield the floor to some more experienced speaker.
But since I have risen, I cannot refuse to attach
a widespread abuse in this city. I refer, of course,
to Corruption at the Bar. Does anyone realize
how many cases there are in Athens' taverns
filled up with water? Heavens to Betsy,* it isn't . . .

PRAXAGORA

Heavens to Betsy, deadhead? Where did you leave
your brain?

FIRST WOMAN

What's wrong? I didn't ask for a drink.

PRAXAGORA

No, but what man swears by *Heavens to Betsy*?
The rest was beautifully stated. Right to the point.

FIRST WOMAN
Oh.
Back into the speech.
—GODDAM IT ALL, it . . .

PRAXAGORA
Snatching back the wreath.

Stop. Enough.
Now get this straight: I won't take another step
toward commandeering Congress unless the strictest accuracy
is observed in everything we do.

SECOND WOMAN
Running back up to Praxagora.

Give me the wreath.
I want another chance to speak. I know
I've got it right this time. All practiced and everything.
Putting on the wreath and striking an attitude.
—It is my pleasure to address you, girls . . .

PRAXAGORA
Snatching back the wreath.

The same mistake again. These are not girls,
they're MEN.

SECOND WOMAN
Pointing to the audience.

It's Epigonos' fault. I saw him sitting
out there and thought I was talking to women.

PRAXAGORA

Scat.
To First Woman.
You too.
To First, Second, and Third Women.

Now sit down over there. You force me
to a hard decision: I'll do the speaking myself.
But first, the wreath.
She puts it on.

I pray the gods will direct
today's deliberations to some successful issue.
A pause, and she begins a formal address.

—My friends: I bear a share no less than yours
in this land of ours, and feel compelled to confess
to a mounting distress. In fact, my grief is great
at the state of our City: Something is rotten in Athens.
Our leaders, our elected officials, are routinely vicious;
if one steps out of line and delivers a day

of honest performance, he balances this with a week
of corruption. Give the job to another, he plumbs
yet deeper depths of depravity. All this indicates
your senselessly finical nature, which makes me despair
of giving you any advice. Your standard behavior
to prospective friends is frightened rejection, the while
you go on your knees to woo potential enemies.
It shakes my faith in government: A few years back,
we never convened the Congress at all, but we knew
one thing for certain: we all agreed Agyrrhios
was a crook.

    But then this crook established a salary
for legislative attendance. So now we convene the Congress . . .
and those of us who get paid are loud in his praise,
while those of us who don't are equally loud
in demanding death for those who pass laws for money.

FIRST WOMAN
Goodness gracious, what a lovely speech!

PRAXAGORA
—Can't you stop that harebrained swearing? *Goodness
gracious* . . . that would sound just peachy in Congress.

FIRST WOMAN
I wouldn't say it there.

PRAXAGORA
       Don't get the habit.

Back to the speech.
    —Or take the current Alliance against the Spartans: *
During debate, it was roundly affirmed that Athens'
future depended upon it; alliance or ruin.
But once we voted it in and the League was established,
reaction arose with a vengeance, so savage and swift
that the man who'd maneuvered acceptance of the longed-for
  League
had to leg it out of the city or lose his life.
—I turn to your wishy-washy stand on seapower:
Should Athens launch a fighting navy?* The poor man
thinks of pay, and votes YES; the rich man thinks
of tax, and votes NO; the farm bloc thinks of reprisals,
and joins the rich man.

      —And Korinth: Only yesterday
you detested Korinth, and Korinth detested you.
Today they're friends and allies; therefore, play
along, about face, be friends and allies too. . . .

The polymath hasn't a brain in his head; the mangiest
moron in town is sporting the name of Sage.
Whoops, there went a glimpse of Salvation . . . but no,
the savior's out of bounds, and nobody calls.*

SECOND WOMAN
This man is profound.

PRAXAGORA
                          (Now, there is proper praise.)
—Of all this higgledypiggledy mixture of moral
incertitude you stand guilty, people of Athens.
You draw a public wage for serving in Congress
with blinders which narrow each man's vision to private
profit, while General Welfare wobbles along
like a drunken cripple.
                          However, All is Not Lost:
Give me your support, and you may yet be saved.
I here propose that we relinquish the State
to a trained managerial class, trustees and directors
of our happy homes—to our wives and daughters—in short,
to the *Women*.

WOMEN
                          Hurray!
                                   —Hurrah!
                                             —Huzzah!
                                                      —Hear! Hear!

PRAXAGORA
The superior nature of the female's behavior pattern
to that of the common male like you or me
is easily shown. Example: Every girl jill
of those women washes her wool in hot water, just like
her mother before her; you never catch them casting
about for a newfangled method.
                          But male-run Athens
has always been *in* hot water, for just the opposite
reason: We men can never resist improving
on something that works; we tinker and innovate the City
right into the ground. Not so the women. Women
are truly conventional, natural-born conservatives:
                  Women kneel to bake their bread,
                    tote their laundry on the head,
                       —just like Mother.
                  Trust a tested recipe,

21

Keep Demeter's yearly spree,*
    —just like Mother.
Nag their husbands till they're dead,
hide their lovers under the bed,
    —just like Mother.
Pad the grocery bill with snacks,
take a drink or three to relax,
prefer their pleasure on their backs,
happy nymphomaniacs,
    —just like Mother.
Therefore, gentlemen, why waste time in debate?
Why deliberate possible courses of action?
Simply hand over the City and let the women
rule. You need convincing? Reflect: Mothers
all, their first desire will be to preserve
their soldier sons.
                Provisions? Who quicker than
the hand that rocks the cradle at filling the mouth?
Finances? Nothing more wily than women at scrounging
a budget—and rest assured that, once in power.
they won't allow embezzlement of public funds;
by dint of training, they themselves are Athens'
finest embezzlers.
                I say no more. Give me
your support, and vote yourselves a life of bliss.

FIRST WOMAN
Lovely, Praxagora darling. Right on the button.

SECOND WOMAN
But where did you learn to talk so beautifully, baby?

PRAXAGORA
During the Terror,* my husband and I hid out
on the Pnyx, where Congress meets. Got lost in the crowd,
and listened to politicians. Learned them all by heart.

FIRST WOMAN
I'm not surprised. You're simply fiendishly clever.
If you can manage to bring your project off,
we'll elect you commander-in-chief on the spot.

THIRD WOMAN
                              But what
if Kephalos starts—worse luck—to call you names?
Can you counter attacks from him in open debate?

PRAXAGORA
I'll say he's deranged.

THIRD WOMAN
So what? Everyone knows that.

PRAXAGORA
A manic-depressive, downhill phase.

THIRD WOMAN
That won't
faze him. Everyone knows that, too.

PRAXAGORA
I'll say
that a man who turns out such tasteless vases would surely
make Athens go to pot.

SECOND WOMAN
But suppose Neokleides
squints his bleary eyes and begins to get nasty?

PRAXAGORA
I'll tell him that sight like his is better suited
for an open-ended probe of a diarrheic dog.

FIRST WOMAN
The members may rise to a point of order. Won't that
stop your flow?

PRAXAGORA
I'm sure I can handle their points.
I have a penchant for twisting things.

FIRST WOMAN
A what?

PRAXAGORA
A knack.

SECOND WOMAN
There's only one danger left. Suppose
the police start dragging you out in the middle—what
can you do?

PRAXAGORA
I'll put my hands on my hips. That way,
my middle is always safe; they'll have to try
for my end.

THIRD WOMAN
We won't sit idle. If they make any
attempt to pick you up, we'll shout them down.

FIRST WOMAN

I think we've got together on a marvelous plan,
but there's still one technical point we haven't worked out.
It's Voting: I know they record their votes by waving
their hands, but how? The only practice we've had
is spreading our legs.

PRAXAGORA

              It isn't an easy procedure;
requires some effort.

Demonstrating.

          First, the right-hand sleeve
is grasped in the left hand, and then shoved back, exposing
the shoulder. The freed right arm is then raised stiffly,
thus.

     That's it.

To the whole crowd of women.

         Now tuck up your dresses. High.
Then on with those Spartan go-to-meeting shoes. And tie
them tight, the way your husband does whenever
he's ready to go to Congress—or wherever else
he says he's going. When this is all in perfect
order, fasten up the beards. Be fussy. Make sure
the adjustment is right in line.

              Next thing, put on
those overcloaks you stole from your men this morning.
Around the shoulders, so.

             And now the canes.
You lean on these when you walk. And while you walk,
you sing. Some antique, elderly melody. Try
to sound like old men tottering in from the country.

FIRST WOMAN

That's beautifully put. But as for us, we'd better
rush on ahead and intercept the girls who are really
coming in from the country. They'll probably go
direct to the Pnyx.

PRAXAGORA

          Then hurry. The rule up there
is In by Dawn, or No Pay. The man who isn't
abreast of the times slinks home without a tittle.

*She exits quickly left, followed by the First,
Second, and Third Women. The remaining women,
fully disguised, are grouped into formation as First
and Second Semichoruses by the First and
Second Koryphaiai.*

FIRST KORYPHAIA

Time to commence
our journey, gents,
and "gents" is the magic word.
The slightest blunder
will send us under;
don't let your gender get blurred.
Our beautiful plot
will come to naught
if you expose your sex;
so, girls, be male
and don't let's fail
unmanned by some damned reflex.

FIRST SEMICHORUS

Singing as they start off.

To Congress, gentlemen. On our way.
to make our country's laws.
The pay's three obols per man per day
but we've got troubles, because:

The authorities state
that the going rate
will only apply
to the sour-faced guy
who arrives half-dead,
unwashed and unfed,
by dawn's early light
just past midnight . . .
He gets his fee;
come later, vote free.

So keep up, Drákês and Smíkythos,
while we rehearse our vote.
Come on, Charitímidês, follow close;
we're dead if there's one false note.

First, we'll check in
before they begin;
next, down we'll flock
and get seats en bloc;
then one of us will
propose a bill
in which we'll concur
and vote for her . . .

A shocked pause.

> Now, there's a gaffe that could be grim:
> Correction, please: we'll vote for *him.*

They move off toward the left, followed by the
Second Semichorus, whose members have cast
themselves as men from the countryside.*

SECOND SEMICHORUS
> Let's shove these townies out of the way.
> This order's preposterous:
> No johnny-come-latelies who vote for pay
> can crowd ahead of *us.*

> When we drew one obol,
> it was too much trouble
> for them to attend;
> they'd chin with a friend
> in the market, and let
> the rest of us sweat
> out the vote. But these days,
> since the recent raise,
> they clog the queue,
> and we can't get through.

> In the golden days of Myrónidês,
> Athens had better men.
> Nobody dreamed of demanding fees
> for being a citizen.

> For statesmanship
> the reward was a sip
> of wine, plus a few
> ripe olives, say two
> small onions, a dried-
> out crust . . . supplied
> at your own expense.
> But that's long since:
> Now Congress is commerce, and politics
> pays just as well as hauling bricks.

They follow the First Semichorus off left.
A pause, and the door of House II opens. Pheidolos
appears, in misery. He wears a skimpy woman's
shift and gaudy house slippers a number of
sizes too small, and walks cramped.

PHEIDOLOS*
What the hell is happening here? It's nearly
sunup, and where's my wife? Disappeared without trace.
She's gone, my clogs are gone, my cloak is gone
and me . . . oooh god, I gotta go. For the last
three hundred years I've been lying in bed, expanding,
trying to find some clothes so I could answer
the hammering at my back door. But Peristalsis won't wait.
I had to settle for this slip of my wife's, and scuff
her Persian mules on over my toes.

He looks around.
Oh, hell.
Damn built-up area. Where's a suitable spot
to shit?
But it's still dark out. Who's to see?
Any old spot'll suit me.

He squats, center stage. The door to House I
opens, and old Blepyros appears, in the same
agony and a different costume. He wears a saffron-
colored shrug over his shoulders, and wobbles
precariously along in Praxagora's wedgies.

BLEPYROS
Goddamitt, OWWW!
I ought to be taken out and flayed alive
for getting married at my age. Don't know what
my wife sneaked out to do, but it's nothing healthy.
Still, on we go. My bowels can't wait on her.

As yet unnoticed by Pheidolos, he stumbles to center
stage and squats, facing the other way. They
remain there, back to back, for a moment,
then Pheidolos turns.

PHEIDOLOS
Who's this? My next-door neighbor Blepyros?

BLEPYROS
God, yes.
The very same.

PHEIDOLOS
What's all that yellow on your shoulders?
Don't tell me Kinesias missed the head again?*

BLEPYROS
How's that? Oh, no. This thing's my wife's. Her shrug.
I had to put something on to come out. She usually
wears it.

27

PHEIDOLOS

   Where's your cloak?

BLEPYROS

         I couldn't say.
I looked all through the covers for it. No luck.

PHEIDOLOS

You didn't ask your wife where it was?

BLEPYROS

           I didn't;
no wife in there to ask. She must have bored
her way out while I was asleep. It doesn't augur
well for the future. She's up to something. Something
radical.

PHEIDOLOS

   Dammit, that's just what happened to me.
My better half took the cloak right off me and left.
Not that I minded that, but she lifted my clogs
as well. At least, I couldn't find them. I'm shoeless.

BLEPYROS

Well, what do you know? So'm I. My go-to-meeting shoes
are gone; the ones I always wear to Congress.
But I had to go, so I wormed her wedgies on
and wobbled out here. It was either that or let it
fly in the nice clean sheets.

PHEIDOLOS

        But what could it be?
Did one of her girlfriends ask her over to breakfast?

BLEPYROS

I'm sure that's it. No hanky-panky from her.
My wife's no whore.
      As far as I know.

PHEIDOLOS

*Rising and gazing down at Blepyros, who
remains squatting.*

          You must
be squeezing out a hawser, instead of shit.
It's time for me to get to Congress. Provided
I locate that cloak. My only one.

BLEPYROS

                       I'm going
to Congress, too, if I ever finish here.
I ate an unripe plum, and it's jammed the passage.
My food's cut off.

PHEIDOLOS

              And pressing your rear. A late
dispatch from the front.*

BLEPYROS

                 You said it; a steady build-up,
restricting freedom of movement.

Pheidolos exits into House II.

                 So what do I do?
Is there no way out? The stoppage is only starting;
what's next? Presuming I keep on eating, where
do I fit the shit? Some green plumber's plugged
my fixtures, and no relief in sight.

To the audience.

                     —Pardon.
Can some one fetch a physician?

                   (But what physician?
It's rather a narrow specialty.)

                Is there a practicing
homosexual here who's free at the moment? Maybe
Amynon?

           (But he won't come. It's not his end
of the business.)

            Antisthenes! That's who I want. A man
who grunts like that can feel what constipation means;
he's always making an ass of himself.

Pause for a reply which does not come.

                  No luck?

Still squatting, he raises his arms toward heaven.

      —Goddess of childbirth, grant my labor some issue
quickly, before I split. Oh, render me corkless
before they stick me under the bed as a comic
prop. My mother didn't raise her boy
to be emptied by hand.

A minor explosion, coinciding with the entrance,
left, of Chremes, who starts to cross to House III,
but stops when he sees Blepyros.

CHREMES

            Can you be taking a crap?

BLEPYROS

Straightening up hurriedly.

Who, me? No more, thank god. Relief at last.

CHREMES

Enchanting costume for it. Your wife's?

BLEPYROS

It was dark
inside the house. I had to take what I got.
And now give me a straight answer: Where've you been?

CHREMES

To Congress.

BLEPYROS

Adjourned already?

CHREMES

Right on the dot
of dawn.

BLEPYROS

That's early.

CHREMES

It is. And oh, the ridiculous
mess they made in rounding up a quorum.

BLEPYROS

You got your pay—three obols?

CHREMES

I wish I had.
This time I came too late. I'm so embarrassed.

BLEPYROS

Ashamed to be late?

CHREMES

Financially embarrassed. I'm broke.

BLEPYROS

But why were you late?

CHREMES

I couldn't get in. The place
was jammed—the biggest crowd since they opened the Pnyx.
A curious bunch. The consensus was, they were cobblers.

BLEPYROS

Cobblers?

CHREMES

They all had that pasty complexion that comes
from indoor labor. Congress appeared to be packed
with anemia victims. Which made me a gratis voter,
me and lots of others.

BLEPYROS

No chance for me
to get paid if I get there now?

CHREMES

No chance for you
if you got there *then*—unless you beat the second
crow of the cock.

BLEPYROS
Mock-tragic, taking off Achilles' reaction at
Patroklos' death in Aischylos' tragedy The Myrmidons.
What bitter blow is this?
Raise not the dirge for dead, departed money;
'Tis I who now must drag out a cashless existence;
O sweet Antilochos, raise the ante for me!
—But what made such a mob assemble so early?

CHREMES
The Executive Board decided to put the question
of Public Safety to a popular vote. Straight off
Neokleides, the local glaucoma king, was trying
to sneak up to speak up first. This raised a general
shout, as you might imagine:
"What a revolting
sight—a man who can't keep his lashes apart
is trying to prescribe a method to hold the State
together." He bleared through the film, and squinted around,
then raised a shout of his own:
"Inform me, friends,
what *is* the remedy?"

BLEPYROS
"A clove of garlic pounded
in an ounce of vinegar; mix in the juice of one Spartan
milkweed; apply the mess to your eyelids at night"—
that's what I'd have told him. If I'd been there.

CHREMES
Euaion was next—a masterful, versatile speaker,
known for his unadorned manner. Came on completely
nude. Or so it appeared; he claimed he was wearing

a cloak. His address was loaded to the lip with appeal:
"Friends," said he, "my obvious lack of savings—
a mere five hundred obols would set me right—
should not disqualify me from showing you
the way toward saving the city and people of Athens.
When winter comes, collect the needy—all those
who get caught short when the nights get long—and take them
to the cleaners.
    And make the cleaners give each one
a woolen cloak off the racks. That way, we'll be saved
from pneumonia. Then, those without beds and covers—save them
a place to sleep after dinner, in the tanners' shops.
And if any tanner locks his door in the winter,
the state will have his hide . . . three hides, in fact,
with the hair left on."

BLEPYROS
     An excellent blanket proposal.
No man would have raised a hand against him, if only
he'd added this: "The Wheat Exchange* will donate dinner—
a peck per pauper per day—or else be soundly
thrashed." One way to make a present profit
from dealers in futures.

CHREMES
     A handsome fellow spoke next,
quite young. And pale—he looked like Nikias does.

BLEPYROS
But *he's* been dead for years.*

CHREMES
       I said the boy
was pale. He jumped up front and began to harangue us.
Insisted our only salvation was placing the state
in the hands of the women. That mob of cobblers applauded
and screamed, Hear, Hear.
    It didn't sit well with the farm bloc,
though. They set up a rumble.

BLEPYROS
     Thus showing brains.

CHREMES
But lacking volume; the young man drowned them out.
He recited a lengthy list of female virtues,
and balanced each one with a vice. To be precise,
a vice of yours.

BLEPYROS
So what did he say?

CHREMES
Well, first
he called you a shyster . . .

BLEPYROS
Not you?

CHREMES
Please don't interrupt.
And then a gangster . . .

BLEPYROS
Just me?

CHREMES
As Zeus is my judge.
And further, a fink.

BLEPYROS
Just me?

CHREMES
As Zeus is my judge . . .

Pointing to the audience.
just you and that mob out there.

BLEPYROS
So what else is new?

CHREMES
But woman, he claimed, is a far superior being,
glutted with judgment, productive of profit in plenty . . .
and buttoned on the lip. The yearly female festivals
preserve unbreached security, but when you and I
serve in the Senate, it's raining classified matter
all over town.

BLEPYROS
By Hermes, God of Liars,
that's true.

CHREMES
Then women, he said, are always lending
each other something—dresses, accessories, cash,
or cups; completely private loans, with never
a witness around—and every item's returned,
no hint of fraud. While most men tend, he claimed,
to filch from their friends.

34

BLEPYROS

                By Poseidon, God of Welshers,
in front of ever so many witnesses, yet.

CHREMES

According to him, the women don't lodge complaints,
or prosecute suits, or plot to destroy democracy;
instead, they bring boundless boons, and bounties, and whatever's
good. He went on for a while, but that was his gist.

BLEPYROS

And how did we vote?

CHREMES

             To entrust the city to women.
By general agreement, that was the only scheme
that Athens had missed.

BLEPYROS

             And that's the vote?

CHREMES

                      The law.

BLEPYROS

The women are now the executive branch?

CHREMES

                    Correct.

BLEPYROS

And all our civic duties. . . ?

CHREMES

                . . . are women's work.

BLEPYROS

So court is not my job any more—it's my wife's?

CHREMES

Support is not your job any more—it's your wife's.

BLEPYROS

No more groaning myself awake at sunup?

CHREMES

No more. From this day forward, leave that to the girls.
Roll over in bed and exchange your groans for blissful
farts.

BLEPYROS

    This could turn nasty. We're not as young
as we were, and with women in the driver's seat . . . Suppose
they put the pressure on and coerce us . . .

35

CHREMES

Into what?

BLEPYROS

Coerce us into coition.

CHREMES

Screw *them.*

BLEPYROS

That's just

what I mean.

CHREMES

But what if we can't?

BLEPYROS

I suppose they'll cut off

our food. We'll die.

CHREMES

Then screw away for dear life.

BLEPYROS

Coition upon coercion. Degrading prospect.

CHREMES

Be firm. A man should be able to stand up under
any disaster for his country's good: An ancient
tradition declares that every idiot blunder
we pass into law will sooner or later redound
to Athens' profit.
                    —O Queen Athene, O
—in fact—all other Members of the Pantheon, *please*
do let this rock redound in the proper fashion.
—I'm leaving. Goodbye, Blepyros.

BLEPYROS

Chremes, goodbye.

Chremes exits into House III, Blepyros into House I.
A pause, and the Chorus enters left. They
are still dressed as men.

FIRST KORYPHAIA

For-WARD, MARCH!

Did anyone notice a Man behind us?

SECOND KORYPHAIA

Rear-WARD, SEARCH! Secure yourselves; these narrow places
are the favorite haunts of the base, unprincipled, sharpeyed male.
So, guard your rear. If enemy eyes should pierce our disguises,
all I can say is that ours would be a sorry tale.

FIRST SEMICHORUS

Singing as they step forward firmly.

March in a masculine manner,
stride with a virile thud.
If a wiggle or sashay
gives our secret away,
we'll be lost to honor,
and our name'll be mud.

Singly as, their resolution breaking, they mill around.

—So close your cloaks. —And don't leave gaps.
—We can't afford the littlest lapse
in our vigilance. —Look left. —Look right.
—Both ways at once! —And keep wrapped up tight.
—If our cover slips, our victory
is canceled,—kaputt,—a catastrophe!

FIRST KORYPHAIA

Speaking, as she tries to rearrange them.

All right, but let's get moving. We've nearly come back safe
and dry to the start of our March on Congress—journey's end.
Look, there's the house of our newly elected Commander-in-Chief,
the girl who conceived the scheme that is now the Law of the Land.

SECOND SEMICHORUS

Singing as they step off firmly again.

Press on ahead—don't loiter,
don't lag along in your beard.
If we're recognized this way
in the hard light of day,
our images will shatter
and our pitch'll be queered.

Singly as they mill around in panic.

—I can't go on in this disguise.
I'm changing. —But where? The walls have eyes.
—Well, this wall doesn't. —Where? —Over here.
—Someone keep a lookout. —I'm shedding this gear.
—A man any more I refuse to be.
—Oh, where is the girl I used to be?

*The Chorus members cluster by House III and
shed their disguises; their leaders try to maintain
some order. The Second Koryphaia looks off left.*

SECOND KORYPHAIA

All right, but don't drag it out so. Look, here comes our Commander
back from Congress, and she and her friends are already dressed
like women again. Don't greet her half-changed; it might offend her.
And strip your jaws of those awful beards, and strip them fast.

The Chorus is still completing its transformation
as Praxagora enters left, followed by the First,
Second, and Third Women. They carry
their male paraphernalia.

PRAXAGORA
Well, ladies, luck has been in attendance upon us;
our venture has fully attained its projected goals.
Sliding into paratragedy.
> But speed is needed, lest some man perceive:
> Doff me your weeds, come bid the lowly clog
> Go footless off, let slack the knotted nodules
> Of Spartan harness . . .

THIRD WOMAN
What'd she say?

FIRST WOMAN
Untie

your shoes.

PRAXAGORA
And chuck those canes.
To the First Koryphaia.
Look here, would you
get them fixed up in something like order? I'd like
to slip inside before my husband sees me
and put his cloak back where I got it—to say
nothing of all this other stuff I took.

FIRST KORYPHAIA
With a wave at the Chorus.
We've carried out all your orders already, and now we need your
advice; we long to be briefed: Just what do we do for a sequel?
You command our complete compliance in any suggested
procedure;
for all-round feminine know-how, I never have seen your equal.

PRAXAGORA
Then wait right here. Be back in a minute to make you privy
to all the problems of this great office to which I'm elected.
You stood shoulder to shoulder with me when the going was heavy;
I'll need your masculine prowess to get my programs effected.
Gear in hand, she starts to enter House I, but is
greeted by the emerging Blepyros, who
is still in her clothes.

BLEPYROS
Well, well. Praxagora. Where've you been?

PRAXAGORA

What business
is that of yours, sir?

BLEPYROS

What business of mine? Now, *there's*
aplomb.

PRAXAGORA

Oh, come. You can't be implying that I've
been sleeping around with anyone.

BLEPYROS

Any one, no.
Any two, any five, any twenty, perhaps.

PRAXAGORA

Still no.
My purity's open to proof. Proceed.

BLEPYROS

Well, how?

PRAXAGORA

A simple sniff of my earlobes.

He complies dubiously.

Well?

BLEPYROS

Well, what?

PRAXAGORA

Well, any perfume?

BLEPYROS

Why, no.

PRAXAGORA

You see? I'm pure.

BLEPYROS

A woman can't be banged with deodorized lobes?

PRAXAGORA

This woman can't.

BLEPYROS

All right, then: Why *did* you snaffle
my cloak and sneak out so early?

PRAXAGORA

                                I was sitting up
with a pregnant friend.
                         She sent for me late last night
when her labor started.

BLEPYROS

                    You might have stopped to explain.

PRAXAGORA

Can you delay a delivery? I had to hurry.

BLEPYROS

Without one word? There's something suspicious here.

PRAXAGORA

Oh no, there isn't. I went as I was. The woman
who came was very insistent.

BLEPYROS

                           Did she insist
that you take my cloak? That you strip your husband's body
and flick this filmy thing on him, and leave him there,
laid out like a corpse? All I needed was a wreath
and a bottle of ritual oil.

PRAXAGORA

                       It was cold out, darling.
I wrapped poor little, delicate me in this cloak
to keep warm . . . as warm as you were, cuddled snug
in all those covers. That's the way I left you.

BLEPYROS

And that's the way my slippers left me, too,
and my cane hobbled off. Just what was the object of *that*?

PRAXAGORA

To ward off robbers. I switched our shoes, and clumped
along flatfooted, just like you, and banged
the cane on the pavement, to throw up a curtain of noise.
It saved you your cloak.

BLEPYROS

                    And lost us eight quarts of wheat—
I couldn't go down to Congress to draw my pay.

PRAXAGORA

Don't worry; nothing miscarried.

BLEPYROS

                      At Congress?

PRAXAGORA

                      Er—no;
my friend—a lovely boy.
            Did Congress meet?

BLEPYROS
You knew damned well it was meeting. I told you last night.

PRAXAGORA
Of course you did. I'd forgotten.

BLEPYROS
                You haven't heard
the latest decree?

PRAXAGORA
        Why, no. Not at all. Not me.

BLEPYROS
Then sit right down in clover and take your ease.
By congressional action, the city is now in the hands
of you women.

PRAXAGORA
        And what do we do with it? Darn it?

BLEPYROS
                      Dammit,
no. You govern.

PRAXAGORA
        What do we govern?

BLEPYROS
              You govern
the government. The entire structure of Athenian society.

*Chremes emerges from House III and
listens unnoticed.*

PRAXAGORA
Aphrodite be blessed, but this is a happy day!
What a Great Society* Athens is going to have!

BLEPYROS
Great? Why great?

PRAXAGORA
           Oh, oodles of reasons. First,
it freely extends to every soul in Athens
a deal that's new, a deal that's fair. The future
holds no place for the Operator's sly maneuvers:
No more false witness, no more informing . . .

BLEPYROS

No more
of this, for god's sake; you're taking away my living.

CHREMES

Crossing to Blepyros.

Kindly shut up and allow your wife to continue.

PRAXAGORA

An end to theft, to keeping up with the neighbors;
an end to the poor, ill-clad, ill-housed, ill-fed;
an end to public slander; an end to foreclosures.

CHREMES

I swear that Great Society's going to be
the absolute end. Provided it all comes true.

PRAXAGORA

I'll demonstrate my programs, point by point. By the time
I'm done, you'll back me all the way, and he

Pointing at Blepyros.

won't have a single argument left to rebut with.

CHORUS

Gathering around Praxagora to urge her on.

Now prod and chivvy
your prudent savvy.
Awake your superhuman acumen.
Let mind and heart
take an equal part
in defending the Day of the Common Woman.
Hone your intelligence;
help our citizens
increase their status without dishonor.
Come, institute
the Welfare State
and make Prosperity turn the corner.
It's time to try
some bold *trouvaille*;
a startling stroke is needed, quick.
But don't essay
some stale cliché . . .
the audience hates a worn-out *shtick*.

FIRST KORYPHAIA

So hurry and start up your plan. Remember the spectators'
standards:
Better early than good, and better never than late.

PRAXAGORA

I'm perfectly sure the advice I have to impart is good, but
the audience makes me anxious; how broad are their minds? how
    modern?
Will they approve of progress, or insist on remaining mired
in extinct tradition?

CHREMES
With a wave which includes the audience.

Don't worry about us, ma'am. We're compulsive
progressives. There's only one tradition left in Athens:
The past is passé; suppress it.

PRAXAGORA
Stepping forward.

I humbly request your attention.
Do not interrupt the proposal, please, before you have heard it,
and kindly refrain from rebuttal until you have grasped the
    concept.*
—Compulsory Universal Community Property is what I propose
to propose; across-the-board Economic Equality, to fill
those fissures that scar our society's face. No more the division
between Rich and Poor; the gap that partitions the squire who lolls
at ease on his acres from the wretch who's pressed to locate a plot
to rot away his final rest in; the gulf that secludes the nabob,
swimming in slaves, from the needy nudnick who can't afford
a second-hand footman.

Such segregation must go!

Instead,
I'll institute total communalization: We'll wear the same clothes,
and share the same food . . .

BLEPYROS

What sort of food will we share?

PRAXAGORA
Furious at the interruption.

Oh, *shit!*

BLEPYROS
So? You can have my share.

PRAXAGORA

No, no, I didn't mean *that.*
AS I WAS ABOUT TO SAY WHEN I WAS SO RUDELY
    INTERRUPTED:
My initial move will be to communalize land, and money,
and all other property, personal and real. From the Common Fund

43

thus created, we women will then proceed to supply you, employing
our talents for Budgeting, Eking Out, and Thinking Ahead.

BLEPYROS
But take the landless man who's invisibly wealthy . . . because
he hides his silver and gold in his pockets. What about him?

PRAXAGORA
He'll deposit it all in the Fund.

BLEPYROS
                              Suppose he keeps it?

PRAXAGORA
                                        Well, then
he'll be guilty of perjury.

BLEPYROS
                    He's guilty already. That's how he got it.

PRAXAGORA
But keeping it simply won't do him any good.

BLEPYROS
                              It won't?

PRAXAGORA
Economic motives, the pressures of want, will cease to exist
when everyone owns everything from bread to cake, from wine
to woolies, from filets to fillets. So where is the profit in *not*
depositing?
          Well?
                    If you find an answer, please expound.

BLEPYROS
Well, these men with money . . . they're all thieves.

PRAXAGORA
                              They *were* . . .
during the obsolete system of the *ancien regime*. But now,
when all the needs and means of existence are common and open
to all, I repeat: Where is the possible profit in *not*
depositing?

BLEPYROS
          Suppose he sees a pretty young piece and decides
to plunge a little. He'll need to dip into private capital
to entice the girl into bed before he puts in for a share
in her assets.

PRAXAGORA

                Pointless. Your man will be able to sleep with her free.
I'm pooling the women, creating a public hoard for the use
of every man who wishes to take them to bed and make babies.

BLEPYROS

You'll start a war. The men will all be shoving to stick
the best-stacked girl in stock.

PRAXAGORA

                      They'll be arranged in rows,
the ugly and snub-nosed right beside the really divine.
The man who wants the latter will have to take a crack
at the gruesome first.

BLEPYROS

                That's quite a layout. But have a heart
for us senior citizens. If we have to dicker with the real dogs first,
we won't have any cock left by the time we've screwed our way
to the raving beauties at the end of the queue.

PRAXAGORA

                            They won't complain.
Don't worry yourself about it. Cheer up. They won't complain.

BLEPYROS

About what?

PRAXAGORA

            About not getting laid.

BLEPYROS

                        That's just what happens with
you.*
—From the women's angle, this seems a remarkable stop-gap
    measure.
There won't be an unplugged loophole left in town. But you haven't
gone to the root of the matter; the men may be left hanging.
The women'll shy away from the ugly ones, and spread
themselves on the handsome.

PRAXAGORA

                    The total losses will keep an eye
on the hero types as they leave dinner, and patrol them in public.
Then, too, we'll enjoin the women from climbing in bed with the
    swell
and the tall before they've raised the spirits and warmed the
    cockles
of the grisly and squat.

BLEPYROS

You mean the flattest nose in Athens*
can hold its head as high as any Adonis?

PRAXAGORA

The pure democratic
ideal. A perfect comedown to all those finicky, ring-fingered,
stuck-up dandies, when a clodhoppered slob can cut in and say,
"Observe the rules of order: As soon as my rider's enacted,
I'll yield her to you to second the motion."

BLEPYROS

A system like this
requires a pretty wise father to know his own children.

PRAXAGORA

But why does
he need to? Age is the new criterion: Children will henceforth
trace their descent from all men who *might* have begot them.

BLEPYROS

A mighty
strain on an overstrung family tie; it should dispose
of every old man in the city. Remember, parricide pays.
These days, at least, a son only strangles the father he *knows*.
But introduce doubt, and the kids will happily work down the list
and, freed from the finer filial feelings, cover their victims
with shit.

PRAXAGORA

Oh, no. The neighbors simply won't permit it.
The old-style laissez-faire father could afford to stand idly by
while the man next door was sapped by his son; he couldn't care less.
But the new, collective father knows, when he hears a howl
of parental pain, that *he* is involved. If he doesn't stop
the slaughter, the boys might get him next.

BLEPYROS

You do have a point.
But I'd be appalled to hear the greeting "Poppa!" slip
from the lips of some of the young punks here—Epikouros, say,
or Leukólophos.

CHREMES

Looks like a worse disaster could happen.

BLEPYROS

Such as?

CHREMES

If that slimy pervert Aristyllos decided that you were his daddy,
and kissed you full on the mouth.

BLEPYROS

Coming from him, that's rape.
I'd make him yell to high heaven.

CHREMES

It's also halitosis, friend;
he'd make you smell like hell.

PRAXAGORA

No fear of a kiss like that:
Aristyllos was born before the act was passed.

BLEPYROS

Saved.
But that was a mighty near thing.

—Who's going to work the land
and produce the food?

PRAXAGORA

The slaves. This leaves you just one civic
function: When the shades of night draw on, slip sleekly down
to dinner.

BLEPYROS

That doesn't dispose of the question of clothes, the source
of supply for cloaks.

PRAXAGORA

The ones you're wearing should last at first;
and then we'll weave you new ones.

BLEPYROS

But a man who loses a suit
in court—where does he find the funds to discharge the judgment?
It wouldn't be right to tap the public till.

PRAXAGORA

To begin with,
the action at law is a thing of the past. No suits.

CHREMES

To Blepyros.

Now, *that*
is a sentence that spells the end of your existence.*

BLEPYROS

Precisely
what I was thinking.

PRAXAGORA

What reason would there be for lawsuits?

BLEPYROS

A raft of reasons. To take just one, let's say a debtor
refuses to pay.

PRAXAGORA

But where did the creditor get the money
to lend? All funds are public; he's ipso facto a thief.

CHREMES

Now, *there* is a lovely piece of deduction.

BLEPYROS

Well, let her deduce me
this one: A communal dinner leads to a mugging. How, pray,
do the guilty parties pay the fine for drunken assault?
I think I've got you stumped.

PRAXAGORA

We'll garnishee the hoodlum's rations
and stamp out that saucy behavior. The way to a man's deportment
is through his stomach.

BLEPYROS

You mean there won't be an honest-to-
goodness
robber remaining in town?

PRAXAGORA

How can you rob yourself?

BLEPYROS

And no more thugs to steal your clothes when they meet you at
night?

CHREMES

Try sleeping at home; you'll be safe.

PRAXAGORA

No need to change your habits.
Sleep wherever you wish. You'll still be safe. Life's little
necessities will be provided for all. If someone starts
to strip you, give him your clothes as a present; don't kick up a
feckless
fuss. There are better clothes for the taking to all who will toddle
down to the public storehouse.

BLEPYROS

But certainly men will still gamble—
a friendly roll of the cubes?

PRAXAGORA

With nothing to feed the poor kitty?

BLEPYROS

What sort of society do you intend to establish?

PRAXAGORA

Communal.
Share and share alike. I'll knock out walls and remodel
the City into one big happy household, where all can come
and go as they choose.

BLEPYROS

And where will you locate the dining room?

PRAXAGORA

I'm converting all the lawcourts. Justice must be served.

BLEPYROS

Then what becomes of the dock?

PRAXAGORA

I'm stocking the dock with crocks
of wine and flasks of water, and packing the bench with relays
of boys to provide entertainment—hymns to our wartime heroes,
interspersed with lampoons on slackers. Enough to shame the
    cowards
away from the dinner table.

BLEPYROS

By Apollo, that sounds attractive.
But what becomes of the urns we used for choosing the juries?*

PRAXAGORA

I'll set them up in the market, and form the citizens in lines
by Harmodios' statue. Each one in turn will draw from the urn
a letter that shows his assignment.

BLEPYROS

Assignment to court?

PRAXAGORA

No, lunch.
Each eating place will bear a different letter. Therefore,
the man who draws Kappa will eat in the Kourt of Klaims; Epsilon,
Equity; Delta, Divorce.

BLEPYROS

And Beta?

50

PRAXAGORA

Probate.

BLEPYROS

But what

about Pi?

PRAXAGORA

We'll let him eat cake in Appeal.

BLEPYROS

And where does this

leave Eta?

PRAXAGORA

He's already eaten.

BLEPYROS

But the poor unlettered chap
who draws a blank—the rest will drive him away from the table?

PRAXAGORA

I rather think you misunderstand.
The State's not going to stint. Its hand
is full and open, its heart is large,
it'll stuff its menfolk free of charge,
then issue them torches when dinner's done
and send them out to hunt for fun.

FIRST WOMAN*

And fun they'll find, in alleys crowded
with women panting, "How's about it?"
with women rustling at their heels
and spinning their heads with sexy spiels:
"Come change your luck. I happen to know
a hot little nymphet who's ready to go."

SECOND WOMAN

Then another one shouts, from a window above,
"Why not try a higher type of love?
The girl up here is an absolute dream,
stacked like a statue, peaches and cream. . . ."

BLEPYROS

Imitating an old woman.

"There's just one thing; before she's free,
you'll have to try a fall with me."

PRAXAGORA

        But that's for the dandies, the gay young blades.
        Priority rating for pretty maids
        goes to the uglies, the awkward crew . . .
        goes, in short, to men like you.
        So when you see some passionate sprout
        go sprinting past you, set up a shout:

THIRD WOMAN

Imitating an old man.

        "Hey, where's the fire? What makes you run?
        Getting there is all the fun
        you're going to have. Just read the decree:
        Revolting, disgusting types like me
        take pride of place in these affairs. . . ."

BLEPYROS

Caught up in the possibilities.

        "But if you want, you can wait downstairs
        and pass the time while I'm inside
        with a little friction, self-applied."

PRAXAGORA

Well, I trust this satisfies you both.

BLEPYROS & CHREMES

        And how.

PRAXAGORA

I'd better be going downtown. Since they elected
me C-in-C, there's so much to *do*. Provide
for receipt of that incoming cash. Procure a girl
with a nice shrill voice to handle public announcements.
And that's not all. I've got to arrange for the dinner.
Your first communal banquet's tonight.

BLEPYROS

        So soon?

PRAXAGORA

You have my word. And then I propose to stamp out
prostitution. Every whore will be forced to shut up
shop.

BLEPYROS

    A broad proposal. But why?

PRAXAGORA

                It's perfectly

plain.

Indicating the Chorus.

    Consider these ladies here.

BLEPYROS

They're perfectly
plain.

PRAXAGORA

Exactly. If whores are left in business,
these ladies won't get a chance at the handsome boys.
I shall also put an end to depilatory practices
by female slaves, a most underhanded ploy
they employ for snatching lovers away from their mistresses.
Henceforth, they're back at scratch, and will choose their bedmates
to fit their proper bracket. Free love should be
for the free.

BLEPYROS

As Praxagora makes to go.

I think I'll follow along with you
and stick by your side. I can feel those admiring glances,
hear those envious whispers: "There goes our Commander's
husband, the man behind a successful woman."

CHREMES

And I'm supposed to deposit my goods and chattels
downtown. But I'd better take stock of my property first.

Chremes enters House III. Praxagora, Blepyros,
*and the First, Second, and Third Women exit right.**

CHORAL INTERLUDE*

. . . .

Chremes, deep in thought, emerges from House III.
During the succeeding sequence, servants keep
coming from the house at his direction, bearing
kitchen utensils which they arrange before him
rather in the fashion of a festival parade.

CHREMES

I love to parade my wares, and such a solemn
occasion calls for a holy procession. But who's
to lead it?
                    Of course.
                              —Dear sister sifter,* hither;
you're to be Queen. (No one's holier than she is.)
Proceed in powdered purity, impeccable product
of bushels of grain. You will refine the whole
procession with your presence. But who will bear your litter?
—Trashbucket outside!
                              You're looking a little pale;

53

your inside's black, in fact. You might have been dyeing
Lysikrates' beard.
                        —Now for a lady-in-waiting.
Waterclock, hurry out here—you've got the time.
—And then someone to carry the ritual pitcher.
That's a tough one . . .
                        Pitcher, get out here!
                                        Contain
yourself, and you may make quite a splash.
                                        —Strike up
the band!

A chamber pot is brought on.
                        You'll get them moving, the way you do me
in the morning, running the gamut from tinkles to roars.
—A coffer for offerings; a cruet to bear the olive;
two tripods to lend some status.
                                —Who'll carry the banner?
The flagon.
            —And now release the weaker vessels
to bring up the rear.
                    But mind you, ladles first.

He surveys the procession happily. Pheidolos,
fuming, bursts out of House II.

PHEIDOLOS
Turn in what belongs to me! That'll be the day.
I'll have to be pretty badly off, without
a brain in my head to call my own.
                                Dammit,
I'll never do it!
                Or first I'll inspect this business
from top to bottom, and see what I can find out.
I've led a thrifty, hardworking life; I refuse
to wash my hands of all that honest sweat
for no good reason. This whole affair needs plumbing.

Seeing Chremes' procession.
                —What sort of crackpot setup is this? You moving?
Or proposing to hock these crocks?

CHREMES
                                Not at all.

PHEIDOLOS
                                        Then why
the formation? A new line of pots for the auction block?

55

CHREMES
You don't understand. I'm making them over . . .

PHEIDOLOS
                                                            Taking
them in for repairs?

CHREMES
                        No, no. I'm making them over
to the City. I'm taking them down to the market and turning
them in. The law's in force.

PHEIDOLOS
                              You really intend
to turn them in?

CHREMES
              I certainly do.

PHEIDOLOS
                              God save you,
you *are* a sap.

CHREMES
              How so?

PHEIDOLOS
                  How so? It's simple.

CHREMES
You mean I shouldn't obey the Law?

PHEIDOLOS
                              You *do*
need help, boy. Law—what law?

CHREMES
                        The law that's in force.

PHEIDOLOS
The law that's in force. Of all the asinine statements.

CHREMES
Asinine?

PHEIDOLOS
          What else? Of all the lackwitted lumps
on earth, you take the cake.

CHREMES
                        Because I do
what I'm told?

PHEIDOLOS
              To do what you're told—is that the Way
of the Wise Man?

CHREMES
Without a doubt.

PHEIDOLOS
It's the Way of the Chump.

CHREMES
I gather you don't intend to deposit yours?

PHEIDOLOS
Well . . . holding off for a little. Waiting to see
the consensus.

CHREMES
But *everyone's* ready to turn in his goods.
The only conceivable consensus.

PHEIDOLOS
Seeing's believing;
I haven't seen a sign of it yet.

CHREMES
They're saying it
on every street in the City.

PHEIDOLOS
Say it, they would.

CHREMES
They pledge to deliver in person.

PHEIDOLOS
Pledge it, they would.

CHREMES
Your irony's wearing me down.

PHEIDOLOS
Iron it, they would.

CHREMES
May god please damn you to hell.

PHEIDOLOS
Damn it, they would.
Can you believe that any Athenian capable
of connected thought will give his goods to the State?
It's not in our culture pattern: We, by god,
are a nation of Takers.
And so, by god, are the Gods.
That's easily seen from their statues; look at the hands.
We pray for a gift from Heaven . . . but there they stand,
hands out, palms *up*. No, they're not planning to give;
they Take.

CHREMES

Sir, you amaze me. But let me get on
with my work. I have to get this packed. Now where
did I put that strap?

PHEIDOLOS

You're truly taking it in?

CHREMES

I swear I am. Watch closely: First, I tie
these tripods together . . .

PHEIDOLOS

But this is lunacy! Why
so hasty? Delay a little. See what action
others take. And then, at length, in the fullness
of time . . .

CHREMES

Do what?

PHEIDOLOS

Well, stall. Defer. And then
you might try Putting Off.

CHREMES

While waiting for what?

PHEIDOLOS

The earthquake, creep!

CHREMES

What earthquake?

PHEIDOLOS

Earthquakes happen.
Or lightning might strike. A polecat could cross your path:
an omen like that is bound to stop these deposits.

CHREMES

It might be a positive blessing if I couldn't find
room to make my deposit?

PHEIDOLOS

Room for a rebate,
you mean. But don't worry. Wait a day, even two . . .
you'll still have room for deposit.

CHREMES

What do you mean?

PHEIDOLOS

Pointing at the audience.

  I know this crew: The fastest voters in Greece . . .
and equally quick to renege on whatever they vote.

CHREMES

Friend, they'll deliver.

PHEIDOLOS

      Supposing they don't turn it in?

CHREMES

Then we'll turn it in.

PHEIDOLOS

     Supposing they won't let you in?

CHREMES

We'll start a holy war.

PHEIDOLOS

     Supposing they win?

CHREMES

I'll chuck my stuff and run.

PHEIDOLOS

       Supposing they sell it?

CHREMES

Drop dead.

PHEIDOLOS

   Supposing I do drop dead?

CHREMES

        I suppose
I'd be in your debt.

PHEIDOLOS

    You persist in this futile yearning
to turn in your goods?

CHREMES

    I certainly do.

Pointing at the audience.

       Just look
at my neighbors here; they're coming across.

PHEIDOLOS

       Oh, sure.
Take Antisthenes there, the well-known theatrical man—
I can see *him* producing. He'd rather do something
tasteful—like sitting on the pot for a month-long run.

CHREMES

Damn *you*.

PHEIDOLOS

Or Kallimachos there, the well-known director:
How much can he manage?

CHREMES

More than Kallias can—
the well-known bankrupt.

PHEIDOLOS

Whatever Kallias has,
he'll waste it himself. He doesn't need help from the city.

CHREMES

All these gibes at our laws—they're hardly fair.

PHEIDOLOS

So what's to be fair? Should I pretend I'm blind,
and haven't seen the dissolving decrees our Congress
turns out? Recall that triumph of planned economy—
the ceiling on salt?*

CHREMES

Well, salt *was* pretty expensive.

PHEIDOLOS

And where is it now?

CHREMES

Well, salt is right out of sight.

PHEIDOLOS

I suppose you've forgotten the copper coinage we voted
when silver was short?*

CHREMES

It caught me shorter. I can't
remember a baser issue. My mouth was stuffed
with the coppers I got for my grapes, and over I went
to the market to use them to buy some barley. And just
as I was holding out my sack to be filled,
the crier cut loose:
"WE'RE OFF THE COPPER STANDARD.
ONLY SILVER IS LEGAL TENDER, EFFECTIVE
NOW!"
It still brings a lump to my throat.

PHEIDOLOS

But don't
neglect our latest winner, that direct assessment
of two-and-a-half percent that was certain to yield
the City forty talents clear. You know,
Euripides' bill.*
And everyone gilded Euripides'
lily . . . until it developed the bill was the usual
blather, and nobody paid, and the mudslinging started . . .
and our guilty Golden Boy turned out to be Tar-Baby.

CHREMES

But all that happened when *we* were in charge. Now things
have changed. The women have taken control.

PHEIDOLOS

And I'll
take care. They may have taken the throne, but they won't
piss on me just to hear it splash.

CHREMES

Now, what does
that gibberish mean?

To House III.

—Hey, boy, bring out the yoke!
A servant obeys, and Chremes continues his packing.
Shortly, Praxagora's newly appointed Town Crieress,
a girl with a very shrill voice, enters right.

CRIERESS

CITIZENS ALL: If you're male, adult, and Athenian,
a word for YOU from our new Commistress-in-Chief:
The word is FOOD!
And it's FREE!
So beat the crowds
downtown and draw for seats! But wherever you sit,
there's PLENTY FOR ALL:
Tables loaded bowlegged
beneath a Complete Selection of Gourmet Goodies!
Luxurious *Couches* smothered in Pillows to ease
the Discriminating Diner! A corps of Winsome *Waitresses*!*
Ready-Blended *Wines* by the bowlful! And FOOD?
There's lots and it's hot: Those tasty *Filets,* that spicy
barbecued *Rabbit,* those bursting-with-goodness *Cakes,*
those crunchy *Sweetmeats* to fill in the chinks . . . PLUS
Party *Garlands* for ALL! AND ALL TOPPED OFF

with a bubbling *Broth* whipped up by charming cookettes
in their very own pipkins!

(All items are tested
by our taster Smoios, who subjects each dish that comes in
to the rigorous probe of his educated tongue. He keeps
the girls in the kitchen right on their toes, I tell you.)

THIS IS A MENU FOR YOU MEN! And age is no object:
The saddest gaffer shucks off his rags and clogs,
and slips on a spruce wool cloak and sumptuous shoes,
as young in heart as the lad who laughs beside him.
SO HURRY! RUSH! The rolls are now being served;
an open mouth at the door ensures satisfaction!

She exits right. A pause.

PHEIDOLOS
I might as well mosey on over. No point in staying
here. After all, it's the will of the City.

CHREMES
You haven't
turned in your property. Where do you think you're going?

PHEIDOLOS
To dinner.

CHREMES
Oh, no. If those women have any sense,
you'll have to make your deposit first.

PHEIDOLOS
I'll make it.

CHREMES
But when?

PHEIDOLOS
I'm hardly the man to keep my Nation
waiting.

CHREMES
Meaning?

PHEIDOLOS
That others are bound to turn
their stuff in later than I do.

CHREMES
And so you'll mosey
on over to dinner regardless?

PHEIDOLOS
                              I have no choice:
At times like these, the truly patriotic man
obliterates his own desires, and does what he can
to aid the State.

CHREMES
                         Supposing they won't let you in?

PHEIDOLOS
I'll butt my way in.

CHREMES
                         Supposing they beat you up?

PHEIDOLOS
I swear I'll sue.

CHREMES
                         Supposing they laugh in your face?

PHEIDOLOS
I'll take a firm stand.

CHREMES
                    On what?

PHEIDOLOS
                              On the stoop, and grab
the food as they carry it in.

CHREMES
                         Then go if you must,
but let me get there first.
To House III.
                              —Sikon, Parmenon,
come get this moving. That's the lot.
Two servants emerge and gather up the utensils.
Chremes leads them off to the right.

PHEIDOLOS
                              Well, look,
I'll help you carry it . . .

CHREMES
                         Not on your life, you won't.
I'm not going to hand this over to our Commistress
only to have you claim it belongs to you.
Exeunt, right, Chremes, his servants, and his
receptacles—with the exception of the chamber pot,
which lies forgotten before his house.

PHEIDOLOS

Oh lord, I need a genuinely subtle gimmick
to wangle a place with those clowns at the public trough
without giving up what's mine.

Now, what?*

His eye lights on the chamber pot.

Of course!
I see it all.

He grabs up the pot.

But I'd better dash. I'll have to
go in to dinner when they do. No time to waste.

Clutching Chremes' chamber pot, he races off right.

CHORAL INTERLUDE
. . . .

*House II is now the home of a Hag, who appears
on the roof and tries, with no success, to
assume an alluring posture. She may be succinctly
described as the third ugliest woman in the world.*

HAG

Why don't the Men get here? They're way overdue.
And here I am, ready and waiting, with all this beauty
going to waste. My complexion's slathered with pancake,
my figure's trim and firm in my best yellow shrug,
I'm humming a song in my heart . . .

but it's not for real.
It needs a *Man*. And so do I—a Man
to snag as he goes by here.

—O Muses, descend
right into my mouth. Bring along an Ionian song . . .
pretty, and not too loud, but pretty lewd.

*A Sweet Young Thing appears on the roof of
House III. Her prettiness matches the ugliness
of the Hag, whom she addresses.*

SWEET YOUNG THING

Oh, look; Dry Rot's set in. My, aren't we up early?
You thought you'd slip in and poach a little while I
was out; inveigle some poor egg upstairs
with your singing. All right, then, sing—and I'll come on
with a song in rebuttal.

Aside.

—I know this antiphonal bit
is liable to bore the audience stiff, but it's really
pleasant enough. No comedy should be without it.

HAG

*Showing a large leather phallos.**

> Here's a friend, little girl; run off and play
> with yourself.
> —MUSIC!

A fluteplayer appears.

> Vamp an accompaniment, honey;
> blow me a tune that does us both some credit.

She sings to the flute's accompaniment.

> If pleasure's your aim, drop into my bed,
> where satisfaction is guaranteed.
> Don't try it with girls—they're limited;
> a Woman responds to your every need.
> Girls are stiff, and they cool down fast;
> girls run off when other men call.
> But Women smolder, and women last:
> Maturity makes it; ripeness is all.

SWEET YOUNG THING

Singing.

> You can't fight nature; don't criticize
> the girls. True sensuous feminine bliss
> buds on their breasts and blooms in their thighs,
> while you spread powder and paint by the pot
> to putty time's craters, and make you the kiss
> of death. Confess it; Ripeness is rot.

HAG

Singing to the same tune.

> I wish you some very unnatural shocks
> when you lie fallow and itch to be plowed:
> I wish you a suddenly vanishing box,
> a suddenly crumbling bed to match,
> and the clammy touch, all curled and cowed,
> of a snake who never comes up to scratch.

The tune changes.

SWEET YOUNG THING

> What shall I do for pleasures?
> My lover hasn't come.
> I'm left to my own resources,
> and Mother isn't home . . .

*She breaks off the song and looks around indignantly,
as if for someone connected with the
production of the play. She speaks.*

> —I'm certainly not supposed to deliver the rest of this?

An obdurate silence. She shrugs resignedly and
returns to the song.

> So Granny, please, a favor:
> Bring up that great reliever,
> the lonely woman's savior
> and send it right on over
> to maneuver
> with me.

HAG

Holding the leather phallos, she sings
*to the same tune.**

> You've caught the fatal itching
> (your lover hasn't come),
> that decadent Eastern letching
> (your mother isn't home) . . .

Speaking.

> —There pants a girl who's ready to put the L in Lesbos.*

Returning to the song, she clutches the
phallos defensively.

> You can't abduct my lover,
> my clever little shaver . . .

SWEET YOUNG THING

> I'm beautiful as ever,
> and that's what you can never
> take over
> from me.

The music ends.

HAG

> Sing all you want. Keep popping in and out
> like a weasel in rut. You can't attract a man
> before he drops in on *me.*

SWEET YOUNG THING

> To pay his last
> respects?
> Confess it, crowbait, that was a new one.

HAG

> Oh no, it wasn't.

SWEET YOUNG THING

> Why waste new jokes on a worn old
> bag like you?

HAG

> My age won't bother you a bit.

SWEET YOUNG THING

What will? That slobbered rouge? That plaster that's plugging
the cracks?

HAG

          This idle chatter is perfectly pointless.

SWEET YOUNG THING

Your presence is perfectly pointless. Why are you perching
there—what's up?

HAG

             Just humming a song for Epígenês—
he's my young man.

SWEET YOUNG THING

          I thought your only man
was eaten by moths years back.*

HAG

               Just wait. You'll see;
my boy'll be here in a bit.

Looking off right.

            And here he comes now.

SWEET YOUNG THING

For you? Oh, no. Whatever he needs, it's not
a case of plague.

HAG

          I'm just what he lacks.

SWEET YOUNG THING

               Like hemlock.
But let him tell you himself. I'm leaving.

HAG

               Me, too.
You'll see that I know what I'm doing. Better than you.

*They disappear into their houses. Epigenes
enters right, carrying a torch, still garlanded from
the banquet. He is very young, very drunk,
and very ithyphallic. He sings.*

EPIGENES

       I want to make sweet music tonight,
         I want my baby in bed.
       I don't want to hump some rickety lump
         or overage eyesore instead.
       I'm Athenian, male, of age, and free;
       I won't put up with sex by decree.

The shutter in House II's window opens, and
the Hag appears. She sings to the same tune,
unnoticed by Epigenes.

HAG

Your vapid lays are out of date;
    the state is calling the tune.
The will of the people chooses your mate;
    you'll hump by the numbers, and soon.
Laissez-faire sex is a losing cause;
    Democracy's only as good as its laws.

Speaking, aside.

I'll go and spy on every move he makes.
She disappears into the house again,
closing the shutter.

EPIGENES

I come here stinking drunk and stuffed with a standing
desire for a certain living doll. Dear Gods:
please let me get her alone.
The shutter of House III's upper window opens,
and the Sweet Young Thing appears.

SWEET YOUNG THING

                          I've pulled the wig
over that damnable granny's eyes. She's gone;
she really thought I'd stay inside.
Seeing Epigenes, who is fidgeting
uncertainly before her door.

                                 Well, look
at this—the very boy we were talking about.
The music starts again, and she sings her
*half of a rather vapid love duet.**

The one way to love
lies this way, my love,
so come this way to love,
    my dear.
With me, up above
in bed, my love,
you'll love away the night
    right here.

I throb with lust   when I see the twist
    and the curl of your well-groomed hair.
The oddest passion   pervades my person;
    my maidenhood's abraded by its wear

                                   and

                               tear . . .

So give way to love,
and don't wait to love,
relieve the weight of love
up here.

The door to House II opens and the Hag emerges.
She watches unnoticed as Epigenes sings his half
of the duet . . . after he has eagerly tried the
door of House III and found it locked.

EPIGENES

There's no way to love;
it's this way, my love:
the way says nay to love,
my dear.
So open, my love,
the doorway hereof,
or I'll cave in and lie
right here.
Love's made me deranged,   my brain is unhinged,
I'm a certified quivering mass.
I'm rabid to rest   on your luscious bust,
and beat a crazy rhythm on your glor-

ious

ass . . .

So give way to love,
and don't wait to love,
relieve the weight of love
down here.

The Sweet Young Thing disappears from her window.
Epigenes waits, then knocks. No reply. Frustrated,
he tries another song.

No words of mine can ever express
the tense extent of my need.
So here's a prayer in my distress
to which I hope you'll take heed:
Please open the door
and give me a kiss.
You got me this way;
don't leave me like this.

He waits, then knocks again. Still no reply.
He tries another verse.

The Goddess of Love gave you her face;
you're a living beauty spot.
You sing like a Muse, you move like a Grace . . .
Darling, what chance have I got?

> Please open the door
> and give me a kiss.
> You got me this way;
> don't leave me like this.

He waits, then knocks as the Hag crosses quickly
to a point just behind him.

HAG

I hear you knocking. Looking for me?

EPIGENES

Turning violently.

> What gives
> you that idea . . . uh, sir or madam, as the case
> may be?

HAG

> You nearly broke down my door. The latch
> is flapping.

EPIGENES

> It wasn't me, lady, I'd die before
> I'd touch your latch.

HAG

> With that torch, you must be looking
> for somebody—who?

EPIGENES

> I'm, uh, trying to deliver a warrant.*

HAG

Pretty nice subpoena you've got. Perhaps
I can serve it for you?

EPIGENES

> I'll handle this myself.

HAG

I know the neighborhood. Lad like you needs help
in these parts.

EPIGENES

> I'd really prefer to pull this off
> alone.

HAG

> Oh, no. I insist. Forget your pride.
> Besides, you can help me with *my* case.

EPIGENES

> But, lady, you're not
> on the docket!

HAG
It's been a while.

EPIGENES
We've built up such
a backlog . . .

HAG
I see.

EPIGENES
. . . that we've had to defer all actions
of more than sixty years' standing till there's another
sitting. We're only opening cases where
the matter at hand is under twenty years old.
I suggest you file your affidavit . . .

HAG
Too tender.

EPIGENES
. . . and wait.

HAG
No, honey. That was the old procedure. Under
this new regime, you have to process our cases
first.

EPIGENES
Oh, no. I can pass my turn. It's like
the rules in craps.

HAG
Did you pass your turn at dinner?
Just can that crap and let's get rolling.

EPIGENES
I'm afraid
I don't understand.
Turning back to the door of House III.
Now, if you'll excuse me, I've got
some pressing business behind this door. I'll knock.

HAG
Grabbing him away and spinning him around.
Enter by the main door only. So bang away
on this.

EPIGENES
But that's a triumphal archway. How
would I know if I'd knocked or not?

72

HAG

'Fess up; you love me.
You're just surprised they let me out.

EPIGENES

I am.

HAG

It's madness. My reputation's ruined. But I don't care.
So pucker up.

EPIGENES

I'm paralyzed; my pucker's stuck.
And what about your lover?

HAG

Lover?

EPIGENES

The eminent artist.

HAG

What artist?

EPIGENES

The still-life man.* The one who lays out
those tasteful arrangements of corpses. Once he catches
you out, you're dead.

Shooing her away.

So quick, now. Back inside.

HAG

Balking.

I know what you're up to.

EPIGENES

And I sure as hell
know what you're up to. And the answer, lady, is no.

HAG

And I sure as heaven got you in the draw. I refuse
to let you go.

EPIGENES

You're out of your head, you relic!

HAG

Poor fevered lad. I'm putting you to bed.
My bed.

EPIGENES

As she drags him toward House II.

           A tip for the handyman: Why waste money
on bucket hooks? Just take a little old lady
(every home has one), let her down in the well
by her ankles, and presto, up comes the bucket, gripped
in a vice.

HAG

           Flattery gets you nowhere, sweetie.
This way. Follow me.

EPIGENES

                Impossible. You haven't paid
the tax.

HAG

     What tax?

EPIGENES

            The use tax.* On this transaction,
one-fifth of one percent of my total value,
or else I don't come across.

HAG

                 There's no withholding,
even on a joint return. You'll do your duty
free. A boy your age goes right to my head.

EPIGENES

And a hag your age goes right to my stomach. You'll never
get my consent.

HAG

Producing a scroll.

           Here's something to make you say yes.

EPIGENES

What's that?

HAG

          A Law, the long and short of which is
that you come along to my place pretty shortly.

EPIGENES

No digests; read me the details.

HAG

                Delighted to do so:

Unrolling the scroll, she reads.

   Be it decreed, by the Women sitting in Congress:
   As Sex is a National Resource, all private parts
   are hereby declared to be public. Free fornication

between adolescents may take place only after
the male adolescent has first applied his resources
to the full satisfaction of a bonafide senile female.
But should said male refuse to fulfill these conditions
and yet persist in attempting to mate with an agemate,
said senile female may then, without let or hindrance,
proceed to take the part of said male—
and pull
as hard as she can until he agrees to give in.

EPIGENES
Talk about stretching the law. That's hitting below
the belt.*

HAG
Still, better obey it. In part and in whole.

EPIGENES
Can't one of my friends or neighbors go bail for me?
My credit's good.

HAG
Credit's abolished. No man
is good for more than he can raise on the spot.*

EPIGENES
I'll claim an exemption. I'll swear I'm unfit.

HAG
You can't
wriggle out of this one.

EPIGENES
I'll plead the pressures of commerce:
This might disturb my business.

HAG
I couldn't care less
if your business drops off completely. You're caught.

EPIGENES
Then what
do I do?

HAG
You come along with me. This way.

EPIGENES
Is there no way out?

HAG
The way out and the way in
are one and the same.*

EPIGENES

Then make your bed ready first:
Strew it with plumes and broken blossoms, drape it
with crepe, bind up your head with fillets, place
the oil before the couch, and set the lustral
jug at the door.
And call the mourners.

HAG

You wait.
There's life in the old girl yet. You'll buy me a wreath
when I'm done with you.

EPIGENES

Don't doubt it. One made of wax—
black wax.* You're liable to fall apart before
you make it inside.

*As they near House II, the Sweet Young Thing
appears at the door of House III.*

SWEET YOUNG THING

Where are you dragging that man?

HAG

I'm taking him home.

SWEET YOUNG THING

Crossing to them.

You sleep with that slip of a lad?
I've heard of mother-love, but this is insane.
You can't be serious. He'd get lost. This law
will give our country an Oedipus complex.* Incest
is now the national family sport.

*She pries the Hag loose from Epigenes
and pushes her away.*

HAG

Just jealous,
that's you, you all-purpose slut. You won't get away
with this.

*Shaking her fist, she exits into House II.
Epigenes turns to the Sweet Young Thing.*

EPIGENES

O god, I'm saved, pulled back from the pit
in the nick of time. My darling, I swell with gratitude;
how can I ever repay you? Tonight I'll go down
on my knees before you and try to discharge my debt.

They start for House III. The door to House II
opens and discloses a Crone—the second ugliest
woman in the world. She scuttles across, grabs
Epigenes, and addresses the Sweet Young Thing.

CRONE
Hey, girlie, where do you think you're taking this?
Trying for a little bedtime tort, you tart?
Stick to the letter of the law: I get first dibs.

EPIGENES
I'm sunk again.
              And where did they dig you up,
you vision of decay?
                —The first was gruesome enough,
but this is catastrophe.

CRONE
              This way, pretty boy. March!
She drags him off toward House II, foiling
efforts by the Sweet Young Thing to save him.
Sadly, the Sweet Young Thing exits into House III.
Epigenes stretches yearningly after her as
the door closes.

EPIGENES
Darling! Don't desert me. Please don't allow
this scarecrow to take me in tow.

CRONE
                It's not me, honey.
You've been hooked by the long long arm of the Law.

EPIGENES
By the long long arm of the Goddess of Acne, all ready
to erupt.

CRONE
        Now be a good boy and come along nice.
No time for talking.

EPIGENES
              Well, first please let me sneak off
to the outhouse and try to recoup my courage, or else
you'll see a yellow streak spread right up my back.

CRONE
Buck up, ducky, and march. I've got a pot
up there. It's perfectly adequate.

EPIGENES

Not for a man
who's scared as shitless as I'll be.

Can't two neighbors
bail me out of this mess? They'll put down a hefty
deposit.

CRONE

You'll make your own deposit. Inside.

The door to House III opens, disclosing, not
the Sweet Young Thing, but a Harridan—
without doubt, the ugliest woman in the world.
She crosses and grabs Epigenes from behind.
He does not turn.

HARRIDAN

And where do you think you're jaunting off to with her?

EPIGENES

Believe me, this is no jaunt. It's more of a drag.

The Harridan pulls him loose from the Crone's
grasp. He still does not turn.

No matter. A million thanks to you, whoever
you are. You've saved me from a fate that's literally
worse than . . .

He turns.

Holy Herakles!

Pan the Paranoid!

Minions of madness!

Kastor!

Pollux!

Help!

Looking from the Crone to the Harridan.

If that one's catastrophe, this is the end of the world.

To the audience.

—Gentlemen, please, a suggestion:

What IS this thing?
A freshly painted baboon just back from a nose job?
An excavated ancestor, up from twenty years
in the cold cold ground?

Or what the hell?

HARRIDAN

Pulling him toward House III.

Flattery gets you nowhere, sweetie. This way.

CRONE

Pulling him toward House II.

You mean *this* way.

HARRIDAN

Don't worry, darling. I'll never

let you go.

CRONE

And neither, lovey, will I.

EPIGENES

Well, somebody better; this is vivisection. Go back
to hell, the both of you!

CRONE

As per the law,

you're coming along with me.

HARRIDAN

Not if a more

revolting old bag turns up.

And here I am!

EPIGENES

Please stop this tugging. If you two ruin me first,
what sort of shape will I be in to see my girl?

HARRIDAN

Well, that's your worry. Right now, you stick to business.

They pull harder.

EPIGENES

I'll stick, I'll stick.

In order to win my freedom

I take on one of you. Which one?

HARRIDAN

No problem.

This way. March!

EPIGENES

Indicating the Crone.

As soon as *she* lets go.

CRONE

You come along with me.

EPIGENES

Indicating the Harridan.

If *she* lets go.

HARRIDAN

I'll never let you go.

CRONE

And neither will I.

EPIGENES

Please, ladies, never go into the ferryboat business.

CRONE

Why not?

EPIGENES

       You'll set your clients ashore on both banks
at once.

HARRIDAN

       Shut up. By the left flank . . .

CRONE

                             Nope. By the right flank.

*The tug-of-war continues, but the advantage is to
the Harridan, and the group is moving
left, toward House III.*

EPIGENES

But this is double jeopardy. I'm standing the same charge
twice. That's half of me for each. Now, how
do I scull two leaky shells with a single oar?

HARRIDAN

A nice aphrodisiac diet does it, dearie:
a bag of truffles, a peck of onions, then back
to the sack.

EPIGENES

       I'm just about at the end of my rope.
One step more to the door.

*The struggling party reaches House III, and
the Crone suddenly relaxes her grip.
She addresses the Harridan.*

CRONE

                 Don't think this means
you win; I'm dropping up to share the wealth.
Three can play at this game.

EPIGENES

                 They've raised the ante
by another granny. And *one* is too much for me.

HARRIDAN

Sonny, whoever told you you had a choice?

EPIGENES

Despairingly, to the audience.

       I'd like to complain to Fate:
                 This is rather too much.
A night and a day of solid humping away

Indicating Harridan.

   on this female compost-heap entitles me

Indicating Crone.

   to proceed to the bumpy embrace of this study in toadskin
   and kiss the worst malocclusion in Greece.

              Unlucky
   isn't the word; I am Cataclysmatically Doomed.
   O Zeus the Savior, do what you can for a seaman
   who's due to cast off soon with a monster cast.
   And if worst comes to worst (and I've got both),
   and my frail frigate sags beneath the weight
   of a couple of slags like these and goes down with all hands,
   then lay my battered body to rest at the inlet's
   outlet, and mark the spot with a monument. Not
   the usual funerary urn, however, nor
   the sailor's solitary oar. Instead, a whore:

Indicating Harridan.

   Take this old bitch, preserve her in pitch, and sink
   her feet in lead right up to the ankles; then set
   her over the grave of one who strove in the breach
   but went down manfully, lost while crossing the gulf.

The Harridan and the Crone
drag him into House III.

   CHORAL INTERLUDE*
    . . . .

The Crieress* staggers on, very drunk. She
has trouble keeping to the point.

   CRIERESS
   O happy people.
       O gladsome native land.
   O blissfullest mistress mine.
         O all you elated
   ladies clustered on your stoops.
          O merry men.
   O radiant neighbors.
        O titillated townsfolk.
            Not
   to mention, O Me. I may be merely a menial,
   but god, do I smell nice. My head is drenched
   in the most expensive scents. But perfume pales
   before the scent of wine. Especially wine
   from Thasos. Comes in little bitty jugs,
   and goes to your head. The smell that tells. The spoor
   that endures. When other odors have flown. (Oh, god.)

So ask for the best. And mix it straight. And breathe
the night away in the blissful bouquet of bottled
beatitude!
>—Oops. Where was I?

To the Chorus.

>—Ladies, where
can I find my mister?
>I mean, of course, my mastress's
husband.

FIRST KORYPHAIA
>Wait here. I think he'll come to you.

CRIERESS
Excellent.

Blepyros enters from House I with a
dancing girl on each arm.

>And here he comes. He's on his way
to dinner.
>—O happy master, topmost tot
of destiny.

BLEPYROS
>Me?

CRIERESS
>Indubitably, you. Who else?
Consider the staggering odds: This city contains
upwards of thirty thousand souls. Above
this mob you stand alone, both fingered by fate
and plucked by luck, the only man who's managed
to miss his dinner.

SECOND KORYPHAIA
>Concisely and clearly put;
they don't make luck like his any more.

Sloughing the dancing girls, Blepyros
starts to the right.

CRIERESS
>Hold on
for a moment. Where are you off to?

BLEPYROS
>Where else? To dinner.

Stopping.

CRIERESS
And, thanks to Aphrodite, you'll be the last in line.
But those were your wife's instructions: To bring you along . . .

Indicating the dancing girls.

Not to forget, of course, this brace of nymphets.
Don't worry; there's plenty left. An excellent vintage
from Chios. Goodies galore.

To the Chorus.

And don't you delay.

To the audience.

And any of you who happen to like our play,
—and any judges who don't let their judgment stray—,
come on along. Provender in plenty. We're loaded.

BLEPYROS
Don't set conditions. Extend admission to everyone
here; no omissions. Inform them it's Liberty Hall
for all, for grandfathers, teenagers, little kids.
A feast awaits them, each and every one,
assembled at startling expense . . .

their own. It's time
to go home for supper.

And as for myself, I'll dash
for dinner.

Grabbing the Crieress's torch.

Taking this torch along, of course.
It's just the thing for after.

CRIERESS

Why fritter away
your time on torch songs? We want dinner music.
You make your exit* and conduct these girls to the table;
I'll start the meal off right with a musical potpourri.

*As Blepyros, bringing the dancing girls, moves to head
the Chorus in its final dance and procession,
the First Koryphaia addresses the audience.*

FIRST KORYPHAIA
I'd like to offer the judges of the comic competition a teeny
admonition, purely in the interests of aesthetic justice.

Gentlemen:
To the Thoughtful Judges—
remember our *Message* and give us the prize.
To the Risible Judges—
remember our *Mirth* and give us the prize.
That covers the panel. In summary, then—

give us the prize.
Also: The draw assigned our play the first production.

Don't let the four plays due to follow us* make you forget us,
but recall your oath of office and assess each chorus fairly.
Avoid the habits employed by the lesser daughters of joy
who only remember the pleasure afforded by the last man in.

CRIERESS
Uh—hey!
The milling Chorus takes no notice of her. She shouts.
AHOY!
They stop dead and turn toward her.
Ahem.
The Time has Come. So ladies, dear ladies—we know what we want;
let's do it correctly. We shall arise and go, and go
to dinner free, and go like bats out of
Crete.*
To Blepyros, as a wild, rapid music begins to sound.
—You, too.

Get those feet moving.

BLEPYROS
Just what I'm doing.

CRIERESS
Then try to convince
those empty bellies in the Chorus that they should keep up with the
dance.
It's time to taste the acme of goodness
that goes by the name of One-Dish Madness!*
*As she rapidly recites the following gibberish to a
strongly accented beat from the music, Blepyros,
his dancing girls, and the Chorus dance
madly and hungrily.*
Its hors-d'oeuvre-dotted-delicious with heart-of-the-briny oysters
and sea-tangy fishlets oh-so-zestfully nestled in clusters
on spry-as-the-morning, utterly udder-fresh goat-good cheese,
caressing a lip-smacking, tooth-tensing medley of goodies like these:
alabaster-bosomed pigeon with bee-sweet-honey-drenched thrush,
do-it-again-love dove and the brown-basted, burst-breasted gush
of thick-thighed chicken, the let-us-be-truly-thankful amen
of gobbet-good bloblets of squab, hard by the hit-me-again
of ever-so-finely-filleted, palate-proud mullet, new-speared,
with gusto-lusty sweetmeats, crunch-yummily kitcheneered
to rush the most reluctant tooth to the gnash . . .
In short, it's Heavenly
Hash.

Pointing to someone in the audience.*

You heard the menu?
I won't detain you;
the play is almost through.
Go get a bowl . . .
then fill it with gruel;
there's nothing here for you.

BLEPYROS

The Chorus is in the throes of famine.

ENTIRE CHORUS

Then upward and onward to supper, women!

As Blepyros leads the entire company off right.

Our play may win, our play may lose;
We'll have to wait and see.
But, win or not, we eat tonight,
And that's a victory,
And that's a victory.

Exeunt omnes, cheering.

Notes

page 9. *three houses:* This is counter to the arrangement favored by most recent scholars, who opt for two houses. My preference for three is
based primarily on my distribution of male parts in the first two-thirds
of the play: Blepyros and Pheidolos emerge from different houses in
the defecation scene; later on, Chremes has his utensils brought *out of
his house* (a point often overlooked) and then confronts Pheidolos
in a scene which will gain nothing but confusion if the audience presumes them to inhabit the same address. Thereafter, Houses II and III
become the working residences of Hag and Crone (II) and Sweet
Young Thing and Harridan (III), while House I remains Blepyros'
home throughout the play, providing him with a place to entertain the
dancing girls. This may appear capricious and prodigal; anyone with
strong objections can certainly reblock this version for two houses.
But the proposal of Miss A. M. Dale, that only one house is required,
involves such strained blocking, particularly in the Epigenes episode,
as to appear dramatically impractical and improbable. Not, of course,
impossible—this play could be done with no set at all or with twenty
houses—but hideously difficult.

9. *an invocation of the sun:* The surprise of the twist from sun to lamp
gains a bit in force when it is remembered that Athenian plays were, of
necessity, produced in broad daylight; but, as often, the precise rel-
evance of the parody to the play as a whole remains a somewhat open
question, not to be answered completely by invoking the comic tension
produced by the contrast between expression and action. Why here,
of all places? A partial answer may be found in Aristophanes' fairly
consistent attempts to unsettle his audience, however slightly, at the
very outset of his plays: *The Knights,* for example, begins with a
scream; *The Acharnians* with a speech delivered by someone who, for
the first twenty lines, appears to be a member of the audience. So here,
the audience may, for some confusing moments, believe that they have
wandered into a tragedy by mistake.

10. *last summer:* The Greek refers specifically to the *Skira,* a festival in
honor of the goddess Athene celebrated by the women on the twelfth
day of the month Skirophorion (roughly, June).

the Congress: The use of this term masks one important difference: The Athenian *ecclêsia* was not a representative body, but the constitutional manifestation of the Athenian people: In theory, all citizens—that is, all male citizens—over the age of twenty were qualified to take part. In practice, a quorum of 6000 was rather difficult to obtain, and payment for attendance, as noted in the Introduction, was instituted early in the fourth century B.C., one of the consequences being this play. The *ecclêsia* held stated meetings forty times during the year at the base of the Pnyx (a hill west of the Acropolis), where it deliberated and passed on legislation proposed to it by the Athenian Senate (*boulê*).

10. *those beery wenches:* According to some rather addled scholia, the name "Phyromachos" is a reference to a certain Kleomachos, possibly an actor, whose habit it was to mix up (*phyrein*) his letters. This individual once, either in a play or when proposing an action in the assembly concerning seating arrangements, pronounced the word *heteras* "others" (= other seats?) as *hetairas* "courtesans." The English approximation here employed was credited to the original Dr. Spooner.

13. *Lamios:* The translation of this desperately obscure joke, identifying Lamios as a drowsy wood-carrier and avoiding any mention of the flatulent ogress Lamia, is based on the text and interpretation given by J. Taillardat in the *Révue de philologie* 38 (1964), 38-42.

13. *a large phallos:* I have introduced this item here to point up the joke, and tie in with its undoubted appearance later. Others may prefer a carding comb.

13. *FIRST WOMAN:* Line assignments in this introductory scene vary widely and are largely arbitrary, depending on what theory is being aired. But at this point Van Leeuwen and earlier editors are clearly correct in following the Aldine edition and giving lines 102-4 to someone other than Praxagora, and my departure from Coulon's text has some precedent.

17. *on your brow:* Speakers in Athenian assemblies were wreathed. So were participants at banquets and drinking parties, a similarity which, in the Greek, prompts the Second Woman's thirst.

18. *Heavens to Betsy:* Literally, "by the Two Goddesses"—i.e., Demeter and Persephone—strictly a woman's oath. The First Woman tries again with a man's oath ("Goddam it all")—literally, "by Apollo."

20. *against the Spartans:* Presumably, the anti-Spartan coalition formed by Athens, Boiotia, Korinth, and Argos in 395, a league shortly thereafter discomfited by Spartan victories in the first year of the Korinthian War —at Nemea in July 394 and at Koroneia in August 394. "The man who'd maneuvered acceptance of the longed-for League" is identified by the scholiast as the Athenian admiral Konon.

page 20. *a fighting navy:* Athens was still recovering from the destruction of its fleet by the Spartans at Aigospotamoi in 405.

21. *and nobody calls:* Reading, with the Aldine edition, *horizetai* in 202. Or, to follow Coulon in adopting Hermann's *orgeizetai,* "Thrasyboulos is violently annoyed that no one calls on him." Whatever the reading, Athens' great (if touchy) hero seems to have been temporarily under a cloud. See Glossary, s. v. "Thrasyboulos."

22. *Demeter's yearly spree:* The Thesmophoria, celebrated by the women of Athens late in October.

22. *During the Terror:* Generally taken as a reference to the rule in Athens of the Thirty Tyrants in 404-403.

26. *from the countryside:* By splitting the chorus in this fashion, and indulging his usual preference for the more conservative countrymen over their urban counterparts, Aristophanes underlines the play's initial motive (the moral decay marked by the payment of congressmen) and comes nearer a conventional appeal to patriotism than at any other point in the play.

27. *PHEIDOLOS:* To William H. Hess's 1963 Princeton dissertation, *Studies in the* Ecclesiazusae *of Aristophanes,* I owe many insights into this play, plus at least one substantial improvement in its text: Hess has proved conclusively, I believe, that the initial speaker in this scene is *not* Blepyros; that lines 311-22 are delivered by another man who has been driven out-of-doors by the same nocturnal motive; that this episode, notorious already, is really a double defecation. I have not followed Hess in his development of the speaker, choosing rather, because of a certain small penuriousness in the character, to identify him with the *pheidôlos*—i.e., the "stingy man"—in the argument over the deposit of property (presumably Chremes' property) which follows Praxagora's presentation of her program.

27. *missed the head again:* While in a lyrical transport, the poet Kinesias seems to have defiled a shrine of Hekate. See *Frogs* 366.

30. *a late dispatch from the front:* In the Greek, Pheidolos replies with a question: "Would that be the plum that Thrasyboulos mentioned to the Spartans?" Concerning this plum, or rather, wild pear, the scholiast remarks: "Thrasyboulos was scheduled to speak against the Spartans who had come to see about a truce, but took a bribe instead. He then alleged that he had eaten wild pears and was too sick to speak." This seems little better than an ad hoc improvisation, though it may be true. I have preferred to develop the military imagery.

33. *the Wheat Exchange:* The Greek refers specifically to one Nausikydes, a profiteer who had made a fortune in wheat during times of war-induced shortage.

33. *dead for years:* An insertion to get some point from a joking allusion, even though a wrong one. Actually, the Nikias referred to here seems to have been pale but still alive, the grandson of the famous Athenian general executed after the Athenian expeditionary force was annihilated in Sicily twenty-two years before.

page 41. *Great Society:* Modern analogues are the blessings and curses of the Aristophanic translator. They often provide a valuable shorthand for him and his audience, broaden and deepen references, focus satire— but they may narrow the result undesirably, import awkward side effects, drastically limit the necessarily brief life of his version. Aristophanes' point of view in this play is certainly reactionary, but to hammer the point home by translating Praxagora into Pedernalese would plug this version as hopelessly into the mid-1960's as a Paphlagonian named McKleon would strand *The Knights* in the mid-1950's. Still, one may be permitted a sidewise glance. . .

43. *until you have grasped the concept:* A number of parallels exist between Praxagora's proposals and the ideal communism—small "c"— propounded in the Fifth Book of Plato's *Republic*: community property, community of women and children, abolition of lawsuits, community feeding. Reinforced by some striking verbal parallels, these have not unnaturally engendered some burning questions, the two most important for our purposes being: (1) What was the relation of the two works? (2) What was Aristophanes' object in treating these ideas? As for question (1), I incline to the hypothesis tendered by J. L. Adam in his edition of the *Republic* (Cambridge 1902; reissued 1963): Utopian thinking was rife in Athenian intellectual circles in the last years of the fifth century and the first years of the fourth; Aristophanes adopted certain of its ideas for his play; Plato, who moved in the same circles and was writing his *Republic* at the time, was sufficiently impressed by the *Ecclesiazusae* to reply obliquely to Aristophanes' satire when, shortly after, he wrote that section of his Fifth Book which discusses the place of women and children in his Ideal State. As for question (2), Aristophanes treats this philosophical communism, not as an enemy to be annihilated, but as source material for comedy. His disapproval is undoubted, but it is not hate; he is content to pick at a few odd points, to run certain peculiarities into the ground, and then move on to the concluding banquet. The objects of his relatively good-natured satire are the Athenians so susceptible to crackpot ideas, not the ideas themselves. *The Congresswomen* is play, not pamphlet.

46. *what happens with you:* The sarcastic little exchange culminating here, implying a less than adequate home life for Praxagora and Blepyros, seems to me the only meaning that can be teased out of two lines of Greek (621-22) which editors have regularly repunctuated, rewritten, and reassigned in an effort to make them yield any sense at all. I follow Coulon's text, but assign the last four words of 622 to Blepyros.

page 47. *the flattest nose in Athens:* See Glossary, s.v. "Lysikrates."

48. *the end of your existence:* As implied earlier by his shocked reaction to his wife's putting an end to legal excesses (lines 561-62), Blepyros makes his living by informing or barratry—possibly both. I believe that his vanishing vocation is the reference here. Accordingly, I have treated lines 657b-58a as byplay between Chremes and Blepyros, inverting the order of Coulon's line assignments.

50. *the urns we used for choosing the juries:* The translation here attempts to counterfeit the humor which must have arisen from the perversion of a phenomenon very familiar to the Athenians and completely alien to moderns. In so doing, it does such violence to the Athenian legal system that I despair of correcting wrong impressions. However, there were ten principal courts in Athens. To facilitate jury assignments, each of these was designated by one of the first ten letters of the Greek alphabet. Each prospective juror drew from the *klêrôtêrion* (here translated as "urn"; really much more sophisticated than that term implies), a bronze check bearing one of those letters, then proceeded to the appropriate tribunal. In adopting this for dinner assignments, Aristophanes has added some acronymic play on locations: A check with a beta on it indicates the Basileion; one with a theta (according to the scholiast), the Theseion. Athenian topography seemed a totally impossible area for communicating humor here; I have therefore had recourse to legal *functions* . . . and have thus graced Athens with a number of separate courts which it never possessed, of which the most disturbing to me is "Delta-Divorce."

51. *FIRST WOMAN:* The distribution of this doggerel among various members of the cast has really no warrant in the Greek, which assigns the whole lot (689-709) to Praxagora. But its quasi-stanzaic structure, as developed in the translation, seemed better served by breaking it up, thus giving some employment to the otherwise mute women who have returned with Praxagora from the Pnyx—and, in Blepyros' interruptions, giving his conversion a bit more expression than the simple assent which follows.

53. *exit right:* Blepyros, when he appears again, enters from House I, and it may well be asked why we do not see him go inside it now or subsequently. The answer is quite simple: I have promoted this awkwardness to point out that it is not really an awkwardness at all. Consistency in those matters extends over very limited areas. Two pertinent points have been established about Blepyros: (1) He wishes to bask in his wife's glory . . . therefore, he leaves for the marketplace with her now; (2) he is fond of tomcatting around . . . therefore, he misses dinner while enjoying himself with the dancing girls later. These are the important considerations, the immediate motivations; others scarcely matter. It is highly unimportant, for example, whether House I remains

his home (as suggested in the first note) or is to be understood, at the play's end, as another house in another part of the city; it is primarily a place where he has been with the girls. Questions on the order of "Does his home have a back door?" belong to another sort of drama.

page 53. *CHORAL INTERLUDE:* As noted in the Introduction, the Greek here reads XOPOY—i.e., *chorou,* "the Chorus's [spot]." It is attractive to think that a complete parabasis, or at least lyrics hailing the Brave New World, might once have existed here, but nothing but naked wishing supports such a theory. A wordless dance seems as much of an *entr'acte* as it is safe to conjecture.

53. *dear sister sifter:* In setting up this well-contained equivalent of a Panathenaic procession, I have kept as close to the Greek as I could while articulating the whole by a series of bad puns. The sifter leads the procession as *arrêphoros* "basket-bearer"—the Maid of Honor who carried the goddess Athene's sacred relics. A pot follows as *diphrophoros* "bench-bearer" to the leader. The lady-in-waiting is unspecified, but Aristophanes employed a water clock in *The Wasps,* and might as well again. Likewise, a pitcher seems a logical pitcher-bearer. The trouble comes with the addition of music—what is to represent the *kitharôidos,* the lyre-player (here transmitted into "the band")? Something which makes a sound in the mornings . . . but the text does not specify. The scholiast points the way toward a handmill; Rogers imported a rooster (rather illogically, given the nature of its companions, though there is one in *The Wasps*); rather deplorably, I opt for the *skôramis,* the chamber pot, already present in the play's fabric through its mention in the defecation scene. Its megaphonic qualities are well known, and, as a way of getting one out of bed, it seems unrivaled.

60. *ceiling on salt:* Evidently, a recent attempt at price control which, the scholiast notes, was passed by the Congress but never put into effect.

60. *when silver was short:* The Spartan occupation of Attika in the later years of the Peloponnesian War shut Athens off from her silver mines at Laurion, forcing a famous if short-lived issue of copper coinage in 406. See *Frogs* 725.

61. *Euripides' bill:* The Euripides mentioned here is not the tragic poet; the date of his attempted direct levy on the citizenry, never executed, is unknown.

61. *Waitresses:* Actually, perfume-girls (*myropôlides*), whose function would be to supply and, possibly, anoint the banqueters with scented oils.

64. *Now, what:* Most editors supply the solution to Pheidolos' problem entirely within the text itself, translating the next two lines (875-76) in some such way as this: "I see precisely what to do [*viz.*]: I have to go along with them to dinner, and not delay." No props are employed; Pheidolos' subtle contrivance, his *mêchanêma,* his gimmick for sharing

food with Chremes and the rest is . . . to go to dinner with them. Given that this is precisely what he is trying to find a way to do, we have the whole scene conclude on the flattest nonjoke in Aristophanes. [Van Leeuwen felt the difficulty and tried to beef up the context by stating that Pheidolos obviously intended to fight his way in. This is (a) not obvious and (b) not much help.] I do not claim truth for what must seem the overuse of my already hypothetical chamber pot, but it does have certain advantages: It supplies Pheidolos with his wished-for gimmick in previously defined terms (a container to carry in the dinner procession); its purpose is clear to the audience; and, in a chamber pot's buying one's way to food, it possesses a certain irony which, however small, is funnier than going to dinner by going to dinner. (I repunctuate the Greek in 875 as follows: half stop or full stop after *orthôs* and a full stop instead of a half stop after *phainetai*.)

page 65. *a large leather phallos:* The precise item indicated by the Hag has been a matter of conjecture for a good many centuries. The dildo seems the best of a number of rather greasy possibilities, if only because its presence is definitely required late in the subsequent exchange of songs . . . where the Greek refers to it (though my English does not) by the proper name "Orthagoras"—i.e., "Mr. Hardon."

66. *to the same tune:* In the Hag's response here, with her echoes of the Sweet Young Thing, I follow the text of 918 ff. as reconstructed by John Jackson (*Marginalia Scaenica,* 109-10). The reassignment of the lines—that is, the shift back to the Sweet Young Thing at 922—is my own.

66. *to put the L in Lesbos:* This rendering, where obscenity is reinforced by obscurity, seems fairly close to the effect of the Greek at 920: "You look to me like a *lambda,* as they say in Lesbos"—or, less likely, "You seem ready to *lambda* in the Lesbian fashion." The scholiast helpfully points out that lambda is the first letter of *leichazein* "lick." Unfairly or not, the island of Lesbos' persistent reputation as a hotbed of female homosexuality arose as a reaction to the life and works of the poetess Sappho.

67. *eaten by moths years back:* To the name Epigenes, "late-born," the Sweet Young Thing counters with *Gerês*—i.e., "Antique." Since the rendering of puns on proper names usually results in Greeks with Anglo-Saxon names, I have tried to work around the problem.—But is the young man's name really Epigenes? When he appears, the mss give *neos* "young (male)"; Coulon follows Brunck and indicates him by *neanias* "young man"; he is never again referred to by name in the text. I have stuck with "Epigenes" to gain a wee bit of particularization; in this play, a named character is worth rubies.

68. *a rather vapid love duet:* This song may be our earliest full example of a noble minor genre, the *paraklausithyron*—the song to be sung by a

frustrated lover before his mistress's closed door—but that is no reason to treat it with reverence. Aristophanes is here parodying pop lyrics, with their reliance on threadbare refrains and their debasement of high-falutin language, and the effect aimed for is bathos. See C. M. Bowra, "A Love-Duet," *American Journal of Philology*, 79 (1958), 376-91.

page 70. *to deliver a warrant:* The original turns on proper-name puns. Epigenes, flustered, pretends a search for a man from the Athenian deme of Anaphlystos (pun on *anaphlan* "masturbate") whose name is not Sebinos (pun on *binein* "screw"). In their stead, I have inserted the warrant-subpoena bit, which should supply the requisite double entendres and at the same time segue logically into the remarks on the crowded court calendar.

73. *The still-life man:* The English here evokes undertaking; the Greek— "the man who paints the *lekythoi* for the dead"—reaches its goal by a different route. These graceful oil bottles, decorated with white-figured paintings, stood at the head of the body while it lay in state and were then buried with it. The painter might have wanted the Hag as prospective user or, more intriguingly, as model for the dead-white figures.

74. *The use tax:* "Sales Tax" might be closer. The reference here seems to be to a fairly recent two-mil impost on all exchanges of property.

75. *hitting below the belt:* In the Greek, Epigenes declares (somewhat illogically, but it's to be expected) that he'll become Prokroustes, or Procrustes—the legendary bandit with the terribly strange bed who stretched or cut his guests to fit it—punning on the sexual sense of *prokrouein* "beat" or "bang."

75. *than he can raise on the spot:* The Greek is more specific and less sexual: "No man's good for more than a bushel now." Under Athenian law, a woman could only make a contract where the value at stake was less than a bushel (*medimnos*) of wheat; the Hag is serving notice, if any were needed, that the tables are turned.

75. *are one and the same:* In the Greek, the Hag informs Epigenes that it is a "Diomedeian necessity" for him to accompany her. This phrase, proverbial for "ineluctable necessity," is of uncertain origin, though it probably refers to Diomedes or Diomede, one of the Greek heroes in the *Iliad*. The scholium here, evidently written by a euhemerist who was trying to explain (1) the proverb, (2) its use in this particular context, and (3) the legend of the man-eating horses of the bandit Diomedes of Thrace (the object of Herakles' Eighth Labor), is clearly wrong, but has its own insane charm: "The Thracian Diomedes' daughters were whores. When strangers came his way, he forced them to make love to his daughters until the girls were satisfied and the men died of exhaustion. The legend called these girls his man-eating horses." With the aim of avoiding this mares' nest, the translation deforms one

of the best-known lines of the philosopher Herakleitos, to whom apologies are due.

page 76. *black wax:* The color is gratuitous misinformation by the translator to reinforce the (possibly incorrect) impression given by the Greek of the existence of such items as waxen funeral wreaths. Conceivably, what is involved is a pun on *kêrinôn* "waxen" and *Kêr* "Death."

76. *an Oedipus complex:* Not nearly the anachronism it might seem. "Carry out that law," goes the Greek, "and you'll fill the country full of Oedipusses."

82. *CHORAL INTERLUDE:* The mss give no indication of it, but some choral action seems probable at this point, and so I follow Bergk and Blaydes in reading XOPOY here.

82. *Crieress:* The character who now appears is feminine and a servant to a woman of some importance. Thus, the mss have named her "Therapaina"—"Maidservant," relating her not at all to any previous character. They are followed by all editors, and I think wrongly. This clearly should be the Crieress, the She-Herald who has appeared before, interrupting the argument between Chremes and Pheidolos to invite the men to dinner. (There, incidentally, since she does not disclose her sex in her announcement, the mss refer to her by the masculine noun *Kêryx* "Herald.") To move even further back, it seems obvious, though unprovable, that the existence of this character, a female Herald who is the servant or functionary of Praxagora, was set up by the Commistress-in-Chief herself, shortly before her final exit, when, at line 713 (p. 50) she noted that she had to procure a Crieress (*kêrykaina*), a "girl with a nice shrill voice to handle public announcements." The difference between the Crieress's mode of speech at her former appearance and now is simply explained: She has been at the banquet and is drunk. Though this may seem a problematical change, it marks the progression of time and gaiety, and provides the play with some sorely needed continuity. It is some comfort in this regard that most scholars persist in considering her Praxagora's servant, and thus identify the tardy husband as Blepyros.

84. *You make your exit:* Those who hold that Aristophanes' theater possessed a platform stage above and distinct from the Chorus' dancing area, the *orchêstra,* may prefer the translation: "You come down [i.e., from stage to orchestra]." But the verb here employed, *katabainein* "descend," is the standard term for "exit"; in leaving the playing area of Athens' Theater of Dionysos, one *descends* by the *parodoi*—its nearest equivalent to wing exits.

85. *the four plays due to follow us:* Early in the fourth century, the number of plays entered in the comic contests at each Athenian dramatic festival was increased from three to five. I have incorporated this intelligence to give the passage here more point, though it may be

inaccurate; records are lacking for 392, the probable year of *The Congresswomen*'s production. The earliest year for which this innovation is noted is 388, when Aristophanes entered his *Ploutos* against Nikochares' *Laconians,* Aristomenes' *Admetos,* Nikophon's *Adonis,* and Alkaios' *Pasiphae.*

page 85. *like bats out of Crete:* In the Greek, instruction is given to dance *krêtikôs* "in the Cretan (or cretic) manner." This is usually interpreted: (1) as a reference to a type of dance, accompanied by music and pantomime, which originated on Crete; or (2) as a rhythmical indication, where the metrical unit specified might not be the usual cretic (— ∪ —), but the so-called "cretic of Aristoxenos," the ditrochee (— ∪ — ∪).

85. *One-Dish Madness:* The dozen lines which follow are an attempt to provide in English something like the effect of the longest word in the Greek language, an original coinage which Aristophanes formed by jamming the names of two dozen items of food into a monstrous compound noun, a melange which reproduces linguistically the hash it describes. Running to seven lines, it looks, in transliteration from Coulon's text, like this:

> *lepadotemachoselachogaleo-*
> *kranioleipsanodrimypotrimmato-*
> *silphiotyromelitokatakechymeno-*
> *kichlepikossyphophattoperistera-*
> *lektryonoptokephaliokinklope-*
> *leiolagôiosiraiobaphêtraga-*
> *lopterygôn.*

Greek's affinity for compounds has been run into the ground, definitively, perhaps in parody of the poet Philoxenos of Leukas, whose gourmet dithyramb, *The Banquet,* abounded in lesser specimens of the art. Unhappily for the translator into English, his language will not agglutinate like Greek or German; a string of English nouns, however connected, remains a string of nouns. I have therefore had recourse to an analogue which is, blessedly, adaptable to food: The building of insane compound premodifiers which so fascinates the advertising industry as it carries out its quickening work.

86. *to someone in the audience:* The Crieress is carrying out Blepyros' instructions and depriving the audience of the huge morsel so lovingly described above. This Indian-giving vis-a-vis the spectators appears to have been a common comic bit, especially toward a play's end (e.g., *Lysistrata* 1043-71, 1189-1215), and should be accorded no especial significance here. Wilamowitz, however, wanted bitterness, and posited Blepyros as the addressee of these verses; the Brave New World thus concludes by cheating the principal male character of his dinner. Eduard Fraenkel went even further in curdling the cream of the jest;

for Blepyros in this scene, he substituted the "dutiful man" (Chremes in this version), whom he chose to describe as the *only* man who had carried out the new directives, and proceeded to cheat *him* of his dinner. Such attempts, however ingenious, are misplaced; they try to pervert an extravaganza into an anticommunist tract by an ill-motivated, unindicated last-minute twist which goes counter to the whole tenor of the text. (As for the use of the singular in an address to the audience, see *Acharnians* 836 ff.)

Glossary

AGYRRHIOS: Athenian demagogue; radical-democrat politician who reached the height of his power and influence in the middle and late 390's, following his introduction of a one-obol wage for assembly attendance and subsequent increase of the rate to three obols. His position as head of the war party did not guarantee him military achievement, however; he succeeded Thrasyboulos as head of the Athenian fleet on the latter's death at Lesbos in 388, but was replaced shortly thereafter. Subsequently, he went to prison for embezzlement. His appearance was evidently effeminate enough to cause comic comment, but Aristophanes may hardly have been unprejudiced: Agyrrhios seems to have been responsible for cutting the pay of comic poets shortly before 405.

AMYNON: A homosexual orator; a pathic.

ANTILOCHOS: Son of Nestor; one of the Greek heroes in the Trojan War, where (Iliad 18.18) he brought Achilles the news of the death of his friend Patroklos.

ANTISTHENES: An extremely wealthy homosexual, very effeminate in appearance.

APHRODITE: Goddess of beauty and sexual love.

APOLLO: God of prophecy, music, healing, and light.

ARIPHRADES: Son of Automenes and a notorious pervert. The creative nature of his perversities (cunnilingual and worse) kept him a standard object of Aristophanic satire for more than thirty years.

ARISTYLLOS: A homosexual of peculiarly disgusting habits. Once identified by the nineteenth-century scholar Bergk, on little better than no evidence at all, as the philosopher Plato. This piece of ingenuity found scarcely any acceptance, and Bergk seems to have thought better of it.

ATHENE: Goddess of wisdom and war; patron of Athens.

CHIOS: Island in the central Aegean, famous for its wine.

CRETE: A large Greek island in the Mediterranean, southeast of the Greek mainland.

DEMETER: The Earth-Mother; goddess of grain, agriculture, and the harvest.

EPIGONOS: A strikingly effeminate Athenian.

EPIKOUROS: A pervert.

EPIKRATES: A hairy politician, whose beard was so bushy that he was called *sakesphoros* "strainer-bearer"; a member of the war party at Athens; once accused of taking bribes while on an embassy to Persia.

EUAION: A most eloquent deadbeat—which is all we can gain from text and scholia. W. H. Hess would identify him with the exceptionally strong brother of Leodamas the Acharnian, mentioned decades later by the orator Demosthenes.

EURIPIDES: (1) Athenian tragedian (480-406 B.C.), whose plays were constantly ridiculed and parodied by Aristophanes. (2) A politician considerably younger than (1)—some conjecture his son—who proposed an unsuccessful levy not too long before 392.

HARMODIOS: Athenian hero who, with Aristogeiton, assassinated the tyrant Hipparchos in 514 and was put to death. Statues to Harmodios and Aristogeiton were erected in the Athenian Agora.

HERAKLES: Hero and demigod, son of Zeus and Alkmene, renowned for his great labors, his prodigious strength, and his gluttonous appetite. The point of his invocation by Epigenes at the sight of the Harridan seems to be partly informational; his twelfth labor took him to the underworld to bring back the three-headed dog Kerberos.

KALLIAS: Son of Hipponikos; a notorious profligate and spendthrift who had run through a fortune.

KALLIMACHOS: An extremely impecunious dramatic poet.

KASTOR: Divinity, son of Leda and Tyndaros, or of Leda and Zeus; twin of Polydeukes (Pollux), with whom he constitutes the Dioskouroi, helpers of men in distress.

KEPHALOS: Son of a potter; a rigidly constitutional democratic politician. A member of the war party, he was instrumental in urging Athens to abandon neutrality in 394 and combine with other Greek states against Sparta.

KINESIAS: A dithyrambic poet with curious ideas of personal hygiene.

KORINTH: A Greek city situated at the narrowest point of the isthmus which bears its name, the neck of land which joins the Peloponneses to the rest of mainland Greece. It was this strategic location which led to constant attacks by invading Spartans in the later 390's and gave the Corinthian War (394-386) its name.

LEUKOLOPHOS: A pervert.

LYSIKRATES: A dark, effeminate, snub-nosed, aging roué who took to dyeing his hair to appear younger.

MYRONIDES: Athenian general of the mid-fifth century. His best-known victory was over the Boiotians at Oinophyta (456). A stock symbol, for Aristophanes, of the Good Old Days when Men were Men and Virtue was Untarnished.

NEOKLEIDES: A blear-eyed politician generally satirized for his ailment, for light-fingeredness, and for alien birth. W. H. Hess theorizes that Aristophanes may use this name to attack Herakleides of Klazomenai, a naturalized alien who was responsible for increasing the legislative pay instituted by Agyrrhios from one obol to three obols. If so, Aristophanes (who attacks "Neokleides" twice in this play and three times in the *Ploutos*) and other poets are untypically coy in avoiding an enemy's real name; but the theory is an attractive one.

NIKIAS: A pale young man, probably the grandson of the ill-fated Athenian general.

PAN: Rural Arkadian god of the flocks and woodlands; associated with sudden madness (hence "panic"). His cult at Athens was instituted by way of thanks for his help to the Athenians at the battle of Marathon.

PHYROMACHOS: According to the scholiast, this name masks Kleomachos, an actor or an orator (or possibly both) with deplorable diction.

POLLUX: Twin of Kastor (q.v.).

POSEIDON: Brother of Zeus and god of the sea.

SMOIOS: A notorious pervert, whose interests seem to have run in the same channels as those of Ariphrades (q.v.).

SPARTA: Capital city of Lakonia, Athens' principal opponent and conqueror in the Peloponnesian War; at this time (392) the greatest single power in Greece, and thus engaged in war against a coalition of lesser Greek powers (Athens, Korinth, Argos, Thebes) while carrying on a naval conflict against Persia.

THASOS: A volcanic island in the northern Aegean, celebrated for the dark, fragrant wine produced by its vineyards.

THRASYBOULOS: Athenian hero, deliverer of the city from the rule of the Thirty Tyrants in 404 B.C. Thereafter, he pursued a moderate course politically, being outmaneuvered by the radical-democratic war party on Athens' entrance into the Corinthian War in 394. Regained much of Athens' northern dominions in 390-389; killed at Lesbos in 388.

ZEUS: Chief god of the Olympian pantheon: son of Kronos, brother of Poseidon, father of Athene.

The Frogs

Translated by Richmond Lattimore
with sketches by Richard Sears

CONTENTS

Introduction

The Frogs was produced at the Lenaia of 405 B.C. and won first prize.[1] The Athenians had been at war most of the time since 431 B.C., and their position now was almost desperate. Since the failure in Sicily, they had indeed won several naval battles and had twice been offered peace by Sparta; they were nevertheless in a position where one defeat would lose the war (this happened six months after *The Frogs* was presented). One great victory might still save them, but only if they used it wisely, as a bargaining point for permanent peace.

This, at least, seems to have been the view of Aristophanes. The champion of peace who spoke in *The Acharnians, Peace,* and *Lysistrata,* is still the champion of peace. It was Kleophon who had forbidden the Athenians to accept Spartan terms, and in this play Aristophanes hates Kleophon as much as ever. But peace cannot now be simply offered or accepted; it must be earned. Aristophanes' program can be summed up as "all hands save ship." All talents and resources, even the doubtful and suspect talents of Alkibiades, must be called on to win one more victory which, if won, must be used as a means to an honorable peace, not as a means to conquest and empire. So, at least, I would read the concluding lines of the play.

In the spring of 405, Athenian literature had suffered too. Aeschylus was dead half a century since, though not forgotten. Euripides and Sophocles, greatest of the moderns, had died within the year. Dionysos, masked though he may be as the preposterous hero of comedy, is also Drama, the spirit and essence of Athenian literature and art. He seeks to bring back good writing to Athens, and with it, the public wisdom which, as Aristophanes maintains against Sokrates, will always be found in the highest poetry.

The first part of *The Frogs,* therefore, takes the form of the Comic Journey beyond the limits of the world, reminiscent in some ways of *Peace* and *The Birds.* During its course, as the Dead are encountered,

---

[1] . . . "It was presented in the archonship of Kallias . . . at the Lenaia. It was placed first; Phrynichus was second with *The Muses;* Plato third, with *Cleophon.* Our play was so much admired because of the parabasis that it was actually given again, according to Dicaearchus." From the ancient *Hypothesis,* or Introduction. The Plato in question is a well-known comic poet, not the philosopher.

these are used to speak the poet's own views and to plead for political harmony. At the end of the Journey, a conversation between the two slaves, Xanthias and Aiakos, introduces the grand final *agon* between Euripides and Aeschylus.

This *agon* is, after suitable introductory exhortation and preparation, disputed on five issues, or in five rounds, as follows:

1. 907-1098. General style, subject matter, and effect upon audiences.

   (1099-1118). Choral interlude.

2. 1119-1250. Prologues, including skill at exposition and the use of iambic metre.

   (1251-60). Choral interlude.

3. 1261-1369. Lyrics and lyric prosody.

   (1370-77). Choral interlude.

4. 1378-1410. The weighing of lines.

   (1411-17). Interlude by Dionysos and Pluto.

5. 1417-65. Advice to the Athenians.

In each round, Euripides attacks first, and in the first three he scores some hits. Nor is his final advice (1446-50) contemptible; at least, it is not unlike the spirit of the poet's own views spoken at 718-37. But Aeschylus, the ultimate winner, has the better position for an *agon,* since the last word is always his.

Briefly, the arguments, round by round, are as follows:

1. Euripides says that Aeschylus is slow moving, undramatic, turgid, obscure, and too militaristic. His own plays are lucid, plausible, and have meaning for all. Aeschylus retorts that he has always maintained a high heroic standard and incited the citizens to virtue, while Euripides, in bringing Tragedy down to earth, has, especially with his morbid interest in sex, dragged her in the dust, and in so doing has unmanned the Athenians.

2. Euripides alleges an obscure and repetitious style. Aeschylus replies with a charge of metrical monotony. In prologue after prologue of Euripides, the main verb is delayed and a subordinate clause completed in such a way that the phrase

   lost his little bottle of oil

which scans

— ‿ — ‿ — ‿‿ —

will now complete both the sentence and the metrical line.

3. Aeschylus having raised the question of metrical monotony, Euripides retorts in kind. The lyrics of Aeschylus are monoto-

nous. For, however he may begin, he constantly ends with the dactylic phrase

$$\smile \_ \smile\smile \_ \smile\smile \_ \smile\smile \_ \_$$

exemplified by his line

> o ho what a stroke come you not to the rescue?

In these metrical criticisms, which are penetrating, the general criticisms of style are repeated, i.e., when Euripides makes sense, he is prosy and pedestrian, when Aeschylus sounds grand, he means little. Aeschylus counters. Euripides writes vers libre, the lyric metres lose their form and the sense loses its coherence. The result is a shoddy, sentimental, drifting sequence, marked in particular by one special fault which Aristophanes loves to detect in Euripides: namely, the unassimilating conjunction of magnificence and homeliness.

4. The weighing of the lines involves a bit of byplay, has been often dismissed as mere fooling, and is mostly that, but nevertheless forwards the constant opinion of Aristophanes (Dionysos): the verse of Aeschylus has more mass, heft, and force than that of Euripides.

5. What shall Athens do? The speakers might represent the poet's own agonizing struggle. Euripides expresses Aristophanes' doubts about the good purposes of the heirs of Perikles, the exponents of naval warfare; but Aeschylus voices Aristophanes' unwilling conclusion, that these men alone have a chance of saving the city.

In this *agon*, Aristophanes has achieved an unfair but telling criticism of Euripides. His Aeschylus, even as parody, fits far less closely the concept which we can form of him from seven complete plays and a number of fragments. Aeschylus was not the Colonel Blimp that Aristophanes makes him. *The Persians* and *The Seven Against Thebes* are not simple glorifications of patriotism and courage. *Agamemnon* condemns war-makers and sackers of cities. The woman's point of view is eloquently stated in every surviving play. And Aphrodite did mean a great deal to Aeschylus; one need only look at the dreaming visions of Helen in *Agamemnon*, or at Klytaimnestra's sadistic ecstasies in the same play. Nor was Aeschylus a reactionary aristocrat. *Prometheus* and *The Eumenides* speak eloquently for progress and reform.

Aristophanes has picked out and exaggerated certain aspects of Aeschylus, not because he was ignorant or blind, but perhaps because he was more concerned with the force of his *agon* than with the inward

3

coherence and validity of his historical persons. The attack is on the moderns. Euripides is their spokesman. Whatever Euripides is, Aeschylus must be the opposite. So, if Euripides is pacific and unmilitary, Aeschylus must be martial. If Euripides is fascinated by the women and writes of their problems from their point of view, Aeschylus must despise sex. And since Euripides was so plainly popular (though not in the sense that he won prizes from the judges), Aeschylus must be in a sense *un*popular, that is, haughty and aristocratic.

A byproduct of the pattern is the unhappy position in which Sophocles finds himself: a second-best Aeschylus. Only two could play this game at once. Aeschylus and Euripides were plainly more fun for the parodist, their peculiarities being a great deal more obvious.

In translating *The Frogs,* I have found myself surprised into breaking away from several principles which I always stuck to when trying to translate serious Greek poetry. Let me, once again, grimly itemize.

1. Notes.   I have generally avoided footnotes on the text of tragedy. But Aristophanes is, as the immortal Stephen Leacock put it . . . "sally after sally, each sally explained in a footnote calling it a sally."[2] I have added some notes.

2. Slang.   The Frogs opens in the manner, though not altogether in the language, of the vaudeville act or minstrel show. My English is much worse than Aristophanes' Greek. But the vernacular seemed to be the only language into which it would translate itself. Frequently, the translation is in very bad taste. And so is Aristophanes.

3. Incongruity.   Comedy does not cultivate appropriateness for its own sake.

4. Rhymes.   Certain metres, such as short iambic lines, and the long ones in iambic and anapaestic, seemed in English to come out rather lame and labored without rhyme, perhaps because English lacks the flexibility and the bold distinction between long and short of polysyllabic Greek. I have left the parabasis (354-71) unrhymed because it seems, in Greek, rather strained and awkward, and is not funny.

Clichés.   In serious verse, these are absolutely obnoxious (in serious *prose,* too!). Awkwardly enthroned out of context, the cliché is of the stuff of comedy. So I have written accordingly. Perhaps the alert reader will find that they have crept into the introduction too.

I have used the *Oxford Classical Text* of Hall and Geldart.

I am deeply indebted to Harry Avery for helpful criticism.

---

[2] Let me point out that, in accordance with modern convention, this quotation from Stephen Leacock must be accompanied by a footnote calling it a quotation from Stephen Leacock. See Stephen Leacock, *Behind the Beyond* (New York: John Lane Company; London: John Lane, The Bodley Head; Toronto: Bell and Cockburn, 1923), pp. 186-87.

Characters in the Play

DIONYSOS

XANTHIAS, *his slave*

HERAKLES

CORPSE

CHARON

CHORUS *(as Frogs; as Initiates;
and as the population of Hades)*

AIAKOS, *the janitor of Hades*

MAID

HOSTESS *of the inn*

PLATHANE, *maid of the inn*

EURIPIDES

AESCHYLUS

PLUTO *(or Hades)*

VARIOUS EXTRAS *(stretcher bearers, dead souls rowing in the
boat, assistants to Aiakos, etc.)*

SCENE: *A Door. Enter Dionysos, on foot; Xanthias, riding a donkey, and with a bundle on his back. Dionysos wears a long yellow robe, but over it the lion skin affected by Herakles, and he carries a primitive knobby club.*

XANTHIAS
Shall I give them any of the usual jokes, master?
You know, the ones that are always good for a laugh?

DIONYSOS
Go ahead. *Any* of them. Except "what a day!"
Don't give them that one. It's gone awfully sour.

XANTHIAS
But something witty, like . . .

DIONYSOS
                                        *Any*thing. Except "my poor back."

XANTHIAS
Well, can I tell the really funny one?

DIONYSOS
                                        Yes, do,
go right ahead. Only don't say *this* one.

XANTHIAS
                                        Don't say what?

DIONYSOS
Don't shift your load because "you need to go to the baffroom."

XANTHIAS
Can't I even tell the people I'm so over-loaded
that unless somebody unloads me I'll blow my —— bottom?

DIONYSOS
No, don't, please don't. Wait till I *need* to vomit.

XANTHIAS
So what did I have to carry all this stuff for,
if I can't pull any of the jokes Phrynichos* pulls,
or what Lykis pulls, or what Ameipsias pulls?

DIONYSOS
Well, just don't do it. When I'm in the audience

and have to watch any of these conscious efforts,
I'm a year older when I leave the place.

XANTHIAS
Poor me. Oh, my poor neck. I think it's broken now.
It won't say anything funny.

DIONYSOS
Now isn't this a sassy slave? I've spoiled him.
Here am I, Dionysos, son of Grapejuice,
wearing out my own feet, and I let him ride
so that he won't get tired carrying the bundles.

XANTHIAS
What do you mean, not carrying them?

DIONYSOS
                                                How can you?
You're riding.

XANTHIAS
                    But I'm carrying.

DIONYSOS
                              How?

XANTHIAS
                                          With an effort.

DIONYSOS
Isn't the donkey carrying what you're carrying?

XANTHIAS
Not carrying what I'm carrying, no, by golly.

DIONYSOS
How can you carry it, when somebody's carrying you?

XANTHIAS
Dunno. I only know my shoulder's falling apart.

DIONYSOS
All right, so the donkey isn't doing any good,
why don't you pick him up and carry him?

XANTHIAS
Why wasn't I in that sea battle,* where they freed the slaves
who fought? Then I could tell you to go jump in the lake.

DIONYSOS
Get down, you bum. Here we are at the door.
This is the place I was trying to find. First stop. Get down.

Knocks on the door.

Hey there! You inside! Hey. Anybody home? Bang bang.

Herakles half opens the door, pokes his head out.

HERAKLES
Who was pounding on my door? Sounded like a Centaur
kicking it or something. What goes on?

DIONYSOS

To Xanthias.

Slave boy!

XANTHIAS
                What is it.

DIONYSOS
                        You noticed, didn't you?

XANTHIAS
                                        Noticed what?

DIONYSOS
How scared he was.

XANTHIAS
                        Yeah, scared. Scared you were going bats.

HERAKLES
Demeter! I have to laugh.
I'm biting my lip to hold it in, but I can't help it.

DIONYSOS
Come here, dear boy. I have a favor to ask of you.

HERAKLES
Wait till I get rid of the giggles. Only I can't stop them.
That lion skin being worn over that buttercup nightie!
Haw haw haw.

                Collapses. Recovers.

What's the idea, this meeting of the warclub and slipper?
Where were you bound?

DIONYSOS

Well, I served aboard a kind of dreamboat
named the Kleisthenes.*

HERAKLES

And did you engage?

DIONYSOS

I did. We sank
a dozen, a baker's dozen, of the enemy craft.

HERAKLES
You two?

DIONYSOS

So help me Apollo.

XANTHIAS

And then I woke up.

DIONYSOS
So then I'm sitting on deck, see, reading this new book:
Andromeda, by Euripides: all of a sudden it hits me
over the heart, a craving, you can't think how hard.

HERAKLES
A craving, huh, A big one?

DIONYSOS

Little one. Molon*-size.

HERAKLES
A craving. For a woman?

DIONYSOS

No.

HERAKLES

For a boy?

DIONYSOS

No no.

HERAKLES
For a, uh, man?

DIONYSOS

Shush shush shush.

HERAKLES

Well, what about you and
Kleisthenes?

DIONYSOS
Don't laugh at me, brother dear. Truly I am in a bad way.
I've got this craving. It's demoralizing me.

HERAKLES
What kind of craving, little brother?

DIONYSOS

I don't know how
to explain. I'll paraphrase it by a parable.
Did you ever feel a sudden longing for baked beans?

HERAKLES
Baked beans? Gosh yes, that's happened to me a million times.

DIONYSOS
Shall I give you another illustration? Expound this one?

HERAKLES
Don't need to expound baked beans to me. I get the point.

DIONYSOS
Well, that's the kind of craving that's been eating me:
a craving for Euripides.

HERAKLES

You mean, dead and all?

DIONYSOS
And nobody's going to persuade me to give up my plan
of going after him.

HERAKLES

Way to Hades', down below?

DIONYSOS
Absolutely. Belower than that, if there's anything there.

HERAKLES
What do you want?

DIONYSOS

What I want is a clever poet
*For some of them are gone. The ones who're left are bad.**

HERAKLES
What? Isn't Iophon* living?

DIONYSOS
He's the one good thing
that's left—that is, if he really is any good.
I don't quite altogether just know about that.

HERAKLES
But if you *got* to resurrect somebody, why
not Sophocles instead of Euripides?

DIONYSOS
No. First I want to get Iophon all by himself
without Sophocles, take him apart, see how he does.
Anyway, Euripides is a slippery character
who'd like to make a jailbreak and come back with me.
Sophocles behaved himself up here. He would down there.

HERAKLES
What happened to Agathon?*

DIONYSOS
Oh, he's left me, gone away.
And he was a good poet, too. His friends miss him.

HERAKLES
Too bad. Where did he go?

DIONYSOS
To join the saints. For dinner.

HERAKLES
What about Xenokles?

DIONYSOS
I only wish he *would* die.

HERAKLES
Pythangelos?

XANTHIAS
And nobody ever thinks of me,
and look at me standing here with my shoulder dropping off.

HERAKLES
Look here, there still are a million and one young guys around.

You know, Tragic Poets
who can outgabble Euripides by a country mile.

DIONYSOS
A lot of morning-glories talking to themselves,
just twitterbirds and free-verse writers, sloppy craftsmen.
One performance, and you never hear of them again.
They sprinkle Drama in passing like a dog at a pump.
You tell me where there's still an honest-to-god poet
to bark me out one good round solid tragic line.

HERAKLES
Honest-to-god like what?

DIONYSOS
                         Honest-to-god like this,
someone with an adventurous style, as who should say:
Bright upper air, Zeus' penthouse* or *the foot of Time,*
or *heart that would not swear upon the holy things*
or *tongue that was forsworn when the heart knew it not.*

HERAKLES
You like that stuff?

DIONYSOS
                         It's absolutely dreamy, man.

HERAKLES
It's bilge. It's awful. Nobody knows it better than you.

DIONYSOS
Rule not my mind. Thine own is thy mind. Rule thou it.*

HERAKLES
No, really, it does seem the most awful slop to me.

DIONYSOS
You stick to food.

XANTHIAS
                         And nobody ever thinks of me.

DIONYSOS
Now, let you tell me why I'm here, wearing all this stuff
that makes me look like you. It's so you can tell me
about your friends who put you up when you went *there*

to fetch the Kerberos dog. Well, I could use some friends,
so tell me about them. Tell me the ports, the bakery shops,
whorehouses, parks and roadside rests, highways and springs,
the cities, boarding houses, and the best hotels
scarcest in bedbugs.

XANTHIAS

          Nobody ever thinks of me.

HERAKLES

You poor idiot. You're really going to try and get there?

DIONYSOS

No more of that stuff, please, just tell me about the roads,
and what's the quickest way to Hades' underhouse,
and don't make it a hot one. Not too cold either.

HERAKLES

Hm. What's my first recommendation? What indeed?
Well, here's a way. You need a footstool and a rope.
Go hang yourself.

DIONYSOS

        Stop stop. That's a stifling sort of way.

HERAKLES

Well, there's a short well-beaten path. *Well-beaten,* I say,
via mortar-and-pestle.

DIONYSOS

          That's hemlock you're talking about?

HERAKLES

Nothing else but.

DIONYSOS

        A chilly way. It makes me shiver.
Your shins go numb.

HERAKLES

Shall I tell you about a downhill road? It's good and quick.

DIONYSOS

That's what I'd like. I'm somebody who hates to walk.

HERAKLES

Well, take just a little walk down to the Potters' Quarter.

15

DIONYSOS

                                                          Yes.

HERAKLES

Climb up the tower, the high one.

DIONYSOS

                             What do I do then?

HERAKLES

Watch for the drop of the signal torch that starts the race,
and when they drop it, all the spectators around
will say "go!" You go, too.

DIONYSOS

                           Go where?

HERAKLES

                                   Over the edge.

DIONYSOS

I'd smash my twin croquettes of brains.
No, I won't go that way of yours.

HERAKLES

                              What *do* you want?

DIONYSOS

The way you went, the deathless way.*

HERAKLES

                               It's a long voyage.
The first thing that you'll come to is a great swampy lake.
It's bottomless.

DIONYSOS

                      Well then, how do I get across?

HERAKLES

There's an ancient mariner with a little tiny boat.
He'll take you across. And you'll give him two bits* for it.

DIONYSOS

Oh, gee.
Those two bits. You can't ever get away from them.
How did they ever get here?

HERAKLES

Theseus* brought them along from
Athens.
After that, you'll see snakes, and armies of wild animals,
monsters.

DIONYSOS
Stop trying to scare me out of this.
You'll never stop me.

HERAKLES

Next comes a great sea of mud
and shitten springs eternal, and people stuck therein,
whoever did an injury to his guest or host,
debauched some child and picked its pockets in the process,
or beat his mother up, or broke his father's jaw,
or swore an oath and broke it,
or copied out a tragic speech of Morsimos.*

DIONYSOS
Don't stop. I've got another one to add to those.
Whoever learned the war-dance by Kinesias.*

HERAKLES
Next a sweet sound of flutes will come upon your ears,
and you'll see a lovely light like the sunlight here above,
myrtles, and solemn troops and sweet societies
of men and women, and an endless clapping of hands.

DIONYSOS
And who are they?

HERAKLES

The blessed, the Initiates.*

XANTHIAS
And I'm the donkey carrying mystic properties,
but I don't mean to keep them for the rest of time.

HERAKLES
Ask them. They'll tell you everything else you need,
for they live closest to the road you have to go.
Their habitation is by Pluto's doors.
So, good luck, little brother.

Herakles disappears, shutting the door.

DIONYSOS

Oh, the same to you!
Keep healthy. You there, Xanthias, pick the bundles up.

XANTHIAS

You mean, before I've put them down?

DIONYSOS

Get a move on.

XANTHIAS

Oh please, please don't make me do it. Why don't you hire
one of these stiffs they're carrying out? There'll be one soon.

DIONYSOS

What if I can't get one?

XANTHIAS

Then I'll do it.

DIONYSOS

Fair enough.
Look, here comes a corpse now being carried out.

Corpse is brought in on a stretcher.

Hey! Hey, you there, the dead one. I'm talking to you.
Want to carry some luggage to Hades?

Corpse sits up.

CORPSE

How much?

DIONYSOS

Showing his hand.

That much.

CORPSE

Give me two bucks*?

DIONYSOS

My god no, that's too much.

Corpse lies down again.

CORPSE

Keep carrying me, you guys.

DIONYSOS

Hey, what's the matter, wait, we've got to work this out.

CORPSE

Two bucks. Put up or shut up.

DIONYSOS

Make it one and a half.

CORPSE

                  I'd sooner come to life again.

Corpse is carried off.

XANTHIAS

Stuck up bastard, isn't he? The hell with him!
I'll take the baggage.

DIONYSOS

             You are nature's nobleman.
Let's go catch a boat.

CHARON

Off stage.

          Woo-oop! Coming alongside!

XANTHIAS

What's going on here?

DIONYSOS

           What indeed. Oh, here, it's the lake
right where he said it would be, and now here comes the boat.

Charon, in a little boat (on wheels) is pushed in.

XANTHIAS

So help me Poseidon, so it is, and Charon too.

DIONYSOS

O carry me Charon o sweet chariot carry me home.*

CHARON

Who wants a cruise? Relaxation from business worries?
The Meadows of Forgetting, or Horsefeatherland?
To go to the Dogs? To go to the Birds? To go to Hell?

DIONYSOS

Me.

CHARON

Get aboard and shake a leg.

19

DIONYSOS

Where d'you think we're bound?
Strictly for the Birds?

CHARON

We sure are, with you aboard.
Get on, get on.

DIONYSOS

Here, boy!

CHARON

No, I won't take a slave.
Only a veteran of our hide-saving sea battle.*

XANTHIAS
I would have made it but I was sick. I had the pinkeye.

CHARON
Then you can just take a little walk around the lake.

XANTHIAS
Where shall I wait for you?

CHARON

By the Stone of Parching Thirst,*
at the pull-off.

DIONYSOS

Got it?

XANTHIAS

Oh, I've got it. Wish I were dead.
What kind of bad-luck-sign did I run into this morning?

*Xanthias trudges off, carrying the bundles. Dionysos
climbs, awkwardly, into the boat.*

CHARON
You, sit to your oar.

Dionysos sits on his oar.

Anyone else going? Hurry it up.

*A few Extras (the ones who carried the corpse),
get into the boat, each taking an oar.*

Hey, *you* there. What d'you think you're doing?

DIONYSOS

With dignity.

              I am sitting
to my oar. Exactly what you told me to do.

CHARON

Rearranging him.

    Well, sit *here,* fatso. Sit like this. Got it?

DIONYSOS

              Okay.

CHARON

Now get your hands away and bring them back.

DIONYSOS

              Okay.

CHARON

Stop being such an ass, will you? Bring your weight forward.
Get your back into it.

DIONYSOS

        What do you want? I never rowed before.
I'm no Old Navy Man. I didn't make the First Crew.*
How'm I supposed to row?

CHARON

        Easily. Just begin to do it,
and you'll get a pretty song to give you the time.

DIONYSOS

          Who's singing?

CHARON

It's a swan song, but the swans are lovely frogs.

DIONYSOS

         Go ahead.
Give me the stroke.

CHARON

OO-pah, oo-pah.

*If he cares to, Charon can go on doing this all
during the following chorus.*

The Chorus appears, in green masks and tights, as
Frogs. They are Frogs only in this rowing-scene.
They dance around the boat.

CHORUS

Brekekekex ko-ax ko-ax,
Brekekekex ko-ax ko-ax,
children of freshwater ponds and springs,
gather we all together now
and swell our lofty well-becroaken chorus,
ko-ax ko-ax

Dionysos' Nysos-song
we sing to the son of Zeus,
Dionysos-in-the-marshes,
when with morning-frog-in-the-throat
the hangover-haggard procession
staggers to the holy Pot-Feast through my dominion,
brekekekex ko-ax ko-ax.

DIONYSOS

I think that I'm beginning to fail,
I'm raising blisters on my tail,
ko-ax ko-ax, I think I am,
but possibly you don't care a damn.

CHORUS

Brekekekex ko-ax ko-ax.

DIONYSOS

I can't hear anything but ko-ax,
go 'way, I'd like to give you the axe.

CHORUS

Of course, you fool, you can't hear anything else,
for the sweet Muses have gifted me with their lyres,
and Pan the horned walker, voice of reed in the woods,
and lyric Apollo himself goes glad for my singing
when with the music of piping my lyrical
song is heard in the pondy waters.
Brekekekex ko-ax ko-ax.

DIONYSOS

My bloody blisters refuse to heal.
My anguished bottom's beginning to squeal.
When I bend over it joins the attack.

CHORUS
Brekekekex ko-ax ko-*ak*.

DIONYSOS
Oh ah ye songful tribe, will you
shut up?

CHORUS
Exactly what we won't do.
Longer stronger
sing in the sunny daytime
as we wriggle and dive in the marsh-
flowers blithe on the lily pads
and dive and duck as we sing,
and when Zeus makes it rain
in green escape to the deep
water our song still pulses
and bubbles up from below.

DIONYSOS
Brepepepeps ko-aps ko-aps
I'm picking the rhythm up from you chaps.

CHORUS
We're sorry for us if *you* join in.

DIONYSOS
I'm sorry for *me* if I begin
to split in two from bottom to chin.

CHORUS
Brekekekex ko-ax ko-ax.

DIONYSOS
And the hell with you. I don't *care* what you do.

CHORUS
Whatever you say we'll croak all day
as long as we're stout
and our throats hold out.

DIONYSOS
Brekekekex ko-ax ko-ax.
There, I can do it better than you.

CHORUS
No, *we* can do it better than *you*.

DIONYSOS
No, *I* can do it better than *you*.
I'll croak away
if it takes all day,
brekekekex ko-ax ko-ax,
and I'll croak you down in the grand climax
brekekekex ko-ax ko-ax.

Frogs slink away. Silence.

Ha ha. I knew I could beat you. You and your ko-ax!

CHARON
Easy, easy. Ship oars now. Coming alongside.
Everybody off. Pay your fare.

DIONYSOS

Two bits for you, my good man.

Charon with his boat is wheeled off.

Xanthias! Hey, Xanthias! Now where's he got to? Xanthias!

XANTHIAS

Off.

Yoo hoo!

DIONYSOS

This way. Over here.

Xanthias appears.

XANTHIAS

Why, hello, master.

DIONYSOS
What's over there?

XANTHIAS

A lot of mud and darkness.

DIONYSOS
Well, did you see those criminal types he was talking
about, the murderers and swindlers?

XANTHIAS

Haven't *you* seen them?

Dionysos stares at the audience and points rudely.

DIONYSOS
Oh, sure, now I know where to look. They're all out there.
Well, what do we do next?

XANTHIAS
                          I think we'd better get out of here.
This is the place he said the wild animals would be,
you know, those monsters he was talking about.

DIONYSOS
                                        Oh, him.
He was just laying it on thick, trying to frighten me.
He knows what a fighting man I am, and it makes him jealous.
There's nobody who's quite as vain as Herakles.
I wish we could have met some terrifying thing,
you know, some ghastly struggle, to make the trip worth while.

XANTHIAS
You know, I think I do hear something moving around.

DIONYSOS
Wh wh which direction?

XANTHIAS
                    Right behind us.

DIONYSOS
                                   Get behind.

XANTHIAS
No, it's in front of us now.

DIONYSOS
                          You better stay in front.

XANTHIAS
I see it. It's an animal—an enormous thing.

DIONYSOS
What does it look like?

XANTHIAS
                      Monster. It keeps changing shape.
Now it's a cow. Now it's a mule. Oh, now it's a girl,
whee-whew, what a beauty!

DIONYSOS

         Let me at her. Where'd she go?

XANTHIAS

Too late. No girl any longer. She turned into a bitch.

DIONYSOS

It's Empousa.*

XANTHIAS

       Whoever she is, she done caught fire.
Her face is burning.

DIONYSOS

      Does she have one brazen leg?

XANTHIAS

She does, she does. The other one is made of dung.
I'm not lying.

DIONYSOS

     Where can I run to?

XANTHIAS

         Where can I?

DIONYSOS

To the priest of Dionysos sitting in the front row.
   Save me, your reverence! We belong to the same lodge.

XANTHIAS

Lord Herakles, we're lost.

DIONYSOS

        Dumb-bell, don't call me that.
Don't give away my name. *Please.*

XANTHIAS

Lord Dionysos then.

DIONYSOS

      No no, that's even worse.
Go on the way you were going.

XANTHIAS

       Here, master, over here.

28

DIONYSOS
    Got something?

XANTHIAS
              Don't be frightened, we've come out all right
and I can speak the line now that Hegelochos spoke:
The storm is over, and the clam has stilled the waves.*
Empousa's gone.

DIONYSOS
          You swear it's true?

XANTHIAS
                  So help me Zeus.

DIONYSOS
Swear it again.

XANTHIAS
       So help me Zeus.

DIONYSOS
              Swear.

XANTHIAS
                Help me Zeus.

DIONYSOS
What a fright. I lost my pretty color when I saw her.

XANTHIAS
Our donkey got a fright too, so you're all in yellow.*

DIONYSOS
Now what did I ever do to have this happen to me?
Looking upward.
Which one of you gods must I hold responsible for this?

XANTHIAS
Bright upper air, Zeus' penthouse? Or the foot of time?
Flute within.

DIONYSOS
Hey, you.

XANTHIAS
      What is it?

DIONYSOS

Did you hear?

XANTHIAS

Did I hear what?

DIONYSOS

Flutes being blown.

XANTHIAS

I heard them too, and there's a crackle
and smell of torches. Seems like it's mysteries going on.

DIONYSOS

Let's just quietly squat where we are, and listen in.

CHORUS

Off.

Iacchos Iacchos*
Iacchos o Iacchos.

XANTHIAS

That's what I thought it was, master. The Initiates.
Remember, he told us, their playground's hereabouts. They sing
the Iacchos song by that noted theologian, Diagoras.*

DIONYSOS

I think you're right, but still we'd better sit quiet here
until we find out just exactly what goes on.

CHORUS

In white, as Initiates.

Iacchos! Well beloved in these pastures o indwelling
Iacchos o Iacchos
come to me come with dance steps down the meadow
to your worshipping companions
with the fruited, the lifebursting,
the enmyrtled and enwreathed garland on your brows, and bold-footed
stamp out the sprightly measure
of the dancing that's your pleasure,
of the dancing full of graces, full of light and sweet and sacred
for your dedicated chosen ones.

XANTHIAS

Demeter's daughter, Persephone, holy lady and queen,
ineffable fragrance wafts upon me. Roasting pigs!*

30

DIONYSOS
If I promise you a handful of tripes, will you shut up?

CHORUS
Let flames fly as the torch tosses in hand's hold
Iacchos o Iacchos
star of fire in the high rites of the night time.
And the field shines in the torch light,
and the old men's knees are limber,
and they shake off aches and miseries
and the years of their antiquity drop from them
in the magical measure.
Oh, torch-in-hand-shining.
Iacchos go before us to the marsh flowers and the meadow
and the blest revel of dances.

*Parabasis. The Chorus advances down stage and
the leader addresses the audience directly.*

LEADER

All now must observe the sacred silence: we ban from our choruses
    any
whose brain cannot fathom the gist of our wit; whose hearts and
    feelings are dirty;
who never has witnessed and never partaken in genuine cult of the
    Muses,
who knows not the speech of bullgobble Kratinos,* who knows not
    the Bacchic fraternity,
who laughs at cheap jokes that should not have been made, who writes
    such stuff at the wrong time,
who stirs up sedition dissension and hate, who does not like the
    Athenians,
who hopes to make money out of our quarrels and lights them and
    fans them to fury,
who holds high office and then takes bribes when the city is tossed in
    the tempest,
who sells out a ship or a fort to the enemy, smuggling our secret
    intelligence
from Aigina over to Epidauros, like any goddam tax-collecting
Thorykion,* with the oarpads and sails and pitch that was meant for
    our navy,
who goes on his rounds and collects contributions to finance the
    enemy's war fleet,
who, humming his cyclical verses the while, uses Hekate's shrine as
    a backhouse,*

who gets up to speak in the public assembly and nibbles at the fees
    of the poets
just because they once made a fool of him in the plays that our
    fathers established.
Such men I forbid, and again I forbid, and again I forbid them a
    third time,
let them get up and go from our choral mysteries.
                                                    All others, strike
    up the singing
and dance of our holy and nightlong revels befitting this solemn
    occasion.

CHORUS

Slowly.

Advance all now, firmly
into the flower strewn hollows
of meadow fields. Stamp strongly
and jeer and sneer
and mock and be outrageous.
For all are well stuffed full with food.

Advance advance, sing strongly
our Lady of Salvation
and march to match your singing.
She promises
to save our land in season
for all Thorykion can do.

LEADER

Come now and alter the tune of the song for the queen of the
    bountiful seasons;
sing loud, sing long, and dance to the song for Demeter our lady and
    goddess.

CHORUS

Demeter, mistress of grave and gay,
stand by now and help me win.
Protect this chorus. It is your own.
Let me in safety all this day
play on and do my dances.
Help me say what will make them grin.
Help me say what will make them think.

Help me say what will make me win
in your own festival today
and wear the victor's garland.

LEADER
Change the tune.
Sing to the pretty god of the time   summon him to join us.
We have a sacred way to go   and he goes with us.

CHORUS
Iacchos, well-beloved spirit of song, o be
my leader and march along with me
this holy way.
Bring me to Eleusis swift and musically.
To you I pray.
Iacchos lover of dancing help me on my way.

You split my shirt to make them laugh and boo.
You cut my cheap little shoes in two.
My rags flap on me.
You know how to make do.
Wartime economy.
Iacchos lover of dancing help me on my way.

I saw a sweet little girl in the crowd down there.
As she leaned forward, her dress, I swear,
bust open a trifle
and I was happy to stare
at a bosomy eyeful.
Iacchos lover of dancing help me on my way.

DIONYSOS
I've always been a fellow who's good
at follow-my-leader; I gladly would
go down and help you play with her.

XANTHIAS
                                   I would if I could.

CHORUS
Shall we now, all together
make fun of Archedemos?*
Seven years he tries to naturalize and still he hasn't made it.

Now he's a leading citizen
among the upworld corpses.
Nobody up there can claim a similar fame—for being a bastard.

And Kleisthenes,* they tell me,
sits mourning among the tombstones,
and tears the hair from his you-know-where, and batters his jawbones.

He was seen, in his usual posture
in tears for his vanished sweetheart—
the dear little friend (of his after-end) Sebinos of Anaphlystos.

And Kallias,* they say,
the son of Ponyplay,
wears a panoply and has gone to sea and the ships with a lionskin
    over his hips.

DIONYSOS
Can any of you guys tell
me where Pluto happens to dwell?
We're visiting firemen. Never been here before.

CHORUS
Stop bothering me so.
You haven't got far to go.
He lives right here. Walk up and knock at the door.

DIONYSOS
Boy! Pick up the stuff again.

XANTHIAS
What's the matter with this guy?
Pick up, pick up, it's nothing but pick up bundles.

CHORUS
Forward, now
to the goddess' sacred circle-dance to the grove that's in blossom
and play on the way for we belong to the company of the elect,
and I shall go where the girls go and I shall go with the women
who keep the nightlong rite of the goddess and carry their sacred
    torch.

Let us go where roses grow
and fields are in flower,
in the way that is ours alone,

playing our blessed play
which the prosperous Fates today
ordain for our playing.

On us alone the sun shines here
and the happy daylight,
for we are Initiates, we
treat honorably
all strangers who are here
and our own people.

The white-robed Chorus file off.

DIONYSOS

Well, tell me, how am I supposed to knock on the door?
How do the natives knock on doors in these here parts?

XANTHIAS

Stop dithering around. Take a good whack at it.
You wear the gear and spirit of Herakles. Act according.

DIONYSOS

Knocking.

Boy! Hey, boy.

AIAKOS*

Inside.

                    Who's out there?

DIONYSOS

                         The mighty Herakles.

AIAKOS

Still inside but he will appear later on.

You hoodlum, did you ever have a nerve,
you bastard, bastard plus, and bastard double-plus.
You were the one who dragged our Kerberos-dog away.
You choked him by the collar and made off with him,
and *I* was on duty. We've got a scissors-hold on *you.*
We've got the cliffs of blackheart Styx* all ready for you,
the blood-dripping rocks of Acheron to shove you off—
or maybe the bloodhounds sniff your trail by Kokytos.
Echidna, our pet hundred-headed viper, waits
to chew your gizzard, and Muraina, eel of hell
shall have your lungs to gnaw on, while your kidneys go
with all the rest of your innards and the bleeding bowels

to the Teithrasian gorgons. Oh, they'll rip you up.
They're straining at the leash. I'll let them loose on you.

Dionysos collapses, doubled up.

XANTHIAS
What's the matter?

DIONYSOS
I can't hold it. Is there a god in the house?

XANTHIAS
You clown. Don't disgrace us. Alley oop! On your feet
before somebody sees you.

DIONYSOS
But I feel so faint.
Be a good chap, put a wet sponge over my heart.

XANTHIAS
Here it is, you put it.

DIONYSOS
Where are we?

*Takes it, searches, and claps it over his lower
anatomy.*

XANTHIAS
O ye golden gods,
is that where you keep your heart?

DIONYSOS
You see, the poor little thing
got awfully frightened, so she crept down there to hide.

XANTHIAS
You're the worst coward of all gods and men.

DIONYSOS
Who, *me?*
Call *me* a coward? Didn't I ask you for a sponge?
Nobody else would have dared do that.

XANTHIAS
What would they have done?

DIONYSOS
Laid there and stunk, that's what a good coward would have done.
I got to my feet again. What's more, united I stand.

36

XANTHIAS
That's manliness, by Poseidon.

DIONYSOS
Goodness gracious yes.

Long pause.
He talked so loud and said such awful things. Weren't you
a little scared?

XANTHIAS
Hell no, I never gave it a thought.

DIONYSOS
Well, tell you what. You win. I guess you're the hero-boy.
So you be me. Here you are. Here's the club, here's
the lion's skin.

Exchange going on.
You're the guy with the fearless guts.
I'll be you, and take my turn with the duffel bags.

XANTHIAS
*I cannot but obey thee.** Gimme. Hurry it up.
Exchange completed. Xanthias parades the stage.
Hey, look at me, everybody. I'm Xanthierakles.
Now see if I'm a sissy, like you.

DIONYSOS
You look like someone
who came from the same ward—but got rode out on a rail.
Well, there's the baggage. Suppose I've got to carry it.

A maid comes out of the door, and squeals with joy.

MAID
Why, *H*erakles! Darling, it's you! Come on inside.
When the Mistress* heard you might be around, she put the buns
in the oven, and lit the stove, and put the pots of beans
to cook, and, oh yes, barbecued you a steer, whole,
and there'll be cakes and cookies too. So come on in.

XANTHIAS
Thanks, it's awfully kind of you, but . . .

MAID
Hear me, Apollo,
I simply won't let you go away. Let's see, we were fixing
some roast chickens, and she was toasting the salted nuts

and mixing the wine—vintage stuff. Here, take my hand
and follow me in.

XANTHIAS
>Awfully nice, but . . .

MAID
>>Don't be so silly.
It's all yours, and I won't let you go. Oh, there's a flute-player-
girl waiting for you inside, she's lovely, and two or three
dancers, too, I believe.

XANTHIAS
>>What did you say? Dancing girls?

MAID
Pretty, just come to flower, all bathed and plucked for you.
Come on, come on, they were just putting the tables out,
and the cook was taking the hot dishes off the stove.

XANTHIAS
*Danc*ing girls! Dancing *girls!* Run on ahead, will you please
and tell those dancing girls of yours I'm coming right in.

Maid disappears.
>Boy, you pick up the baggage there, and follow me.

DIONYSOS
Hey, wait a minute. You didn't think I was serious,
did you, when I got you up as Herakles, for fun?
Xanthias, will you kindly stop being such an ass?
Here's your baggage again. Take it. It's all yours.

*During the following dialogue, the Chorus come
back on. They are no longer Initiates specifically,
but simply represent an ideal audience, the population of Hades.*

XANTHIAS
What is this, anyway? Are you thinking of taking back
What you gave me?

DIONYSOS
>>I'm not thinking of it, I'm doing it.
Give me that lionskin.

XANTHIAS
>>Witnesses! Make a note! I'll sue!
I'm putting this in the hands of my—uh—gods.

DIONYSOS

                                        What gods,
you stupid clown, thinking you could be Herakles
Alkmene's son, when you're human, and a slave at that.

XANTHIAS
Oh, the hell with it. Here, take it, take it.

Re-exchange.

                                        Maybe, though,
if God so wills, you'll find you need me after all.

CHORUS
There's an *adaptable* guy.
Must have been in the navy.
He's been around. He'll never get drowned.
Always knows where the gravy
is. The ships on her beam,
he's on the side that's dry.
He's got supersensory vision
like our glorious politician
Theramenes.* Just call him galosh
or any old boot you can easily put
on either your right- or your left-hand foot.

DIONYSOS
Here's what would have been funny.
Picture it like this.
Here's Xanthias and his honey
ready to kiss.
But he needs to go. Here's me,
and I hold the pot for him, see?
I make a pass at the girl's—well
anyway, he's on to me,
so he hauls off and socks
me one in the teeth, and knocks
the spots out of Attic Tragedy.

Hostess comes out the door.

HOSTESS
Plathane! Plathane! Come out, come out. Here's that awful man!
Remember the one who came to our hotel one time
and ate up sixteen loaves of our bread?

Plathane, the maid, emerges.

PLATHANE
                              Heavens yes
it's him, it's him.

XANTHIAS
                    Somebody's going to be sor-ry.

HOSTESS
That wasn't all. He made away with twenty pounds
of roast beef too.

XANTHIAS
                    Somebody's going to get hu-urt.

HOSTESS
And a lot of garlic.

DIONYSOS
                    Woman, you're crazy in the head.
You don't know what you're talking about.

HOSTESS
                                        I don't, don't I?
You thought I wouldn't know you in your tragic boots?
Well, what about it? I didn't even mention the herrings.

PLATHANE
You didn't even mention our poor white feta cheese.
He ate the lot, boxes and all.

HOSTESS
Then, when I asked him please if he would pay for it,
he just glared at me, fighting mad. He bellowed at me.

XANTHIAS
Yes, that's exactly like him. He always does like that.

HOSTESS
Pretended he was out of his mind, and pulled a sword.

PLATHANE
You poor thing, so he did.

HOSTESS
                              He frightened us girls so
we had to run away upstairs and hide.
He charged away. Took our rush mats along with him.

XANTHIAS
Yes, that's him all the way.

PLATHANE

Let's do something about it.

HOSTESS
Run and get us a dead Politician. Kleon* will do.

PLATHANE
Bring the whole subcommittee. Bring Hyperbolos.
We'll fix him, once for all.

HOSTESS

You horrid gourmet, you,
I'd like to take a rock to you and break those teeth
you ate me out of house and home with.

PLATHANE

And I'd like
to throw you in the ditch they bury criminals in.

HOSTESS
I'd like to find that carving knife you used
to cut our sausages up—and carve your neck with it.

PLATHANE
I'll go get Kleon. If we ask him he'll come today
and pull the stuffings out of this guy, bit by bit.

Women rush off. Long pause.

DIONYSOS
Dear Xanthias. How I love him. Wonder if he knows it.

XANTHIAS
I know what you're thinking about. You stop right there.
I will *not* be Herakles again.

DIONYSOS

Sweet little Xanthias
say not so.

XANTHIAS

Tell me, how can I be Herakles,
Alkmene's son, when I'm human, and a slave at that?

DIONYSOS
I know you're cross, my Xanthias. I don't blame you a bit.
You can even hit me if you want, I won't say a thing.
I tell you: If I ever make you change again
I hope to die, with my whole family: my wife:*
my kiddies:* throw in bleary Archedemos too.

XANTHIAS
I note your oath, and on these terms I will accept.

Re-exchange going on, Xanthias becoming Herakles.

CHORUS
Now you've got his costume on you.
Now you've got a reputation
to live up to. Better do
a transformation.
Remember the kind of god*
you're supposed to be.
Act accordingly
with masculinity.
Be rough and tough
or you'll be reduced to the bottom roost
and have to carry the stuff.

XANTHIAS
Gentlemen, you are not so
far off the mark, but, you know,
I thought of that too.
If it's anything bad this lovely lad
hands it to me: anything good
he'd take it back if he could.
I'll chew brave herbs* and I won't take fright,
so fight fight fight
for Xanthias. Yea!
And it's time for it, boys. I hear a noise.
The doors! Trouble coming this way.

*Aiakos rushes out, followed by two unprepossessing
assistants.*

AIAKOS
There's the dog-stealer. Get him, fellows, tie him up
and take him away. We'll fix him.

DIONYSOS

Somebody's going to be sor-ry.

*Xanthias waves the club of Herakles and holds
them off.*

XANTHIAS
The hell with you. Keep away from me.

AIAKOS

So you'll fight, will you?
Hey Ditylas hey Skeblyas hey Pardokos,
out here. Fight going on! Come along, give us a hand.

The reinforcements rush on.

DIONYSOS
Tut tut. Shocking, isn't it, the way this fellow
steals from you, then assaults you?

AIAKOS

He's too big for his boots.

DIONYSOS
Outrageous, shouldn't be allowed.

XANTHIAS

So help me Zeus
and hope to die if I ever was in this place before
or ever stole a hair's worth of goods that belonged to you.
Here, I'll make you a gentlemanly* proposition, my man.
Here's my slave-boy. Take him, put him to the torture;
then kill me, if you find I did anything wrong.

AIAKOS
What tortures?

XANTHIAS

Oh, try them all. Tie him on the ladder,
hang him up, beat him with a whip of bristles, take his skin off,
twist him on the rack, pour vinegar up his nose,
pile bricks on him. Just give him the works—only please excuse him
from anything gentle, like soft onion-whips, or leeks.*

AIAKOS
Why, fair enough. And if I hit your slave too hard
and cripple him—the damages will be paid to you.

XANTHIAS
Never mind paying me. Take him away and work on him.

AIAKOS
I'll do it right here, so he'll confess before your eyes.
Here, put that luggage down. Be quick about it. See that you don't
tell me any lies.

DIONYSOS
                    I protest. I'm warning everybody
not to torture me. I'm a god. If you touch me
you'll have yourself to blame.

AIAKOS
                                        What are you talking about?

DIONYSOS
I am immortal Dionysos, son of Zeus.
Pointing to Xanthias.
And *he*'s the slave.

AIAKOS
                        You hear that?

XANTHIAS
                                    Oh, I hear it. Sure.
That's all the better reason for him to get a whipping.
If he's really a god, he won't feel anything.

DIONYSOS
Well, you're claiming you're a god too. So what about it?
Shouldn't you get the same number of strokes as me?

XANTHIAS
That's fair enough too. Whip us both, and if you see
either of us paying any attention, or crying in pain
at what you're doing, you'll know that one isn't a god.

AIAKOS
You must be a gentleman. Can't be any doubt about it,
the way you love a trial scene. Well, strip, both of you.
Xanthias and Dionysos bare their backs.

XANTHIAS
How are you going to make this even?

AIAKOS

Picking up a whip.

Easy.
Hit one of you first and then the other, and so on.

XANTHIAS

Okay.

AIAKOS

Hitting him.

There!

XANTHIAS

And when you hit me, see if I move.

AIAKOS

I did hit you.

XANTHIAS

Like hell you did.

AIAKOS

Hm. Must have missed him.
Well, here goes for the other one.

Hits Dionysos.

DIONYSOS

When are you going to hit me?

AIAKOS

I did hit you already.

DIONYSOS

Oh? Why didn't I sneeze?
I do when I'm tickled.

AIAKOS

Dunno. Let's try this one again.

XANTHIAS

You supposed to be doing something?

Aiakos hits him.

Oh my gosh!

AIAKOS

My gosh?

That hurt, did it?

XANTHIAS

Nyet. Just thought of something. Time for my feast at Diomeia,* and the enemy won't let us hold it.

AIAKOS

The man's too religious. Can't get to him. Try the other one.

Hits Dionysos.

DIONYSOS

Wahoo!

AIAKOS

What's the matter?

DIONYSOS

There go the cavalry. That's their call.

AIAKOS

But there're tears in your eyes.

DIONYSOS

Got a whiff of their onion rations.

AIAKOS

Didn't feel anything?

DIONYSOS

Nothing that would bother me.

Aiakos goes back to Xanthias.

AIAKOS

I'd better go back to this one and try again.

Hits Xanthias.

XANTHIAS

Owoo!

AIAKOS

What's the matter?

Xanthias holds up his foot.

XANTHIAS

Take this thing out, will you? Thorn.

AIAKOS

Where am I getting to? Try this other one again.

Hits Dionysos.

DIONYSOS
*Apollo who art lord of Delos and Pytho.**

XANTHIAS
That hurt him! Didn't you hear?

DIONYSOS
                                    It did not. I was
simply going over a line of verse by Hipponax.

XANTHIAS
You aren't trying. Give him a good hard whack in the ribs.

AIAKOS
Thanks. Good idea. Here, turn your belly. That's the **way.**

Hits Dionysos in the belly.

DIONYSOS
Owoo Poseidon . . .

XANTHIAS
                            Somebody did get hurt that time.

DIONYSOS

Singing.

*Who dost hold sway
over Aigaion's promontories,
or in the depths of the sea's green waters.**

AIAKOS
Demeter. I can't tell
which of you two is a god. You'd better go on in.
The master will know who you are, anyway,
and Persephone the mistress. They're real gods, those two.

DIONYSOS

Struck.

                        You're absolutely right, only I wish you'd thought
of that first. Then you wouldn't have had to whack me.

*The principals enter the door, leaving the stage to
the Chorus.*

CHORUS
Muse of the holy choruses come to us, come, make all **enjoy my**
    music,
cast your eyes on this multitude of wits here seated
sharper than Kleophon,* that sharper, on whose **no-spik-Athenian**
    beak

mutters bad pidgin-Attic,
Thracian swallowbird he
perched on a barberry blackball bush
singing his mournful nightingale threnody, how he must hang, though
    the votes come out equal.

LEADER
It's the right and duty of our sacred chorus to determine
better courses for our city. Here's the first text of our sermon.
All the citizens should be equal, and their fears be taken away.*
All who once were tricked by Phrynichos, caught and held and led
    astray,
ought to be allowed to join the rest of us, who slipped away.
Amnesty. Let's all forgive them for mistakes made long ago.
Nobody in our community ought to lose his civic rights.
Isn't it unfair that, just for having been in one sea fight,
slaves should have Plataian status,* and be over men once free?
Please, I'm not against their freedom in itself. I quite agree.
They deserve it. That's the only thing you've done intelligently.
Still, there are those others, men who also often fought at sea,
by your side, whose fathers fought for us, akin by blood to you.
Let their one fault be forgotten. Let them know your mercy, too.
Oh, Athenians, wise beyond all other men, forget your rage;
any man who fights at sea beside us, let him be our friend,
take him as a citizen, honored kinsmen; let all hatred end.
Now our city fights the storm and struggles in the grip of the waves,
surely this is not the time for your old hard exclusive pride.
Some day, you'll regret it, if you leave unsaid the word that saves.

CHORUS
If I have true discrimination to judge a man and his sorrows to come,
not long will our current baboon be here to bother us.
That is little Kleigenes,*
cheapest of all the lords of the babble-whirlpool-bath where soap's
    without soda.
What they really use
is the clay of Kimolos.
He won't be around very long, and he knows it,
but he carries a club against robbers whenever he goes on one of his
    drunken strolls.

LEADER
We've been thinking much of late about the way the city treats
all the choicest souls among its citizens: it seems to be
like the recent coinage as compared with the old currency.*

We still have the ancient money: finest coins, I think, in Greece,
better than the coins of Asia; clink them, and they ring the bell,
truly fashioned, never phony, round and honest every piece.
Do we ever use it? We do not. We use this wretched brass,
last week's issue, badly minted, light and cheap and looks like hell.
Now compare the citizens. We have some stately gentlemen,
modest, anciently descended, proud and educated well
on the wrestling ground, men of distinction who have been to school.
These we outrage and reject, preferring any foreign fool,
redhead slave, or brassy clown or shyster. This is what we choose
to direct our city—immigrants. Once our city would not use
one of these as public scapegoat.* That was in the former days.
Now we love them. Think, you idiots. Turn about and change your
    ways.
Use our useful men. That will look best, in case of victory.
Hang we must, if we must hang; but let's hang from a handsome tree.
Cultured gentlemen should bear their sufferings with dignity.

Aiakos and Xanthias come out of the door.
Xanthias is in his slave's costume.

AIAKOS
This master of yours, by Zeus the savior, he's a man
of parts, a gentleman.

XANTHIAS
                        That's a logical conclusion
if trencherman plus wencherman means gentleman.

AIAKOS
But he didn't have you on the mat and beat you up
even when you said you were the master and he was the slave.

XANTHIAS
He'd have been sorry if he had.

AIAKOS
                        Good slavemanship
that. Well played. Exactly the way I like to do it.

XANTHIAS
Come again, please. You like what?

AIAKOS
                        Seeing myself in action
when *I* get off where he can't hear, and curse my master.

XANTHIAS
What about sneaking out of doors after a good beating
and muttering at your master?

AIAKOS
                                   I enjoy that too.

XANTHIAS
And poking into his business?

AIAKOS
                              Can you think of anything nicer?

XANTHIAS
My brother, by Zeus! How about listening at the keyhole
when masters are gossiping?

AIAKOS
                              Just about sends me crazy, man.

XANTHIAS
And spreading secrets you listened in on? Like that?

AIAKOS
                                             Who, me?
That's more than crazy, bud, that's super crazy plus.

XANTHIAS
Phoebus Apollo! You're one of us. Give me the grip,
and kiss me, and let me kiss you, and then tell me, please,
in the name of Zeus-of-the-slaves, who wears his stripes with us,
what's all this racket and yelling and screaming? What goes on
inside?

AIAKOS
        One's Aeschylus and one's Euripides.

XANTHIAS
Aha!

AIAKOS
Oh, it's a big business, it's a big business:
great fight among the corpses: this high argument.

XANTHIAS
What's it all about?

AIAKOS

We have a local custom here,
sort of award for literature and humanities,
and the one who wins top rating in the work he does
gets to eat dinner in the capitol and sits
in a chair next to Pluto, see?

XANTHIAS

I see.

AIAKOS

That's until somebody else comes along who's better
at it than he is. Then he has to move over.

XANTHIAS

I don't see
Aeschylus having anything to worry about.

AIAKOS

He held the Chair of Tragedy.
He was the best at writing them.

XANTHIAS

So who is now?

AIAKOS

Well, when Euripides came down, he exhibited
before the toughs, the sneak-thieves, and the pickpockets
and the safecrackers and the juvenile delinquents,
and there's a lot of that in Hades, and they listened
to his disputations and his wrigglings and his twists
and went crazy, and thought he was the cleverest writer.
That all went to his head, so he challenged for the chair
where Aeschylus was sitting.

XANTHIAS

Didn't they throw him out?

AIAKOS

They did not. The public cried out for a contest
to see which one really was better than the other.

XANTHIAS

You mean, the criminal public.

AIAKOS

Sure. They yelled to heaven.

XANTHIAS
But wasn't there anyone on the side of Aeschylus?

AIAKOS
Honesty's scarce. The same down here; the same up there.

XANTHIAS
Well, what's Pluto getting ready to do about it?

AIKOS
He's going to hold a contest, an event, that's what,
and judge their skills against each other.

XANTHIAS
                                        But how come
Sophocles didn't make a bid for the Tragic Chair?

AIAKOS
He never even tried to. When he came down here,
he walked up to Aeschylus, kissed him, and shook hands with him,
and gave up his claim on the chair, in favor of Aeschylus.
His idea, Kleidemidas* was telling me,
was to sit on the bench as substitute. If Aeschylus wins,
he'll stay where he is; if Aeschylus loses, then he means
to fight for his own art against Euripides.

XANTHIAS
So the thing's coming off?

AIAKOS
                        Zeus, yes, in just a little while,
and all the terrors of tragedy will be let loose.
They're going to have a scale to weigh the music on.

XANTHIAS
What's the idea of that? Short-changing tragedy?

AIAKOS
And they'll bring out their rulers and their angled rods,
and T-squares, the kind you fold.

XANTHIAS
                        Bricklayers' reunion?

AIAKOS
Wedges and calipers. You see, Euripides says
you have to wring the gist from tragedy, word by word.

XANTHIAS
I guess all this is making Aeschylus pretty mad.

AIAKOS
He lowered his head and glared, like a bull on the charge.

XANTHIAS
Who's going to judge this?

AIAKOS
                              That was sort of difficult.
They found the intellectuals pretty hard to find.
Aeschylus didn't go down so well with the Athenians.

XANTHIAS
Maybe he noticed most of them were bank robbers.

AIAKOS
Besides, he thought it was pretty silly for anyone
but poets to judge poets. Then your master came
along, and they handed it to him. He knows technique.
We'd better go inside. When the masters get excited,
you know what happens: screams and yells of pain—from us.

Aiakos and Xanthias go in the door.

CHORUS
Fearful shall be the spleen now of Thundermutter withinside
when the riptooth-sharpening he sees of his multiloquacious
antagonist to encounter him. Then shall ensue dread
eyewhirl of fury.

Horse-encrested phrases shall shock in helmtossing combat,
chariots collide in whelm of wreckage and splinter-flown action,
warrior beating off brain-crafted warrior's
cavalried speeches.

Bristling the hairy mane on his neck of self-grown horsehair
bellowing he shall blast the bolts from compacted joinery
banging plank by plank nailed sections of verse in
stormburst gigantic.

Next, mouthforged tormenter of versification, the slim-shaped
tongue unraveling to champ on the bit of malignance
wickedly shall chip and chop at its tropes, much
labor of lungwork.

Enter from the door Aeschylus and Euripides,
Dionysos, (in his proper costume, without the gear
of Herakles or Xanthias), and Pluto. The poets
stand one on each side of the stage. Three chairs
are placed. Pluto sits in the middle, Dionysos on his
right, and the chair on his left is empty.

EURIPIDES
I won't give up the chair, so stop trying to tell me to.
I tell you, I'm a better poet than he is.

DIONYSOS
You heard him, Aeschylus. Don't you have anything to say?

EURIPIDES
He's always started with the line of scornful silence.
He used to do it in his plays, to mystify us.

DIONYSOS
Now take care, Aeschylus. Don't be overconfident.

EURIPIDES
I know this man. I've studied him for a long time.
His verse is fiercely made, all full of sound and fury,
language unbridled uncontrolled ungated-in
untalkable-around, bundles of blast and boast.

AESCHYLUS
Is that so, child of the goddess of the cabbage patch?*
You, you jabber-compiler, you dead-beat poet,
you rag-stitcher-together, you say this to me?
Say it again. You'll be sorry.

DIONYSOS
                    Now, Aeschylus, stop it.
Don't in your passion boil your mortal coils in oil.

AESCHYLUS
I won't stop, until I've demonstrated in detail
what kind of one-legged poet this is who talks so big.

DIONYSOS
Black rams, black rams, boys, run and bring us black rams, quick.
Sacrifice to the hurricane. It's on the way.

AESCHYLUS

Why, you compiler of Cretan solo-arias,
you fouled our art by staging indecent marriages.

DIONYSOS

Most honorable Aeschylus, please stop right there.
And as for you, my poor Euripides, if you
have any sense, you'll take yourself out of the storm's way
before the hail breaks on your head in lines of wrath
and knocks it open, and your—*Telephos* oozes out—
your brains, you know. Now, gently, gently, Aeschylus,
criticize, don't yell. It's not becoming for two poets
and gentlemen to squabble like two baker's wives.
You're crackling like an oak log that's been set ablaze.

EURIPIDES

I'm ready for him. Don't try to make me back down.
I'll bite before I'm bitten, if that's what he wants,
with lines, with music, the gut-strings of tragedy,
with my best plays, with *Peleus* and with *Aiolos,*
with *Meleagros,* best of all, with *Telephos.*

DIONYSOS

All right, Aeschylus, tell us what you want to do.

AESCHYLUS

I would have preferred not to have the match down here.
It isn't fair. We don't start even.

DIONYSOS

                              What do you mean?

AESCHYLUS

I mean my poetry didn't die with me, but his
did die with him; so he'll have it here to quote. Still,
if this is your decision, then we'll have to do it.

DIONYSOS

All right, bring on the incense and the fire, while I
in the presence of these great intelligences pray
that I may judge this match most literarily.
You, chorus, meanwhile, sing an anthem to the Muses.

CHORUS

Daughters of Zeus, nine maidens immaculate,
Muses, patronesses of subtly spoken acute brains

of men, forgers of idiom, when to the contest they hasten, with care—
sharpened wrestling-hooks and holds for their disputations,
come, o Muses, to watch and bestow
potency on these mouths of magnificence,
figures and jigsaw patterns of words.
Now the great test of artistic ability goes into action.

DIONYSOS
Both of you two pray also, before you speak your lines.

AESCHYLUS

Putting incense on the fire.

Demeter, mistress, nurse of my intelligence,
grant me that I be worthy of thy mysteries.

DIONYSOS
Now you put your incense on, too.

EURIPIDES

Excuse me, please.
Quite other are the gods to whom I sacrifice.

DIONYSOS
You mean, you have private gods? New currency?

EURIPIDES

Yes, I have.

DIONYSOS
Go ahead, then, sacrifice to your private gods.

EURIPIDES
Bright upper air, my foodage! Socket of the tongue!
Oh, comprehension, sensory nostrils, oh
grant I be critical in all my arguments.

CHORUS
We're all eager to listen
to the two great wits debating
and stating
the luminous course of their wissen-
schaft. Speech bitter and wild,
tough hearts, nothing mild.
Neither is dull.
From one we'll get witty designs
polished and filed.

The other can pull
up trees by the roots for his use,
goes wild, cuts loose
stampedes of lines.

DIONYSOS
Get on with it, get on with it, and put your finest wit in all
you say, and be concrete, and be exact; and, be original.

EURIPIDES
I'll make my self-analysis a later ceremony
after having demonstrated that my rival is a phony.
His audience was a lot of louts and Phrynichus* was all they knew.
He gypped and cheated them with ease, and here's one thing he used
    to do.
He'd start with one veiled bundled muffled character plunked down
    in place,
Achilleus,* like, or Niobe, but nobody could see its face.
It looked like drama, sure, but not one syllable would it mutter.

DIONYSOS
By Jove, they didn't, and that's a fact.

EURIPIDES
                            The chorus then would utter
four huge concatenations of verse. The characters just sat there mum.

DIONYSOS
You know, I liked them quiet like that. I'd rather have them deaf and
    dumb
than yak yak yak the way they do.

EURIPIDES
                        That's because you're an idiot too.

DIONYSOS
Oh, by all means, and to be sure, and what was Aeschylus trying to do?

EURIPIDES
Phony effects. The audience sat and watched the panorama
breathlessly. *"When will Niobe speak?"* And that was half the drama.

DIONYSOS
It's the old shell game. I've been had. Aeschylus, why this agitation?
You're looking cross and at a loss.

EURIPIDES

He doesn't like investigation.
Then after a lot of stuff like this, and now the play was half-way
    through,
the character would grunt and moo a dozen cow-sized lines or two,
with beetling brows and hairy crests like voodoo goblins all got up,
incomprehensible, of course.

AESCHYLUS

You're killing me.

DIONYSOS

Will you shut up?

EURIPIDES

Not one word you could understand . . .

DIONYSOS

No, Aeschylus, don't grind
    your teeth . . .

EURIPIDES

. . . but battles of Skamandros, barbicans with ditches underneath,
and hooknosed eagles bronze-enwrought on shields, verse armed like
    infantry,
not altogether easy to make out the sense.

DIONYSOS

You're telling me?
Many a night I've lain awake and puzzled on a single word.
A fulvid roosterhorse is please exactly just what kind of bird?

AESCHYLUS

It was a symbol painted on the galleys, you illiterate block.

DIONYSOS

I thought it was Eryxis, our Philoxenos's fighting-cock.

EURIPIDES

Well, should a rooster—vulgah bird!—get into tragedy at all?

AESCHYLUS

Tell me of *your* creations, you free-thinker, if you have the gall.

EURIPIDES

No roosterhorses, bullmoosegoats, nor any of the millions
of monsters that the Medes and Persians paint on their pavilions.

When I took over our craft from you, I instantly became aware
that she was gassy from being stuffed with heavy text and noisy air,
so I eased her aches and reduced the swelling and took away the
    weights and heats
with neat conceits and tripping feets, with parsnips, radishes, and
    beets.
I gave her mashed and predigested baby-food strained from my books,
then fed her on solo-arias.

DIONYSOS

                  Kephisophon* had you in his hooks.

EURIPIDES

My openings were never confused or pitched at random. They were
    not
difficult. My first character would give the background of the plot
at once.

DIONYSOS

         That's better than giving away your personal background, eh,
what, what?

EURIPIDES

Then, from the opening lines, no person ever was left with nothing to
    do.
They all stepped up to speak their piece, the mistress spoke, the slave
    spoke too,
the master spoke, the daughter spoke, and grandma spoke.

AESCHYLUS

                          And tell me
    why
you shouldn't be hanged for daring that.

EURIPIDES

                     No, cross my heart and hope
    to die,
I made the drama *democratic*.

DIONYSOS

To Aeschylus.

                You'd better let that one pass, old sport;
you never were such a shining light in that particular line of thought.*

EURIPIDES
Then I taught natural conversational dialogue.

AESCHYLUS

                            I'll say you did.
And before you ever taught them that, I wish you could have split in
    middle.

EURIPIDES

Going right on.

Taught them delicate tests and verbalized commensuration,
and squint and fraud and guess and god and loving application,
and always how to think the worst of everything.

AESCHYLUS

                              So I believe.

EURIPIDES

I staged the life of everyday, the way we live. I couldn't deceive
my audience with the sort of stuff they knew as much about as I.
They would have spotted me right away. I played it straight and
    didn't try
to bind a verbal spell and hypnotize and lead them by the nose
with Memnons and with Kyknoses with rings on their fingers and bells
    on their toes.
Judge both of us by our influence on followers. Give him Manes,
Phormisios* and Megainetos and sundry creeps and zanies,
the big moustachio bugleboys, the pinetreebenders twelve feet high,
but Kleitophon is mine, and so's Theramenes, a clever guy.

DIONYSOS

I'll grant your Theramenes. Falls in a puddle and comes out dry.
The man is quick and very slick, a true Euripidean.
When Chians are in trouble he's no Chian, he's a Keian.

EURIPIDES

So that's what my plays are about,
and these are my contributions,
and I turn everything inside out
looking for new solutions
to the problems of today,
always critical, giving
suggestions for gracious living,
and they come away from seeing a play
in a questioning mood, with "where are we at?,"
and "who's got my this?," and "who took my that?."

DIONYSOS

So now the Athenian hears a pome
of yours, and watch him come stomping home
to yell at his servants every one:
"where oh where are my pitchers gone?—
where is the maid who hath betrayed
my heads of fish to the garbage trade?
Where are the pots of yesteryear?
Where's the garlic of yesterday?
Who hath ravished my oil away?"
Formerly they sat like hicks
fresh out of the sticks
with their jaws hung down in a witless way.

CHORUS

To Aeschylus.

See you this, glorious
Achilleus?* What have you got to say?
Don't let your rage
sweep you away,
or you'll never be victorious.
This cynical sage
hits hard. Mind the controls.
Don't lead with your chin.
Take skysails in.
Scud under bare poles.
Easy now. Keep him full in your sights.
When the wind falls, watch him,
then catch him
dead to rights.

DIONYSOS

O mighty-mouthed inventor of harmonies, grand old bulwark ot
balderdash,
frontispiece of Hellenic tragedy, open the faucets and let 'er splash.

AESCHYLUS

The whole business gives me a pain in the middle, my rage and
resentment are heated
at the idea of having to argue with *him*. But so he can't say I'm
defeated,
here, answer me, you. What's the poet's duty, and why is the poet
respected?

63

EURIPIDES

Because he can write, and because he can think, but mostly because he's injected
some virtue into the body politic.

AESCHYLUS

                      What if you've broken your trust,
and corrupted good sound right-thinking people and filled them with
    treacherous lust?
If poets do that, what reward should they get?

DIONYSOS

                             The axe. That's what
    we should do with 'em.

AESCHYLUS

Then think of the people *I* gave him, and think of the people when he
    got through with 'em.
I left him a lot of heroic six-footers, a grand generation of heroes,
unlike our new crop of street-corner loafers and gangsters and
    decadent queer-os.
Mine snorted the spirit of spears and splendor, of white-plumed
    helmets and stricken fields,
of warrior heroes in shining armor and greaves and sevenfold-oxhide
    shields.

DIONYSOS

And that's a disease that never dies out. The munition-makers will
    kill me.

EURIPIDES

Just what did you do to make them so noble? Is that what you're
    trying to tell me?

DIONYSOS

Well, answer him, Aeschylus, don't withdraw into injured dignity.
    That don't go.

AESCHYLUS

I made them a martial drama.

DIONYSOS

                     Which?

AESCHYLUS

Seven Against Thebes, if you want to know.
Any man in an audience sitting through that would aspire to heroic endeavor.

DIONYSOS

That was a mistake, man. Why did you make the Thebans more warlike than ever
and harder to fight with? By every right it should mean a good beating for you.

AESCHYLUS

To the audience.

Well, *you* could have practiced austerity too. It's exactly what *you* wouldn't *do.*
Then I put on my *Persians,** and anyone witnessing that would promptly be smitten
with longing for victory over the enemy. Best play I ever have written.

DIONYSOS

Oh, yes, I loved that, and I thrilled where I sat when I heard old Dareios was dead
and the chorus cried "wahoo" and clapped with their hands. I tell you, it went to my head.

AESCHYLUS

There, there is work for poets who also are MEN. From the earliest times
incitement to virtue and useful knowledge have come from the makers of rhymes.
There was Orpheus first. He preached against murder, and showed us the heavenly way.
Musaeus taught divination and medicine; Hesiod, the day-after-day
cultivation of fields, the seasons, and plowings. Then Homer, divinely inspired,
is a source of indoctrination to virtue. Why else is he justly admired
than for teaching how heroes armed them for battle?

DIONYSOS

He didn't teach Pantakles, though.
He can't get it right. I watched him last night. He was called to parade, don't you know,

and he put on his helmet and tried to tie on the plume when the
   helm was on top of his head.

AESCHYLUS

Ah, many have been my heroic disciples; the last of them, Lamachos
   (recently dead).
The man in the street simply has to catch something from all my
   heroics and braveries.
My Teucers and lion-hearted Patrokloses lift him right out of his
   knaveries
and make him thrill to the glory of war and spring to the sound of the
   trumpet.
But I never regaled you with Phaidra* the floozie—or Sthenoboia* the
   strumpet.
I think I can say that a lovesick woman has never been pictured by me.

EURIPIDES

Aphrodite never did notice you much.

AESCHYLUS

                              Aphrodite can go climb a tree.
But you'll never have to complain that she didn't bestow her attentions
   on you.
She got you in person, didn't she?

DIONYSOS

                              Yes, she did, and your stories came
   true.
The fictitious chickens came home to roost.

EURIPIDES

                              But tell me, o man with-
   out pity:
suppose I did write about Sthenoboia. What harm has she done to
   our city?

AESCHYLUS

Bellerophon-intrigues, as given by you, have caused the respectable
   wives
of respectable men, in shame and confusion, to do away with their
   lives.

EURIPIDES

But isn't my story of Phaidra a story that really has happened?

AESCHYLUS

So be it.

It's true. But the poet should cover up scandal, and not let anyone
    see it.
He shouldn't exhibit it out on the stage. For the little boys have
    their teachers
to show them example, but when they grow up we poets must act as
    their preachers,
and what we preach should be useful and good.

EURIPIDES

But you, with your
    massive construction,
huge words and mountainous phrases, is that what you call useful in-
    struction?
You ought to make people talk like people.

AESCHYLUS

Your folksy style's for the
    birds.
For magnificent thoughts and magnificent fancies, we must have
    magnificent words.
It's appropriate too for the demigods of heroic times to talk bigger
than we. It goes with their representation as grander in costume and
    figure.
I set them a standard of purity. You've corrupted it.

EURIPIDES

How did I do it?

AESCHYLUS

By showing a royal man in a costume of rags, with his skin showing
    through it.
You played on emotions.

EURIPIDES

But why should it be so wrong to awaken
    their pity?

AESCHYLUS

The rich men won't contribute for warships.* You can't find
    one in the city
who's willing to give. He appears in his rags, and howls, and com-
    plains that he's broke.

68

DIONYSOS

But he always has soft and expensive underwear under the beggarman's cloak.
The liar's so rich and he eats so much that he has to feed some to the
fishes.

AESCHYLUS

You've taught the young man to be disputatious. Each argues as
long as he wishes.
You've emptied the wrestling yards of wrestlers. They all sit around
on their fannies
and listen to adolescent debates. The sailormen gossip like grannies
and question their officers' orders. In my time, all that they knew
how to do
was to holler for rations, and sing "yeo-ho," and row, with the rest
of the crew.

DIONYSOS

And blast in the face of the man behind, that's another thing too
that they knew how to do.
And how to steal from the mess at sea, and how to be robbers ashore.
But now they argue their orders. We just can't send them to sea any
more.

AESCHYLUS

That's what he's begun. What hasn't he done?
His nurses go propositioning others.
His heroines have their babies in church
or sleep with their brothers
or go around murmuring: *"Is* life life?"*
So our city is rife
with the clerk and the jerk,
the altar-baboon, the political ape,
and our physical fitness is now a disgrace
with nobody in shape
to carry a torch in a race.

DIONYSOS

By Zeus, you're right. I laughed till I cried
at the Panathenaia* a while ago,
as the torch-relay-runners went by.
Here comes this guy;
he was puffed, he was slow,
he was white, he was fat,
he was left behind,

and he didn't know where he was at,
and the pottery works gang
stood at the gates to give him a bang
in the gut and the groin and the ribs and the rump
till the poor fellow, harried
by one cruel thump
exploded his inward air
and blew out the flare that he carried.

CHORUS
Great is this action, bitter the spite, the situation is ripe for war.
How shall the onlooker judge between them?
One is a wrestler strong and rough;
quick the other one, deft in defensive throws and the back-heel stuff.
Up from your places! Into the ring again!
Wit must wrestle wit once more in fall upon fall.
Fight him, wrestle him, throw the book at him,
talk at him, sit on him, skin him alive,
old tricks, new tricks, give him the works.
This is the great debate for the championship. Hazard all.

Never hold back any attack for fear you may not be understood.
You have an audience who can follow you,
don't be afraid of being too difficult.
That could once have happened, but now we've changed all that.
  They're good
and they're armed for action. Everyone's holding
his little book, so he can follow the subtle allusions.*
Athenian playgoers, best in the world,
bright and sharp and ready for games
waiting for you to begin.
Here's your sophisticated audience. Play it to win.

EURIPIDES
All right, I'll work on your prologues first of all, because
they come at the beginning of every tragedy.
I'll analyse this great man's prologues. Did you know
how murky you were in getting your action under way?

DIONYSOS
How are you going to analyse them?

EURIPIDES
                              Lots of ways.
First, read me the beginning of your *Oresteia.**

DIONYSOS
Silence all. Let no man speak. Aeschylus, read.

AESCHYLUS
Hermes, lord of the dead, who watch over the powers
of my father, be my savior and stand by my claim.
*I have come back to my own soil. I have returned.**

DIONYSOS
Find any mistakes there?

EURIPIDES
                              Yes, a dozen. Maybe more.

DIONYSOS
Why, man, the whole passage is only three lines.

EURIPIDES
But each of them has twenty things wrong with it.
Aeschylus growls.

DIONYSOS
Aeschylus, as counsel I advise you: keep quiet,
or you'll be mulcted, three lines of blank verse, plus costs.

AESCHYLUS
I have to keep quiet for *him?*

DIONYSOS
                              That's my advice to you.

EURIPIDES
He made one colossal howler, right at the beginning.

AESCHYLUS
To Dionysos
Hear that? *You*'re crazy.

DIONYSOS
                              Fact has never bothered me much.

AESCHYLUS
What kind of mistake?

EURIPIDES
                    Take it again from the beginning.

AESCHYLUS
Hermes, lord of the dead, who watch over the powers

EURIPIDES
Well, look, you've got Orestes saying this over the tomb
of his father, and his father's dead. That right?

AESCHYLUS
That's right.

EURIPIDES
Let's get this straight. Here is where his father was killed,
murdered in fact, by his own wife, in a treacherous plot.
You make him say Hermes is *watching over* this.

AESCHYLUS
I don't mean the Hermes you mean. He was talking to
the Kindly Hermes of the world below. He made that clear
when he said he was keeping his inheritance for him.

EURIPIDES
Why that's a bigger and better blunder than I hoped.
It makes his inheritance an underworld property.

DIONYSOS
Orestes then would have to rob his father's grave?

AESCHYLUS
Dionysos, the wine you're drinking has bouquet. It stinks.

DIONYSOS
Read the next line. Watch for errors, Euripides.

AESCHYLUS
of my father, be my savior and stand by my claim.
I have come back to my own soil. I have returned.

EURIPIDES
Ha! The great Aeschylus has said the same thing twice.

DIONYSOS
Twice,   how?

EURIPIDES
Look at the sentence. Or better, I'll show you.
I have come back, he says, but also *I have returned.*
I have come back means the same as *I have returned.*

DIONYSOS
You're right, by golly. It's like saying to your neighbor:
"Lend me your kneading-trough, your trough to knead things in."

AESCHYLUS
You two jabberwocks, it is not the same thing at all.
The diction's excellent.

EURIPIDES
Show me. Tell me what you mean, will you, please.

AESCHYLUS
Come back just means getting back home again, arrival
without further context. If he gets there, he arrives.
The exile arriving *comes back;* but he also *returns.*

DIONYSOS
That's good, by god. What do you say, Euripides?

EURIPIDES
I say Orestes didn't *return,* if *returned* means
restored. It wasn't formal. He sneaked past the guards.

DIONYSOS
By god, that's good. (Except I don't know what you mean.)

EURIPIDES
Go on. Next line.

DIONYSOS
                    Yes, Aeschylus, better go on.
Keep at it. You, keep watching for anything wrong.

AESCHYLUS
And by this mounded gravebank I invoke my sire
to hear, to listen. . . .

EURIPIDES
                    Saying the same thing twice again.
To hear, to listen. Same thing twice. Perfectly clear.

DIONYSOS
Of course, you fool, he has to; he's talking to the dead.
We call to them three times,* and still we don't get through.

AESCHYLUS
How do you make *your* prologues, then?

EURIPIDES

I'll give you some,
and if you catch me saying the same thing twice, or padding
my lines, without adding to the sense—spit in my eye.

DIONYSOS

Speak us some lines then, speak them. There's nothing else for it
than to listen to your prologues and criticize the verse.

EURIPIDES

*Oedipus at the outset was a fortunate man . . .***

AESCHYLUS

By god, he was not. He was most *un*fortunate
from birth. Before birth, since Apollo prophesied
before he was even begotten, that he would kill his father.
How could he have been, at the outset, *fortunate?*

EURIPIDES

. . . But then he became the wretchedest of humankind.

AESCHYLUS

He didn't *become* the wretchedest. He never stopped.
Look here. First thing that happened after he was born
they put him in a broken pot and laid him out in the snow
so he'd never grow up to be his father's murderer.
Then he went to Polybus, with sore feet, wasn't that luck?
and then he married an old lady, though he was young,
and also the old lady turned out to be his mother,
and then he blinded himself . . .

DIONYSOS

That would have saved his life
if he'd been a general along with Erasinides.*

EURIPIDES

You're crazy. The prologues that I write are very fine.

AESCHYLUS

By Zeus! I'm not going to savor you, word by word
and line by line, like you, but, with the help of the gods,
I'll ruin your prologues with a little bottle of oil.

EURIPIDES

Ruin my prologues with a bottle of oil?

AESCHYLUS

> Just one
bundle of fleece or *bottle of oil* or *packet of goods.*
The way you write iambics, always there's just room
for a phrase the length of one of those. I'll demonstrate.

EURIPIDES

Demonstrate? Poof.

AESCHYLUS

> I say I can.

DIONYSOS

> Read us a line.

EURIPIDES

Aigyptos, as the common tale disseminates,
with all his sea-armada and his fifty sons
*coming to Argos**

AESCHYLUS

> lost his little bottle of oil.*

DIONYSOS

A naughty little bottle. It'll be spanked for that.
Give us another line, I want to see what happens.

EURIPIDES

Dionysos, who, with thrysos and in hides of fawns
appareled on Parnassos up among the pines
*dances on light feet**

AESCHYLUS

> lost his little bottle of oil.

DIONYSOS

*Ah me, again, I am struck again,** with a bottle of oil.

EURIPIDES

He hasn't done much to me; here's another prologue
I'll give him, where he can't tag on his bottle of oil.
There's been no man who's had good fortune all his days.
For one was born to fortune, but his goods are gone.
*One, born unhappy**

AESCHYLUS

> lost his little bottle of oil.

DIONYSOS
Euripides.

EURIPIDES
What?

DIONYSOS
Maybe you'd better strike your sails.
That little bottle of oil is blowing up a storm.

EURIPIDES
Demeter be my witness, it doesn't mean a thing.
Here comes a line to smash his little—uh—property.

DIONYSOS
Go ahead, read another, but look out for that bottle.

EURIPIDES
*Kadmos, son of Agenor, once upon a time
sailing from Sidon**

AESCHYLUS
lost his little bottle of oil.

DIONYSOS
My poor dear friend, you'd better buy that bottle of oil
or it'll chew up all our prologues.

EURIPIDES
You mean that?
You're saying *I* should buy from *him?*

DIONYSOS
That's my advice.

EURIPIDES
I refuse to do it. I have lots of prologues left
where he can't tag on any little bottle of oil.
*Pelops the son of Tantalos reaching Pisa plain
with his swift horses**

AESCHYLUS
lost his little bottle of oil.

DIONYSOS
You see? Once more he makes the little bottle fit.
Now be a good fellow. It isn't too late yet, buy one quick.
For only a quarter you can get one, nice and new.

EURIPIDES

Not yet, by god, not yet. I still have plenty left.
*Oineus, from his land**

AESCHYLUS

lost his little bottle of oil.

EURIPIDES

Hey, wait a minute. Let me get a whole line out.
*Oineus from his land choosing out a store of grain
and sacrificing*

AESCHYLUS

lost his little bottle of oil.

DIONYSOS

In the middle of his sacrifice? Who found it for him?

EURIPIDES

Let me alone, please. See what he can say to this:
*Zeus, as the most authentic version hath maintained . . .**

DIONYSOS

He'll do you in. Zeus lost his little bottle of oil.
That bottle of oil is in your prologues everywhere
and multiplies like scabs of sickness in the eyes.
For god's sake, change the subject to his lyric lines.

EURIPIDES

Good idea. I've plenty of material to show
he's a bad lyric poet. It all sounds alike.

CHORUS

What can be the meaning of that?
Think as I will, I can not conceive
any thing he can say
against the man who can boast
the loveliest lyrics and the most
of any until today.
Much I wonder, what charge he can make
good against the great master
of tragic verse. He courts disaster.
I fear for his sake.

EURIPIDES

Wonder is right, if you mean his prosody. You'll see.
One little cut, and his metres all come out the same.

DIONYSOS

The same? Give me a handful of pebbles. I'll keep count.

Flute music off.

EURIPIDES

Phthian A - chilleus as you hear in the slaughter of heroes
   oho what a stroke come you not to the rescue?*
Hermes ances - tral, oh how we honor you, we of the lakeside*
   oho what a stroke come you not to the rescue?

DIONYSOS

There's two strokes scored against you, Aeschylus.

EURIPIDES

Greatest Achaian, At - reus son who art lord over multitudes hear
 me*

    oho what a stroke come you not to the
    rescue?

DIONYSOS

Another stroke, dear Aeschylus. That makes the third.

EURIPIDES

Quiet, all. O bee-keepers - now open the temple of Artemis nearby*
    oho what a stroke come you not to the
    rescue?
  I am enabled - to sing of the prodigy shown at the way-
  side*

    oho what a stroke come you not to the
    rescue?

DIONYSOS

Oh what a mess of strokes, lord Zeus, I'm on the ropes.
Stroke upon stroke has got my kidneys black and blue.
I think I'd better go and take a soothing bath.

EURIPIDES

Wait till you've listened to my next melodic line-up.
We will now take up the music written for the lyre.

DIONYSOS

Go ahead. But leave the strokes out, will you please.

EURIPIDES

How the twin-throned — power of Achaia and manhood of Hellas*
   di tum di tum di tum di tum
  Sends forth the — sphinx who is princess of ominous hell-
  hounds*
   di tum di tum di tum di tum

> *hand on the — spear and embattled, the bird of encounter**
> di tum di tum di tum di tum
> *giving assault — there to the hovering hounds of the air-*
> *ways**
> di tum di tum di tum di tum.

DIONYSOS

Where did you get this tum diddy stuff? From Marathon?*
It sounds like water-pulling-from-the-well-up music.

AESCHYLUS

My source is excellent, if that's what you mean, the result
excellent too. I only tried not to be seen
reaping the same Muse-meadow Phrynichos had reaped.
But this man draws from every kind of source, burlesque,
Meletos'* drinking-ditties, all that Karian jazz,
dirges, folksongs. Here, let me show you. Bring me a lyre
somebody. Wait! No, don't. What's the use of a lyre
for this stuff? Where's that girl who uses oyster shells
for castanets? Hither, Euripidean Muse.

*A scantily clad girl comes on. Aeschylus bows to her
with mock ceremony.*

To thee, onlie begetter of these melodies.

DIONYSOS

So that's the Tenth Muse is it? Well, she ain't no Sappho.
That's a man's woman if I ever saw one.*

AESCHYLUS

*Halycon-birds who in the sea's ever-streaming**
billows twittering
dabble wings in the flying spray
dipping and ducking feathery forms:
you in the angles under the roof
finger-wee-hee-heeving embattled
handiwork of your woof-warp-webs,
singing shuttle's endeavor
where the flute-loving dolphin leaps
next the cutwater's darkened edge
oracular in her pastures,
gleam and joy of the grapevine
where clusters of heart's ease curl and cling.
Circle me in your arms, o my child.

Breaking off in disgust.

Just look at that line.

DIONYSOS

     I'm looking.

AESCHYLUS

And look at *that* one.

DIONYSOS

     I'm looking.

AESCHYLUS

And you the writer of lines like that
dare to say that my verse is bad.
Yours is made like a whore displayed
in all the amorous postures.

So much for your choral metres. Now I'll demonstrate
the composition of your lyric monodies.*

O darkness of night, shining
in gloom, what vision of dream
bring you poor me
fished from the occult depths,
envoy of Hades
spiritless spirit possessing,
child of the sable night,
ghastly grim apparition
in dark trappings of death
and bloodily bloodily glaring,
and her nails were long they were long.
Help me, my handmaidens, light up the lanterns and
run with your pitchers and fetch from the river and heat up the water
that I may wash this vision from me.

O spirit of the sea
that was it. Heigh-ho housemates
behold, here are portents.
Glyke has stolen my rooster away,
and lo, she is gone.
O ye nymphs of the mountains,
Mania, arrest her.

Soft you now. I was sitting
plying my humble tasks
at the loom filled with its flax
wee-hee-hee-hee-hee-hee-heeving
with my hands, spinning a veil

so I could take it at dawn
to market to market it there,
and he fluttered he fluttered away
on gossamer wings to the air
and sorrows sorrows he left me
and tears tears from my eyes
I shed I shed. Poor me.

But o Kretans, nurselings of Ida,
seize your bows and come to aid me,
prithee, shake your leaping legs and surround me the house,
with you Diktynna, and Artemis—pretty child—
holding her puppies in leash let her search the premises,
and you, Zeus' daughter, in both hands upholding
your brightest twin torches, appear, o Hekate,
at Glyke's house, that I may
get her with the goods. (My ravishéd rooster.)

DIONYSOS
That will be all for the lyric verse.

AESCHYLUS
                              I've had enough.
I want to bring him out and put him to the scales,
for that alone will show our poetry's true weight.
Weigh phrase with phrase, for their specific gravity.

DIONYSOS
Bring out the scales then, if my duty is to judge
two master poets like a grocer selling cheese.

CHORUS
Devious is the great intellect.
Here is a portent of poetry
beyond what anyone could expect.
Who could have thought of this, but he?
Had anyone else proceeded
to such invention
I would have said he needed
medical attention.

*Scales are brought. As each poet speaks one of the
lines of verse, he drops, I think, a scrap of papyrus
into the scale pan.*

DIONYSOS
Now take your places by the weighing pans.

AESCHYLUS AND EURIPIDES

Ready.

DIONYSOS
Each of you hold his line while he is speaking it.
Don't drop it in the pan until I say "cuckoo."

AESCHYLUS AND EURIPIDES
We have them.

DIONYSOS

Say and lay a line upon the scale.

EURIPIDES
*I wish the Argo's hull had never winged her way.**

AESCHYLUS
*River Spercheios with your cattle-pastures near.**

DIONYSOS
Cuckoo! Let go.
The slips drop, and the scale of Aeschylus descends.

Aha. The scale of Aeschylus
is far the heavier.

EURIPIDES

What can be the cause of that?

DIONYSOS
He put a river in it, the wool-merchant's trick,
and soaked his words in water as they do their wool.
But you put in a winged word, a feathery line.

EURIPIDES
Have him speak another one. Match us again.

DIONYSOS
Take your next lines.

AESCHYLUS AND EURIPIDES

We're ready.

DIONYSOS

Speak them.

Same business as before.

EURIPIDES
*Persuasion has no shrine except within the word.**

AESCHYLUS
*Death is the only god who is not moved by gifts.**

DIONYSOS
Let go, let go. Aeschylus has the weight again.
He put Death in. There's nothing more *depressing* than that.

EURIPIDES
But I put in Persuasion. That's a handsome word.

DIONYSOS
Persuasion she's a scatterbrain, a featherweight.
Better see if you can't turn up a heavier line,
something massive and bulky, that will give you heft.

*Euripides frantically rummages through a pile of
papers, muttering to himself.*

EURIPIDES
Now where on earth did I put my lines like that?

DIONYSOS
                                                    Here's one.
"Achilleus threw the dice, and shot a deuce and a four."
All right, ready with your lines. This is the final test.

EURIPIDES
*His right hand seized the spear heavily shod with steel.**

AESCHYLUS
*Chariot piled on chariot and corpse on corpse.**

DIONYSOS
Aeschylus fooled you again.

EURIPIDES
                            How?

DIONYSOS
Threw in a couple of chariots and two dead men.
A hundred Egyptian coolies couldn't lift that load.

AESCHYLUS
Don't do it line by line, now. Let him climb in the scale
with his children and his wife, I mean Kephisophon,
and all his books, and hold them in his lap. I'll speak
only two lines of verse, and still I'll sink the scale.

DIONYSOS
Gentlemen, my friends. I can not judge them any more.
I must not lose the love of either one of them.
One of them's a great poet. I like the other one.

PLUTO
You mean, you won't do what you came down here to do?

DIONYSOS
And if I do decide?

PLUTO
                    Then take the one you want
and go; we must not let your journey be in vain.

DIONYSOS
To Pluto.
                    Bless your heart.
To the poets.
                              Very well, then. Answer me this.
I came down here to get a poet. Why? To help
our city survive, so it can stage my choruses.
The one of you who has the best advice to give
for saving the city is the one that I'll take back.
Alkibiades is a baby who's giving
our state delivery-pains. What shall we do with him?
That's the first question.

EURIPIDES
                    How does the state feel about him?

DIONYSOS
It longs for him, it hates him, and it wants him back.
Speak your minds both, and tell us what we are to do.

EURIPIDES
I hate the citizen who, by nature well endowed,
is slow to help his city, swift to do her harm,
to himself useful, useless to the community.

DIONYSOS
Good   answer,   by   Poseidon.
To Aeschylus.
                    Now, what about you?

AESCHYLUS
We should not rear a lion's cub within the state.
[Lions are lords. We should not have them here at all.]*
But if we rear one, we must do as it desires.

DIONYSOS
By Zeus the Savior, I still can't make up my mind.
One answer was so clever. The other was so clear.
Give me one more opinion, each of you.
How can we save the city?

EURIPIDES
Give Kleokritos Kinesias* to serve as wings;
let him be airborne over the vast sea's expanse.

DIONYSOS
Well, that would be amusing. Would there be some point?

EURIPIDES
They could be armed with vinegar-jars, and bomb
the enemy at sea with vinegar in their eyes.
Embarrassed pause.
No, really, I do know what to do. Let me speak.

DIONYSOS
                                                          Speak.

EURIPIDES
When that we trust not now, we trust, and trust no more
what now we do trust—we shall win.

DIONYSOS
                                        How's that again?
Please be a bit more stupid, so I'll understand.

EURIPIDES
If we mistrust those citizens whom now we trust,
and use those citizens whom we do not use now,
we might be saved.
If we are losing using what we use, will it
not follow we might win by doing the opposite?

DIONYSOS
Ingenious, o my Palamedes, soul of wit.
Did you think that up yourself, or was it Kephisophon?

EURIPIDES
All by myself. The vinegar was Kephisophon.

DIONYSOS
Well, Aeschylus, what is your view?

AESCHYLUS
                                          First tell me this.
Which men *is* Athens using? Her best?

DIONYSOS
                              Her best? Where've *you* been?
She hates them like poison.

AESCHYLUS
                        Does she really like her worst men?

DIONYSOS
She doesn't *like* them. Uses them because she has to.

AESCHYLUS
How can you pull a city like that out of the water
when neither the fine mantle nor coarse cloak will serve?*

DIONYSOS
Better find something, or she'll sink and never come up.

AESCHYLUS
I'd rather tell you up there. I don't want to down here.

DIONYSOS
Oh please, yes. Send your blessings up from underground.

AESCHYLUS
They shall win—
when they think of their land as if it were their enemies',
and think of their enemies' land as if it were their own,
that ships are all their wealth, and all their wealth, despair.

DIONYSOS
Good! But the jurymen will eat up all that wealth.

PLUTO
Decide.

DIONYSOS
        Out of their own mouths have they spoken it.
For I shall choose the poet that my soul desires.

EURIPIDES
Do not forget the vows you swore by all the gods,
to take me home with you. Choose him who loves you best.

DIONYSOS
*My tongue swore, not my heart.** I'm taking Aeschylus.

EURIPIDES
Can you do this, and look me in the face for shame?

DIONYSOS
*What's shameful?—unless it seems so to the audience?**

EURIPIDES
And wilt thou leave me thus for dead? Say nay, say nay.

DIONYSOS
*Who knows if life be death indeed or death be life,**
or breath be breakfast, sleep in fleece be comforter?

PLUTO
Go all inside now, Dionysos.

DIONYSOS
                              Why, what for?

PLUTO
So I can feast you before you sail away.

DIONYSOS
                                        Good news.
I am not discontented with my morning's work.

CHORUS
Blessed he
who has such wisdom and wit.
Many can learn from it.
Through good counsel he won the right
to return home again
for the good of the cause and state,
for the good of his fellow men,
to help them fight the good fight
with his great brain.

Better not to sit at the feet
of Sokrates* and chatter,
nor cast out of the heart
the high serious matter
of tragic art.
Better not to compete
in the no-good lazy
Sokratic dialogue.
Man, that *is* crazy.

PLUTO
Go forth rejoicing, Aeschylus, go,
save us our city
by your good sense and integrity.
Instruct the foolish majority.
Here is a rope to give Kleophon,
here's one for the revenuers,
Myrmex and Nikomachos,
this for Archenomos,*
tell them their hour
has come; they are waited for here, today,
and if they delay
I, in person, will go brand them, sting them,
sling them each in a thong
and bring them
here to Hades', where they belong.

AESCHYLUS
All this I will do. Here is my Chair
of Tragedy. Give it to Sophocles there
to keep for me until I come down
once more, for I judge him to be
the greatest of poets—after me.
But mind: never give My Chair
over to the vile uses
of this pseudo-poet, this lying clown.
Not even if he refuses.

PLUTO
Torches, this way.
With holy illumination light him
and with his own songs and dances delight him
as you escort him away.

CHORUS

First, o divinities under the ground indwelling, we pray you,
grant fair journey to the poet as he goes back to the daylight:
grant him success in all the thoughts that will prosper our city.
So at last may we find surcease from sorrows we suffer
through war's encounters. Let Kleophon and all similar aliens
who love to fight go home and fight—in the lands of their fathers.

Notes

page 7. *Phrynichos, Lykis, Ameipsias:* Comic poets, rivals of Aristophanes.

8. *sea battle:* The battle of Arginousai, fought in 406 B.C., the summer before this play. Slaves were then used in the Athenian navy for the first time, and these slaves were set free after the victory.

11. *Kleisthenes:* Aristophanes makes him a synonym for effeminacy and homosexuality throughout his plays (see also page 34 in this play) and uses him as a character in *The Thesmophoriazusae.*

11. *Molon:* An actor apparently, who was either very little or very large.

12. *For some . . . are bad:* From the lost *Oeneus* of Euripides.

13. *Iophon:* The son of Sophocles. The point here and in the following lines was that the younger man had been helped by his father.

13. *Agathon:* A tragic poet whose works are lost but who had a good reputation as a poet and seems to have been personally very well liked. There are portraits of him in Plato's *Symposium* and Aristophanes' *Thesmophoriazusae,* and though the latter teases him for a ladylike manner and appearance, the teasing is done without Aristophanes' usual cruelty. The reader would think Agathon had died. He had not. At some time not long before this play, he left Athens and joined a group of celebrities at the court of King Archelaos in Macedonia. The thought is, that for Athenian audiences he might just as well have quitted this world for the Islands of the Blest at the end of the world. Little is known about Xenocles and nothing about Pythangelos.

14. *Bright upper air, Zeus' penthouse:* All these lines are Euripidean. "Bright upper air, Zeus' penthouse" seems to be adapted from a phrase in the lost *Clever Melanippe.* "The foot of Time" is from the lost *Alexander.* The *heart that would . . .* and *Tongue that was . . .* are an adaptation from *Hippolytus* 612.

14. *Rule thou it:* This line is Euripidean, but the scholiast's ascription of it to *Andromache* is wrong.

16. *the deathless way:* As the Greeks conceived it, death is the separation of the soul or *psyche* (life, breath, ghost, or image) from the body. The body decays. The soul, such as it is, goes to the house or realm of Hades, or

to Hades (Hades is Plouton or Pluto, a person rather than a place). Usually, *but not always,* Hades is imagined to be under the ground. An alternate thought is to put the land of the dead, sometimes of the blessed dead only, at the end of the world. So certain special heroes pass to the other world merely by going further than natural means could have taken anyone: they do not go underground, their psyche is not torn out of their body, *they do not die.* Odysseus makes a long voyage and returns. Herakles went, and came back alive, so he must have gone by the roundabout way (Tainaron, land's end of the Peloponnese, the jumping-off place). In *The Metamorphoses* (*The Golden Ass*) of Apuleius (6. 17-18), Psyche must do an errand in Hades and return. She climbs a high tower and is about to jump. But the tower tells her not to, for if her spirit is broken out of her body she will go to the deepest place and never come back. Instead, she should go the long way, via Tainaron. Apuleius wrote in the second century A.D., but he helps to show what Dionysos is here talking about. In this play, the ferryboat on the Styx is combined perhaps with the far-voyaging ship, such a one as carried Odysseus. But one should not go too far in quest of intelligibility, since this is a funny play, not theology.

page 16. *two bits:* Literally, two obols. The *diobelia* or "two-obol payment" was a notorious but mysterious payment, probably some kind of dole, instituted by the demagogue Kleophon.

17. *Theseus:* The Athenian hero also made the trip to Hades and back.

17. *Morsimos:* A tragic poet, great-nephew of Aeschylus.

17. *Kinesias:* A writer of dithyrambs.

17. *Initiates:* Those initiated in the Eleusinian Mysteries expected a blissful life after death.

18. *bucks:* Literally, drachmas.

19. *carry me home:* The Greek here has a punning sequence only a little less idiotic than the translation.

20. *sea battle:* See the note to page 8.

20. *Stone of Parching Thirst:* (*Auainou lithos*). This would be a landmark in the country of the dead. Refreshing *water* from the Well of Memory stands for immortality ("may Isis give you cold water" on many Greek-Egyptian epitaphs): so being dried out would be a preliminary torment.

21. *First Crew:* Literally, "I am asalaminious." This could mean, "I am not a Salamis man," that is "I didn't fight at the battle of Salamis." But it could also mean "I am not a Salaminia man." The "Salaminia" was a consecrated ship, used for sacred and special missions. Its crew would doubtless be picked men. Since the sea fight of seventy-five years earlier is quite remote from this part of the play's action, I prefer the second interpretation.

28. *Empousa:* A bogey to frighten children with.

page 29. *the clam has stilled the waves:* In Euripides *Orestes* 279 the line runs:

ἐκ κυμάτων γὰρ αὖθις αὖ γαλήν(α) ὁρῶ.

The storm is over and the *calm* has stilled the waves.

But the actor, Hegelochos, spoke it:

ἐκ κυμάτων γὰρ αὖθις αὖ γαλῆν ὁρῶ.

The storm is over and the *cat* has stilled the waves.

Since "cat" (or "weasel"?) makes no plausible confusion in English, I have taken a slight liberty. In this, I find I have been anticipated by Mr. Dudley Fitts.

29. *all in yellow:* This seems the likeliest interpretation, though it is difficult to have the donkey on stage for so long.

30. *Iacchos:* Both Dionysos *and* the companion of Demeter and Persephone (that the god is eavesdropping on his own rituals is part of the fun). In the choral passage to come, and in the parabasis, the features of the Mysteries are combined with the worship of the Muses—which is drama.

30. *Diagoras:* A poet notorious for his atheism.

30. *Roasting pigs!:* Pigs were sacrificed at the Mysteries.

31. *Kratinos:* A distinguished comic poet, older contemporary (no longer living at the time of this play) of Aristophanes.

31. *Thorykion:* A tax-collector, evidently. Nothing is known about him except what is alleged here.

31. *shrine as a backhouse:* This seems to mean Kinesias. See page 17.

33. *Archedemos:* The demagogue who instituted proceedings against the generals after the battle of Arginousai (see the note on page 39). Non-Athenian birth is a frequent charge brought against demagogues by the comic poets.

34. *Kleisthenes:* See page 11. He is supposed to be mourning for a lost boy friend, like a wife for a husband killed in the war. Mourners tore out their hair (from their heads) and beat their faces.

34. *Kallias:* Member of a very rich family in Athens. Then as now only the rich raced horses.

35. *Aiakos:* In epic and saga a great hero, grandfather of Achilleus, head of that heroic line, the Aiakidai, so dear to the Aiginetans and Pindar and, according to some, made for his uprightness a judge of the dead in the underworld. Here he is a slave, plainly the janitor or porter.

35. *Styx, Acheron, Kokytos:* The rivers of the underworld. But Styx, often personified, is here hinted at in her true and ancient form, a waterfall dribbling off a huge black cliff on the northern face of Mount Chelmos, between Arkadia and Achaia.

37. *I cannot but obey thee:* This sounds like a tragic tag, but I cannot place it.

37. *Mistress:* Persephone.

39. *Theramenes:* A well-known politician of the time. Having in mind his own schemes for reform, he would join whatever party seemed temporarily to be most likely to further them, and then change sides at dis-

cretion. He showed the same kind of "adaptability" after the victory at Arginousai (see page 8). Bad weather prevented the victorious Athenians from picking up many survivors and floating corpses after the battle. The assembly was out for blood, and things looked bad for the captains of the ships, of whom Theramenes was one. He saved himself by adding his voice to the clamor, but putting the blame on the admirals of the fleet, who were condemned to death. Such maneuvers won Theramenes the nickname *kothornos,* which means "tragic buskin," or a military boot, or, more important for our purpose here, any boot which would fit either foot. The nickname is attested by Xenophon *Hellenica* 2. 3. 31. It does not appear in our text. I apologize for crowding it in; it seemed to me to make clear the well-known character of the man Aristophanes was attacking.

page 42. *Kleon:* If you have read the early plays, especially *The Knights,* you know all about Kleon. Hyperbolos was his successor, and of the same sort.

43. *my wife:* He hasn't any.

43. *my kiddies:* He hasn't any.

43. *the kind of god:* Herakles, as brother of Dionysos, is treated mostly as a god in this play.

43. *brave herbs:* Oregano. It was supposed to put one in a fighting mood.

44. *gentlemanly:* Athenian law permitted the torture of slaves in order to make them give evidence. This could not be done to free men, or "gentlemen," so it is a "generous" and "gentlemanly" gesture on the part of Xanthias when he offers his *slave* to be tortured for evidence concerning *himself.*

44. *or leeks:* A master might ask that his slave be excused from tortures too injurious or painful, either for the slave's own sake, or with thoughts of his future uses.

47. *Diomeia:* This feast of Herakles was held outside the walls and could not be celebrated while the enemy occupied Attica.

48. *Apollo . . . Pytho:* A line of verse by Hipponax, the iambic poet.

48. *Who . . . green waters:* The lyric is said to be from the lost *Laocoön* of Sophocles.

48. *Kleophon:* Politician, leader of the popular party, which was also the war party, detested by the comic poets, and attacked as being of non-Athenian (Thracian) birth. See the last lines of this play. Swallow and nightingale (Philomela and Prokne) are associated with Thrace (see *The Birds*), and the twittering of birds is often used to describe barbarian speech. The point is apparently something like this: Kleophon must stand trial at some time, and though in Attic law even ballots mean acquittal, Kleophon is so awful that an exception ought to be made.

49. *fears be taken away:* What follows is a plea for amnesty, and the restoration of full citizens' rights to all those who had lost them for political

reasons, particularly for supporting Phrynichos in the revolution of 411 B.C.

page 49. *Plataian status:* Plataia, a city of Boiotia, had been the most steadfast and devoted of the allies of Athens. When in 427 B.C. the city was destroyed by the Spartans and Thebans, the survivors were granted Athenian citizenship (with a few limitations).

49. *Kleigenes:* This bathman was doubtless also a politician, but we know nothing more about him.

49. *currency:* The Spartan occupation of part of Attica had cut off access to the silver mines at Laurion. This resulted in a debasing of the coinage.

50. *scapegoat:* Or *pharmakos.* This was a condemned criminal on whom was loaded all the accumulated guilt of the city. His execution, therefore, amounted to an act of public sacrifice and expiation.

53. *Kleidemidas:* Perhaps a son of Sophocles, perhaps only a friend.

55. *cabbage patch:* Aristophanes is fond of saying that Euripides' mother maintained a truck garden.

59. *Phrynichus:* The earliest of the great tragic poets, active in the first decades of the fifth century (not to be confused with the comic poet mentioned on page 7).

59. *Achilleus:* References are to lost plays, *The Phrygians* (or *The Ransoming of Hector*) and *Niobe.*

61. *Kephisophon:* Euripides' secretary, supposed, here, to have done some ghostwriting for him.

61. *line of thought:* Aristophanes portrays Aeschylus as a haughty patrician who disliked the common people. See the Introduction.

62. *Phormisios:* A "reactionary" politician. Of Megainetos and Manes (this may be a nickname) nothing is known. Kleitophon, who appears in the dialogue of Plato which bears his name, seems to have belonged with Phormisios, as does Theramenes (see note 39 on page 95). Euripides' disciples seem to be distinguished from those of Aeschylus not so much for their views as for their characters and methods.

63. *See you . . . Achilleus?:* The opening of the lost *Myrmidons* of Aeschylus.

65. *Persians:* This seems to be a slip of memory on the part of Aristophanes. *The Persians* is reliably dated 472 B.C., *The Seven Against Thebes* 467 B.C.

66. *Phaidra:* See Euripides, *Hippolytus.*

66. *Sthenoboia:* The heroine of a lost play named after her. Her story is similar to that of Phaidra, insofar as she made advances to Bellerophon, her husband's guest, was refused, and told her husband that Bellerophon had tried to seduce her.

68. *warships:* No one is willing to be a *trierarch.* The *trierarchy,* a special duty or liturgy imposed on rich citizens, involved the outfitting and upkeep of a *trireme* (war galley), as well as the nominal command of the vessel on active service.

69. *His nurses . . . life?:* The nurse-procuress could be Phaidra's nurse in

Hippolytus. In *Auge,* the heroine gave birth in the temple of Athene. In *Aeolus,* Makareus and Kanake, brother and sister, are involved in a love affair. For musings on life, see the fragment from the lost *Polyeidus:*

> Who knows if life be not thought death, or death be life in the world below?

There is a similar thought in the lost *Phrixus.*

page 69. *Panathenaia:* The pan-Athenian festival.

70. *subtle allusions:* We are told that *The Frogs* was so well received that a second performance was given during the poet's lifetime. This stanza may conceivably have been written for this second performance, when "the book was out." But an annotated edition, by which the audience could identify allusions, is something absolutely unexampled for this date.

70. *Oresteia:* The title is here used for the play we call *The Choephori,* or *The Libation Bearers.*

71. *Hermes, . . . I have returned:* These lines are missing from our mss. of Aeschylus. I have discarded my previous translation for a more literal one, in order to make the use of synonymous phrases, real or apparent, more obvious.

73. *three times:* At the last rites for the dead, the name was called three times.

74. *Oedipus . . . man:* This and the fifth line below are the first two lines of Euripides' lost *Antigone.*

74. *Erasinides:* A general at the time of the battle of Arginousai. Had one of these generals lost his sight, he would have been excused from military service, and so would have escaped the fate that befell Erasinides and his colleagues. See the note on Theramenes on page 95.

75. *Aigyptos . . . Argos:* Said to have been the first lines of the lost *Archelaus,* but the opening of this play is also given in another form.

75. *little bottle of oil:* The *lekythion,* or little oil bottle, was part of the traveler's regular luggage.

75. *Dionysos . . . feet:* Opening of the lost *Hypsipyle.*

75. *Ah me, . . . again:* This line combines the two death cries of Agamemnon, Aeschylus *Agamemnon* 1343, 1345.

75. *There's been . . . born unhappy:* Opening of the lost *Sthenoboea.*

76. *Kadmos . . . Sidon:* Opening of the lost *Phrixus.*

76. *Pelops . . . horses:* Opening of *Iphigeneia in Tauris.*

77. *Oineus, from his land:* Opening of the lost *Meleager.*

77. *Zeus . . . maintained:* Opening of the lost *Clever Melanippe.*

78. *Phthian . . . rescue?:* Two lines from the lost *Myrmidons,* the second repeated as a refrain by Aristophanes.

78. *Hermes . . . lakeside:* From the lost *Psychagogi.*

78. *Greatest Achaian . . . hear me:* From either *Telephus* or *Iphigeneia* (both lost).

78. *Quiet, all . . . nearby:* From *The Priestesses* (lost).

78. *I am . . . at the wayside:* *Agamemnon* 104.

page 78. *How the . . . of Hellas: Agamemnon* 108.

78. *Sends forth . . . hellhounds:* From the lost *Sphinx.*

79. *hand on . . . of encounter: Agamemnon* 111.

79. *giving assault . . . airways:* Provenance unknown.

79. *From Marathon:* The next Aeschylean line, *which leaning on Aias,* is meaningless here, since unmetrical, and I have omitted it.

79. *Meletos':* A poet of indifferent reputation, better known as the accuser of Socrates.

79. *That's a man's woman . . . one:* Literally, Dionysos says: "This Muse was never a Lesbian, not at all." Rogers, reading the Greek so as to obtain "The Muse herself" instead of "This Muse," translates: "The Muse herself can't be a wanton? No!" I do not find this convincing. Outraged indignation does not suit Dionysos, and the expression "be a Lesbian" should not mean "be a wanton" in any general sense. If Sappho had ever, at this time, been called "The tenth Muse," the point would be perfect. She was so called, but I do not find it earlier than *Palatine Anthology* 9. 506. This is attributed to Plato, and therefore could, by an exceedingly strenuous stretch of the imagination, have been current before *The Frogs* was written. But attributions in the *Anthology* are frequently suspect, and this epigram does not sound Platonic to me. Still, "Tenth Muse" could have been a tag already applied to Sappho, and the allusion to Lesbos ought to be accounted for in the translation.

79. *sea's ever-streaming:* This sequence seems to be a patchwork of Euripidean passages, but not all can be identified. The first four lines are said to be from *Iphigeneia,* but do not appear in our extant texts for either of the plays so called. Other identifications are: the eighth line, *Meleager;* ninth and tenth, *Electra;* eleventh to fourteenth, *Hypsipyle.*

81. *monodies:* The monody is a solo for the female character (played of course by a male actor). Unlike the patchwork demonstration of "Euripidean lyric" above, this is a true parody, done "in the manner of Euripides" but without (apparently) direct quotations.

83. *I wish . . . her way:* The opening line of *Medea.*

83. *River . . . near:* From the lost *Philoctetes.*

83. *Persuasion . . . the word:* From the lost *Antigone.*

85. *Death . . . by gifts:* From the lost *Niobe.*

85. *His right hand . . . steel:* From the lost *Meleager.*

85. *Chariot . . . on corpse:* From the lost *Glaucus.*

87. *[Lions . . . all]:* The authenticity of this line, omitted by two good mss., is highly doubtful, so I have left it in square brackets. The allusion to the lion's cub may be to *Agamemnon* 716-36, but there is no direct quotation. Lions are constantly associated with kingship. There would be a hint at Alkibiades' suspected ambitions toward tyranny. I have read this thought into my translation. To the question, what shall we do about Alkibiades, the answers may be paraphrased thus: Euripides: He is

selfish and therefore unreliable: Aeschylus: True, but he is our only promising leader, and we should put ourselves in his hands.

page 87. *Kleokritos* and *Kinesias:* see *The Birds* 877, 1372.

88. *will serve?:* I hope I am right in this interpretation. Neither the mantle of the rich nor the sackcloth of the poor is satisfactory. These articles of clothing are, I believe, thought of as emergency life preservers. Cp. *Odyssey* 5. 346-50.

89. *My tongue . . . heart:* See *Hippolytus* 612.

89. *What's shameful? . . . audience?:* Adapted from the lost *Aeolus*. It should read: "What's shameful, unless it seems so to those who do it?"

89. *Who knows . . . life:* See note 69 on page 97.

90. *Sokrates:* The word *sophia* stands sometimes for literary skill, sometimes for wisdom. The ambiguity shows that the Greeks did not always distinguish between the two as sharply as we do. Aristophanes, acknowledging perhaps that the clever Sokrates does possess some kind of *sophia*, rejects it as the wrong kind. The objection is based, clearly, on certain antiliterary views of Sokrates which are attested again and again in the works of Plato.

90. *Archenomos:* They were involved in the collection of taxes.

Selected Ann Arbor Paperbacks
Works of enduring merit

For a complete list of Ann Arbor Paperback titles write:
THE UNIVERSITY OF MICHIGAN PRESS ANN ARBOR